For Kerri

2018 Rabbooks Publishing First Edition

ISBN-13: 978-1541299122

ISBN-10: 1541299124

Book Design and Illustration by Alex James

www.rabbitstudios.blogspot.com
www.facebook.com/rabbitstudiosbigpush

FLAMING JACKASS
Returns

Alexander G. J.

ACKNOWLEDGMENTS

Special thanks to all the people who helped in one way or another, either by inspiration or perspiration, to place this book in your hands.

A special thanks to Melissa Ehman and Luke Neher for their tireless editing and support.

CONTENTS

Part One

Jet Lag

Friday, February 12, 1999

"Pauvre con!"

Erin's French was bad, but even she knew the cab driver who'd almost run her over had just called her an asshole. She racked her brain to remember how to reply in French. She settled for the American version and the accompanying sign language: "Fuck you! Pedestrians have the right of way, dickhead!" When she lowered her bird hand she noticed three elderly madams also sharing the traffic island near the Place de Bastille structure. They stared at her as if she was the ugliest of ugly Americans "Désolé," Erin apologized.

The women turned to one another and muttered something in French as they scurried to the sidewalk. *Yes, I know, even in Paris I'm a horrible, horrible person. Don't worry, I'll be gone soon.* She rubbed her buzz-cut orange hair. It felt good and calmed her, like stroking a pet. Putting the incident with three strangers she'd never see again behind her, she dragged her luggage down the street and around the corner to the brasserie. Her heart started pounding and her hands shook—the same three old ladies were leaning on the bar, drinking Oranginas and smoking. One of them gestured to her. *Goddamn it, give me a break!* She took a deep breath and checked out the rest of the room. Only two people sat at the little round tables near the window. *I need to make it clear that I'm going to sit down.*

"Bonjour," the large, aproned man behind the counter said as he approached her.

Crap—I forgot to say 'bonjour' first, and after all those nasty looks thrown at me each time I forgot that part of the game. "B-bonjour..." she stuttered. "...J-je voudrais, une...un café, and uh...ah pâtisserie? S'il vous plaît?"

"Pâtisserie? Vous voulez commander un croissant?"

1

The man spoke fast, and Erin almost broke out into a sweat. *'Croissant' rings a bell. He's asking me if I want a croissant!* "Yes—er-ah, oui! La croissant—merci—And café."

The man smiled and shook his head a little as he poured Erin a cup of coffee and put a croissant onto a plate. He rattled off an amount in Euros. Erin couldn't follow numbers, but her trick was to look at the register. The price reminded her she was supposed to have mentioned eating at a table. She poked her finger in the direction of the tables near the window. "For er-ah—pour la table? S'il vous plaît? Merci?"

The man handed her the items. "Oui, vous pouvez les manger à la table." From his open-handed gesture she guessed he had either already charged her a table price or was too nice or lazy to ring her up again. She put some Euros on the counter and he gave her change, which she didn't bother counting.

"Merci."

"Merci, Mademoiselle. Bonjour," he said, turning his attention to the old ladies who had started smoking their second cigarettes.

At her little table, her heart slowed back to normal and her hands became less sweaty. She looked out the window at the Parisians traveling to work, on scooters, in tiny cars and little trucks that sped past in an anarchistic traffic pattern, and at the people, mostly in black, talking on cell phones, cleaning the streets, going to school and jaywalking. *So similar to rush hour in Neopolitan.* She sighed. *Tomorrow at this time, I'll be back in my own zone. There will be coffee, croissants and French people, but it won't look, sound or taste the same.* She lit up a cigarette, knowing a new law back home wouldn't allow her to light up in restaurants and bars. *What crap. I can understand restaurants, but why do people go to bars if they don't want to be around smokers?* She took a sip of coffee. It was extra good. *Intellectually, I know it's not necessarily the special African beans they use or whatever, just my idolization of everything Parisian. I'm used to Europe, and my taste buds are telling me not to go. Yes, here bartenders make fun of my horrible Dutch, French, and Italian, but people in Neopolitan made fun of me without me having to speak.*

A familiar figure in a long black coat approached the window and waved. When Madam Marie Callier came in, Erin stood so they could kiss cheeks. The bangs of her shoulder length, dark black hair hid her sullen features.

"Bonjour, ma chère petite. How did you do?" Marie asked. She removed her long purple silk scarf.

"Terrible, I said patesserie instead of croissant."

"Ooh." Marie winced

"I just tense up whenever I have to talk to anybody."

"Il n'est pas grave…don't worry about it, at least you tried. You just need to be more confident." She patted Erin's shoulder and walked away. "Bonjour," she called as she went to the counter and, in a much more effortless fashion than Erin, ordered a coffee. She returned and sat across from Erin and also lit a cigarette.

How does she smoke so much more elegantly than I do? She always looks bored, tired and older than thirty-nine, but I practice that look in the bathroom mirror and can't look that sexy. "Man, I'm gonna miss this."

"Paris or eating croissants?"

"Both. I'm not ready to go back."

"Ah, poor Eir-on. You can stay another week, non?"

"No, I can't. I have a crap-load of things I need to take care of."

"Oui, responsabilité—c'est bon."

"Plus, I'm sure you're sick of me sleeping in your spare room."

"Don't worry about me. I like having your company. But you miss your home by now, no?"

"Some of it. I miss my friends and my mom. I miss my dog and I do like Neo. But I just don't like all the loose ends."

"Loose ends?"

"It means things I left behind, that I didn't solve."

Marie rolled her eyes. "Oui, I know the saying 'loose ends'. I mean, what loose ends you have? You will stay away from those troublesome boys, you will talk to your mother about your brother, and you do not have that awful pizza job, non?"

"Yes, but I still have to get a new job to pay off the big fat bill coming from my brother, and my dad covered my rent, so he's blackmailing me into signing up for art school as payment. It's gonna suck."

"It is good that you are going to school. You are very talented. Look, see, I am wearing your necklace." She drew aside her coat collar to reveal a pendant of small, turquoise-colored turtles and tiny gold fish.

"I noticed. You know, buying the supplies in the arts and craft shop was even harder than ordering coffee."

"The first time you were here, you were getting over a boy. Now it is Steiner-Kevin. Am I only to see you again when your heart is breaking?"

"Oh, no-no-no! I hope not. I mean, I hope that's not the only time I come to Europe. That's funny, in England Mr. Humphrey said the same thing."

"Well, you know you are always welcomed. I like all of my friends from Nopolitón."

"I tried to call Salome, but she apparently moved, and Bob and Larry never gave me their numbers."

"That is too bad." Marie took a slow drag on her cigarette and gazed sideways at Erin.

Erin looked down. *That trying-to-look-at-my-soul expression always makes me feel weird.*

Marie put her hand on Erin's head. "Très orange." She finished her coffee and looked at her watch. "Tant pis. I have to go. Time to go see Danielle about some fabrics." She caressed Erin's hands. "I wish you could stay, ma chère petite."

"Me, too." Erin's heart sank and she almost felt like crying.

"You will e-mail me when you get home, oui?"

"Oui, definitely!" They stood and kissed each other's cheeks more than once. Marie departed for her job as a buyer/seller/shop owner. Erin actually never understood what Marie did for a living. She made tons of money, took long lunches, usually set her own hours, and had tons of friends who also had vague, high-paying jobs with long lunches and flexible hours.

As Erin looked out the window at the beautiful, cold February day, she tried to psych herself up for her homecoming.

If you have to go home after a long vacation, I guess there's no place better to return to than Neopolitan.

#

"Goddamn fucking-son-of-a-bitch!" Erin muttered as the plane hit an air pocket and dipped so much the flight attendant in the isle crouched to keep from falling. Erin held her breath to stop the roller coaster feeling. *Am I the only passenger freaking out over this? Everybody else is talking, laughing, reading and sleeping. Must be Neopolitans.* She looked out the window at the wall of fog and rain, whisking past and glowing red every time the lights on the wings blinked. She panicked. *If I can see no further than 30 feet, how is the pilot flying through this?* The captain's voice instructed the flight attendants to sit down because the plane will be landing in 15 minutes. *Landing where?* She still couldn't see the mountains or the river, only the gray wall. The guy next to her was asleep. *How can you sleep through this shit?* The plane dipped again, causing the baby that had been crying for six hours, to start up again. The lights flickered for a second. *Oh shit, this is it! This is what I get for leaving town and running away! Perfect, Erin. You try to go away and clear your head and they'll be no one to appreciate the new, improved version. Maybe I should pray.* She did the Catholic sign of the cross. *Oh God, please don't let me die on this plane! I promise I'll try to be better. I'll try to do charity or something, Amen!*

There was a whining noise under the plane and a bright light on the wings. *Fire? It was the landing lights; the whining sound was the tires coming down. Landing? How can we be landing? There's no runway? There's no ground. Shit! Are we making an emergency landing? Maybe the pilot's passed out?* She moved her head to see if the carpet of clouds showed any sign of terra firma. The plane sank into the clouds and visibility was zero. People around her, continued to talk, sleep and read airplane magazines. Erin took out her copy of Learn French Fast she had purchased in Paris. She noticed a phrase she should have used in a shop when she was in Dijon. *Bottles is bouteilles? Shit! I said where are the boots of wine? I suck.* The plane banked hard to the left. *Fuck! What are we avoiding a mountain?* She put the book away and closed her eyes. *Perhaps if I can't see what's going on, then it wont exist.* The trick worked for a few seconds until someone cried: "What's that?" Erin looked through the window for a fire or a mountain obstacle. The object was the Victoria River, expanding like a big gray snake under a blanket of rain clouds. *Okay, there's the river, where's the airport? Is this pilot using the river as a road map? At this height, won't we crash into the bridge? Shit! Is this it? Great, I'm gonna die without showing people how different I've changed. I was looking forward to seeing Kevin or Steiner again and just ignoring them, or maybe going by F.J. Pizza and telling Ed: "I'm glad you fired me, because I had a blast in Europe and soon I'm gonna get a job that'll make yours look like shit."*

The plane banked again to the right and started descending lower. *Okay we're heading in the wrong direction. Damn it! What's this pilot doing? God, what if he's a crazy hijacker? Great, my claim to fame will be passenger 18 on flight whatever from Dallas!* The view disappeared again in a sea of fog as the plane got lower and lower. *Dude! What the fuck?* She squeezed the hand rest. *If that was the river then we're heading into the mountains!* She kept looking through the window. Farmland came into view and then power lines and factories. The plane got so low she could see cars and motorcycles. *No wait, that's not mountains. Where the hell are we?* The ground turned into thick heavy woods and fields. *Are we crash landing in a field? Shouldn't they warn us? Damn airline!* The plane slowed. The engine sounded like it was cut off and then a moment later, came on again. Fog and mist streamed over the wings like smoke. The plane descended into another low cloud. She said a silent prayer. The ground appeared and was so close she could see the texture of the grass. *Okay, I see grass, grass, fence, grass, grass, cow—hello! Where's the motherfucking runway? Goddamn it!* Two seconds later a platform of black asphalt and lights rolled underneath the back tires, the plane touched down with a thump and the front came down three seconds later with a bump. The engines made a revving noise, the front of the wings flapped up and the plane slowly braked until it was taxiing speed. Erin exhaled. The inside of the plane was quiet; *All of the people who pretended to be so cool were probably panicking as much as I was.*

The pilot made an announcement: "I'd like to welcome you all to the Neopolitan International Airport, local time is 3:47 PM. We apologize for being 40 minutes behind schedule. Weather report: Temperatures are in the low 60s. Rain today and Saturday with a chance of clearing by Sunday. We do remind you that as of January first, there is no smoking allowed inside the airport."

Lame. Erin craved a smoke after the many hours of withholding.

The plane stopped at one point and waited for another plane to cross its path. *I feel like we've been sitting here for years.* Eventually they made if to gate 38B. The pilot gave everyone a warning about remaining seated and keeping their seat belts buckled, but half were already standing and pulling their bags from the overhead. The jetway was cold. The rain pounded the outside shell. *I didn't expect the weather to be this bad.* At the gate exit, lots of people were being greeted by their friends and family members. Erin looked for Lashell. *She's nowhere in sight I bet she waited for 10 minutes and then left.* "Damn it, Shell!" she mumbled, craning her neck around the crowd. There wasn't any sign of her friend. *Maybe she went to baggage claim.* Riding on the moving walkway, she studied the artwork on the wall of the tunnel. *I've been spoiled by the artwork of all the museums. To me, these abstract paintings of fish and bridges are about as artistic as the signs telling me where the restrooms are.*

She made it to the baggage claim just as her plane's luggage was making its appearance through the flap-covered hole in the wall, randomly spitting their bags onto the conveyer belt of luggage roulette. She got to relax as the other passengers with expensive bags kept picking up the wrong ones and putting them back, over and over. *There's no way anyone else would have something covered in so many tacky stickers as mine.*

She heard a familiar voice say: "I'm in baggage claim…no, I haven't seen her…"

Is that Lashell? Looking around, Erin saw the back of someone's head that could be her. She was Black, had the same build, but the hair was different—instead of long braids, she now had straight black hair that turned into orange curls. *Did we walk right past each other?* Erin moved around so she could look at her face. It was Lashell, talking on a cell phone, something else that was new.

"I went to the gate but their plane was 40 minutes late!" Lashell complained. "I went to the bathroom and when I came out they were…" Lashell looked over at Erin. As part of a joke, Erin didn't look at her. "No way! she's here, talk to you later." She hung up. "No fuck'n way!" Erin smiled coyly and turned toward her. "Oh my god! What the hell did you do to yo dreads?"

"Hi, Shell," Erin laughed and ran her fingers through her own new hairstyle. They screamed, laughed and hugged each other. Erin wanted to kiss her on the cheek but held back.

"Oh my god, what did you do, you crazy bitch?" Lashell asked again.

"I cut if off?"

"Oh my god! It's fuck'n orange!"

"What about you? I didn't recognize you, you're orange, too?…And you got a cell phone you yuppie bitch!"

"No, I'm redhead. Your head is fuck'n orange! You look like a match! And girl, I got to have my phone."

Erin noticed her bag and removed it from the rotating lineup. "So, You like it?"

"The bag, or yo' Woody Woodpecker head?"

"Hair."

"Girl, I didn't like that blonde rat's nest Rasta wig you had before. What make you think I'm gonna like that?" She reached over and ran her hand through Erin's buzz cut. "Short hair, huh? It's kinda cute. I thought for sure you'd worry about people thinking you're a lesbian. You didn't come back all gay, did you?"

"I'm quite straight, thank you. Women in Paris all had short hair; very in." They started to walk to the exit.

"Did you get some ass in Europe?"

"Well… I'll talk about that later."

"Oh my god! You got some ass?"

"Later. How about you? How are you doing? Did you ever get my graduation present?"

"Oh, oh, subject change, eh? Yeah I did. Don't know what country-ass European town you sent that from, but that motherfucker arrived, <u>after</u> your Christmas present."

"What did you do for New Year's?"

"I just hung out with my sisters."

"No New Year's nookie?"

"Oh please, I don't have time for that shit."

"My mom work'n you huh?"

"I don't work for your mom. I'm way on the other side of the campus."

"Oh, so I guess you don't hang out or anything?"

"I saw her, once in the cafeteria. Hanging out with doctor Dan."

"Geez! Are they still dating?"

"What? You didn't keep in touch with your mama?"

"I did, but I never wrote her about anything personal. It was all: Dear Mom, saw a guy pee in another guy's mouth today."

"Whoa! Whoa! Hold up! You saw what? In the who now?"

"This art show in Amsterdam—I couldn't watch—bleah! Can we talk about something else?" Erin shivered.

"Dang, girl, seems like a lot you don't wanna talk about. You sure you had a good time?"

"I had a great time. I'm just trying to readjust to a normal life. It feels so weird to be back. It's like I haven't touched the earth since November and now I have to walk on hard ground, you know what I mean?"

"Back to reality."

"Exactly: no more English tea, French coffee, artsy Dutch porn shows and Italian...whatever's."

"I'm gonna ask you about that Italian whatever later."

"Yes, much later. Oh! Let me use your phone and call my mom." Lashell gave instructions on how to use it. Erin called the administration office and left a message on her mother's voicemail that she would call again tomorrow.

Outside, the rain had subsided into a cold drizzle. As they walked across the busy loading zone under Lashell's umbrella, Erin looked at Lashell and tried to adjust to her new appearance. *I bet Lashell is having the same if not more of a difficult time with my own change.* She took out a cigarette and lit it.

"You still on those?" Lashell complained fanning her nose.

"Can't smoke anywhere else. When did all this anti smoking shit start?"

"Girl, you better make sure you finished before you get in my car. Ain't nobody smoke'n in my baby."

"Oh, oh, you're one of those."

"Ain't no way I'm gonna let my car smell like your ol' punk rock mobile."

"My poor car. I guess I'm gonna have to get another one or something."

"Not without no job and no money."

"Speaking of no jobs, been to F.J. Pizza, lately?"

"You kid'n? When I quit I swore I'd never step foot in there again. You know they fired Doug, right?"

"You told me. Sleeping on the job or something?"

"Yep, dumb-ass. What kind of delivery guy drives somewhere and sleeps?"

"Well, he has his band thing and the baby keeping him up at night."

"Whatever. He started working at some warehouse."

"So you stay in contact with the gang?"

"Not really. I saw Tracy and her crew at the mall, probably shoplifting. Only reason I know about Doug is I ran into him at the movies. I think I told you about Ed."

"Yeah, They should have fired his ass instead of moving him to the new place. I guess that's good news for everyone else. That mean's Jeannie is the manager and Tracy and that bitch Barbara are assistant manager's."

"You'd think, but just Barbara's the assistant manager."

"Oh my god, that blows! Tracy's been there like, forever!"

"She knows what situation she's in—here we are." Lashell pointed to her new car, a powder blue '78 Mustang.

"Cool! A Mustang, good find!" They put Erin's bags in the

trunk and she politely snuffed her cigarette out before getting in. Erin wanted to pay for parking, but all she had on her were a couple of Euro coins. In the time it took to travel to one of the three bridges, Lashell talked about her new job at the University of Neopolitan Medical Center and her family. She did administrative and receptionist work all day, which seemed kind of boring to Erin, but Lashell really liked the people and the pay was almost three times as much as F.J. Pizza. Her sister and niece had finally moved out, giving Lashell, her little sister and their mom a little extra space. Lashell was now being pressured to move out on her own. After seeing what Erin went through trying to find an affordable place in the North, Lashell was more content to look more in the South side.

They patiently merged into the lane to take them to the West Side Bridge. While driving across, Erin felt chills. *The last time I was here was my big car accident and arrest.* The fogged and wet windows mostly obscured the view of the approaching downtown area. In spite of the rain and the traffic, Erin was a little glad to be back. *This is my home. I don't understand why I wasn't gonna come back.* Several turns and red lights later, they arrived at Erin's shared house in Grand View. *This Neighborhood reminds me of Europe: rainy narrow streets containing black clad hipsters, drinking in cafes and hanging out in its over priced shops.* "Book…store," she read to herself. It took her a second to get used to reading signs without having to figure out what they meant. *Being in Europe was like being dyslexic.*

After parking behind a BMW SUV, they walked up the steps of the salmon and white colored Queen Anne style rental. At this time, at least one of her roommates should be home. Erin felt a bit nervous about seeing them again. She had made sure that her share of the rent was taken care of, but unlike her communications with Lashell, she hadn't e-mailed them as often. On the porch, Erin tried to hold her bag while fumbling around for her house keys. Lashell returned dirty looks at the yuppies walking their golden retriever. "Hurry up, people think we're trying to break in or something," Lashell commented.

"Probably—Goddamn it, where's that fucking key?" Behind the door, her dog Buster started to bark. "Hey, boy! I'm almost there, baby. Just hold on." Erin found the right key and tried to flip it around into her hand. Suddenly the door swung open. Erin made a short squeal. There in the doorway stood Roger Gaines. It didn't surprise Erin he had opened the door—after all, he was Fabrianne's ex-boyfriend, and the last Erin knew, they were still friends—what did surprise her was he was wearing gym shorts and no shoes. Buster ran around Roger and jumped on her. He wagged his tail and tried to lick whatever exposed skin she had, howling and barking for joy. Erin petted and hugged her dog.

"Hey! Whoa! The hair!" Roger said, pointing at Erin.

"Roger. What the hell are you doing in my house?"

"Uhh, I live here?"

Erin dropped her bag on the floor, narrowly missing his feet.

"Very funny. No, you don't, you got your own place."

"Not anymore."

"What? You're serious? What happened? You got evicted?"

"Bingo."

"Where's Fabrianne and Tawnee?— Fabrianne! Tawnee!" Erin yelled, rushing past Roger to have a word or two with her roommates about letting someone move in without telling her.

"They went to get some food for your homecoming."

"When did this happen? Where are you sleeping? It better not be in my room, 'cause there's gonna be a gallon of blood in your future."

"Chill, so violent! I've been crashing on the sofa."

"How long? Why would Fabrianne let you move in here? You guys broke up!"

"It's only been a couple of days. My landlord decided to sell my house, that asshole."

"So, didn't that give you at least a month to find some place to live?"

"Are you kidding? Fuck'n yuppies jacked up rents everywhere. I can't find anything I can afford."

"What the hell-ever, I found a place, you can too!"

"Sh-yeah right, you lived with Mary Jo and then this place. You didn't have to live with some strange weirdos."

Erin laughed, remembering how Mary Joe walked around naked and had a garbage bag full of pot. Lashell and Roger chuckled a little.

"Okay, maybe not Mary Joe, but everyone I know, either has a roommate or they've graduated and left town."

"Boo fucking hoo, Roger. When I was looking for a place, your sorry ass wouldn't let me move in. Now you expect me to let you live here?"

"Hey! I couldn't let you move in because one of my roommates was going through some bad times and still had her shit up stairs. I wasn't gonna put her out."

She noticed Roger had piled a bunch of boxes in the hallway next to the stairs. "...That's not the reason why. You wouldn't let me move in 'cause you didn't like me."

"That's not true."

"Yes it—" The front door swung open. Fabrianne Faulkner came in carrying a plastic bag full of Chinese takeout containers. She screamed when she saw Erin. "Oh, my god! Your hair! Your hair!" She put the bags down, ran over and gave Erin a big hug. *She let her hair grow out a little. What's with the conservative pantsuit she's wearing?* Following behind Fabrianne, Tawnee Fitzgerald carried two bottles of plum wine. She wore all black, had Goth makeup and her hair in long skinny braids that ran down to her shoulder blades. *She hasn't done anything different with her appearance in the four months since I saw her.* Like Fabrianne, she screamed, put everything down and hugged Erin, adding a kiss on the cheek. Erin forgot what she was yelling about until Fabrianne told Roger to put on some pants. Roger went into the hallway and started digging through his box of clothes. Erin grabbed Fabrianne and Tawnee's arms and led them into the kitchen. Lashell stayed behind to keep Buster from eating the bags of food.

"Okay. What the hell is he doing here?" Erin asked

"Love the hair. When did you do it?" Tawnee complimented.

"Don't change the subject! Are you guys back together?"

"N-no. He got evicted. We're just helping out," Fabrianne answered.

"But guys, I don't really get along with Roger."

"We know, that's why we told him to be out before you returned, but the market is pretty tight right now for cheap apartments."

"Fabe, I know it's tough out there. Believe me, I spent the night in my car, remember? But the longer he's here, the more crazy things are going to get—it's' disruptive! Like bringing in too much masculine energy into a feminine house!"

Tawnee pointed to Fabrianne. "Ah-ha! That's exactly what I said to her, 'cept I said cock in a hen house."

Fabrianne picked up one of the bottles of wine and opened it. "You guys, I know it can be a problem, but what can I do? Put him out on the streets? He's our friend?"

"Not our problem!" Erin said. "If it were me, you know he wouldn't let me move in. No, wait—He didn't let me move in. that's why we got our own damn house!"

"It's only for a short period. I told him that."

"Are you sure you're not fawning over him?"

"No, I've moved on."

"So, you've started dating someone else?"

"Not yet, but who knows? The point is, it's over."

"So if you start—"

"Better?" Roger interrupted, pointing to his long, grungy camouflage sweat pants.

Oookay, maybe they won't get back together.

Erin thought the mock Peking duck from Yakie Chan's Chinese Food was pretty good. Its taste was accented by the two glasses of plum wine.

"I'm surprised you started drinking again," Lashell commented.

"Are you kidding? Wine is sooo cheap in Europe. Could get a whole bottle for less than five bucks."

"You still a vegetarian?" Tawnee asked.

"I am now. Paris cooked their potatoes in goose fat; it was

deadly! So, what have you girls been up to, besides letting a homeless guy move in?"

"Hey!" Roger protested. "I'm not some homeless bum!"

Before Erin could counter with an insult, Fabrianne volunteered information about her life. "I got a job as a designer at a company that prints sporting event stuff like beer cozies, T-shirts and those giant #1 foam fingers..." She preempted Erin's question "...and yes they do a giant middle finger version as well.

"Tawnee ?" Erin asked

"Still working at Ripped to Threads. Trying to finish my portfolio so I can graduate in March. And, get this, me, Lisa Ann and Annette just started renting a small art space at the Cannery so we can sell our art stuff."

"That's awesome! Congratulations!"

"You still at F.J. Pizza?" Erin asked Roger.

"Yep."

"Didn't you graduate?"

"With a useless communications degree."

"You should get a better job so you can have more money and move out."

"Thanks, Mom."

"Anyway..." Fabrianne interrupted Erin's potential retort.,"...where did you go? I only know about France."

"First a layover in Newark to visit my family and suffer through a fancy-ass dinner with them, then I flew to Paris for a couple of days, flew over to Manchester where I met up with Pat and Mimi. Trained it to London, over and up to Amsterdam, where my friends Paul and Suzette moved to. Down to Antwerp, Paris again, over and down to Florence where Lisa Ann and her so called 'platonic friend' Tony were staying, down to this little town called Siena and then back to Paris for the remainder."

"Dang, girl, you been everywhere!" Lashell commented.

"Not really. I was planning on going to Spain but my credit card was getting to its limit, plus I didn't know anyone down there."

"So, was it all worth it?" Fabrianne asked.

"It was. I mean, I'm sorry I left without saying goodbye to you guys, but I really needed to do it."

"Sometimes you have to do stuff like that," Tawnee said.

"I feel so bad, though, that I missed Lashell's graduation, I missed Fabrianne's. Lashell got my gift 400 years later, did you?" Erin asked Fabrianne.

"Oh! Oh! Oh!" Tawnee yelled getting off the floor where she had been sitting.

"What is it?" Roger asked.

"Erin's Christmas present!" she yelled and headed out of the room to the back door.

"Oh yeah!" Fabrianne said. "I forgot all about that. Thanks by the way for the earrings."

"No prob, where is she going?" Erin's question was answered a minute later when Tawnee pushed an old, red and Silver Schwinn bicycle from the back.

"Merry Christmas, ho, ho, ho!" Tawnee yelled.

"Holy Shit! You didn't!" Erin jumped up and ran over to the bike. "You guys spent too much!"

"Naw. Got a good deal at Mr. Mike's Bikes." She put her hand next to her mouth and whispered "It's used" as if telling a secret to the whole room.

"Oh, my god! this is fuck'n awesome!" Erin hugged Tawnee and then ran back and hugged Fabrianne. She was about to hug Roger. "You didn't have anything to do with this, did you?"

"Sh-yeah, right," he said sarcastically. "You guys giving her a hint that she needs to loose weight?" Erin glared angrily at him. Lashell laughed.

"You got a hell'a lotta balls for someone staying in _my_ house," she responded. Roger quieted like a slapped dog.

"No, it's not an exercise thing," Tawnee answered tooting the horn attached to the handlebars. "We figured since Erin totaled her car, she'll need this to get around"

Erin tooted the horn. "You guys rule!"

Lashell went home at 11:47. At 2:35AM, everyone else called it a night and retired to their bedrooms. Due to the time change, Erin wasn't sleepy. She spent her time sorting through her 50 plus e-mails and 39 physical ones. She sent Madam Callier a short note communicating a safe arrival. She looked in the French Fast book and was able to write Je suis arrivé à Neopolitan.

In the morning, Erin had 'Grandma's House Syndrome'. It was a condition in which she would spend the night in a relative's house, and in the morning have no idea where she was.

It took her a second to realize she was in her bedroom, that furry, white thing sleeping in the corner was her dog and that noise coming from the living room was Roger, watching Saturday morning cartoons. She grumbled and mumbled, looking for a pair of pajama pants to cover her purple panties under the white T-shirt. *I have no interest in giving Roger a free show of any kind.*

She opened the door and yelled: "Hey! Can you turn that down, it's like..." She looked at the clock expecting six in the morning, it was 9:30, "...too early to be up on a Saturday!" Roger obliged and turned the TV down. On her way back to her room she looked back at him and noticed him staring at her butt. *Even in a pair of pajamas. What a pig!*

Erin didn't get any extra sleep. Thirty minutes after she returned to her room, Tawnee knocked on the door and was invited in. She sat on the edge of the bed.

"Bonjour, Erin. Comment allez-vous?"

"Say what? Oh—tres bien...or some shit. Merci, et vous... or is it tu?"

"Sorry, that's the extent of my high school French."

"You know more than I do. I struggled with just finding the bathroom in a bar–Ou est les salle de bains?"

"Er-ah, I think you just asked for the kind of bathroom where you can take a bath and stuff, not the restroom."

"Great, I was asking where I can take a shower, in a bar." Tawnee laughed. Erin giggled.

"So, you're adjusting?"

"So far–do you mean time change or having Roger in the

living room?"

"Both, I guess."

"The time one, will be gone by today. The Roger thing is a lot more complicated. It just seems like Fabrianne should have been tougher with him."

"She is. He's our friend, yours too. We can't have him on the streets."

"It'd do him some good. He want's to be all political radical guy. Nothing makes you more political radical than sleeping on a park bench."

Tawnee laughed. "You're cold."

"I'm serious. How long are we supposed to let him stay? Until he sees me naked or I catch him masturbating?"

"Perhaps at the same time." They laughed. "I really feel for him though, your girlfriend and house in the same season."

"Whatever. If he does one weird thing…" Tawnee grabbed one of Erin's cigarettes off the milk crates night stand and lit it up. "Go ahead, Tawn, I don't mind."

"Hey, I'm helping you cut down."

"No chance of that, I'm back to three or four a day."

"That's bad."

"I know. When I left, I tossed all of my fasting out the damn window."

"What about the man thing? You get any?"

"Gee-zus! What's up with you and Lashell and me getting some?"

"That a no?"

"No, it's—there are other things to do on vacations besides get laid! What about you? You get laid while I was gone?"

"Matter of fact I did–but back to you. Who was it?"

"If I told you, I'd have to kill you."

"He was that ugly?"

"Sure, why not."

Fabrianne entered the room. "Morning, guys…" She lay on the bed and put her head on Erin's stomach. Erin started to play with the stripe in her hair. "…What were you talking about?"

"Erin won't tell me about her man action."

"Tawnee won't tell me about her man action, either."

"Oookay, what do you sluts want to do about breakfast?" They all laughed.

"Let's go to Buck Buck, Oink," Erin suggested

"That place is so crowded on Saturdays. I have no interest in waiting outside in the rain," Tawnee complained.

"Psychicmondogrooverama has started serving breakfast on weekends," said Fabrianne.

"Uhh," Erin said with uncertainty. *All of the people I want to avoid, all showing up at the popular cafe.* "Won't that be crowded, too?"

"I don't think so, they haven't advertised it yet. It's kind of on the down low, 'cause they don't exactly have a license to serve food yet."

I guess I'm supposed to be indifferent and confrontational to the troubles of my past. "Sure, whatever."

#

Fabrianne's old yellow Nova automobile transported the girls and guy to Psychicmondogrooverama. The rain apparently hadn't deterred others from making the journey to the packed cafe. Erin looked around at the many artistic decorations, some by her ex-roommate, Mary Joe. The tables were painted in wacky neon colors and patterns and looked more vibrant in the daytime.

Even though the rumor was they serve breakfast, they seem to offer nothing more elaborate than muffiny things. As much as I enjoy this scone, I'd rather have a cheese blintz or huevos rancheros. Erin scanned the room for enemies. The only person she recognized was a hippie girl that had hit her up for money in the park. She was able to relax. Tamara Etcheverria, Donna's sister and cafe owner, came from the back. *With the exception of the curly blonde hair, I can't see any family resemblance. Tamara has more of a longish face and a beak-like nose. Donna's face is a lot rounder and prettier, yet, Steiner pursued Tamara and shunned Donna's affection. They're such polar opposites. Maybe they don't really get along. Tamara's Bohemian lifestyle and Donna's trend-following uses their dead parent's money like*

Yin and Yang. Tamara's life would be my template if I came across large amounts of money, although there's something appealing about Donna's carefree highlife.

Fabrianne took out a cell phone.

"Holy shit! Not you too?" Erin complained.

"What? I'm not calling anyone, I'm just checking my messages."

"No, I mean you and Lashell both have cell phones! All of my friends have gone yuppie!"

"Tawnee has one too," Roger added. Tawnee gritted her teeth at Roger.

Erin opened her mouth and looked shocked. *He might as well had said she was actually a man.* "Oh-my-God, you too Bluto?"

"I think it's et tu Bruté," Fabrianne corrected while giggling.

"What ever! Who's ever heard of a goth yuppie?"

"Hey! I only got it to keep in touch for the business I'm starting. And look…" Tawnee took out the phone. It was black with a Halloween skeleton pattern on it. "…I'm still goth."

"What ever, my girlfriends are yuppies! What's next an SUV?"

"Fabrianne was looking at this used one that this guy down the street was selling." Roger snitched again.

This time Fabrianne sneered at him. "I was only interested because it was for a good price."

Erin put her head on the table." Oh, my lord, my girlfriends have become the enemy."

"Hey! I'm still down," Fabrianne complained. "Look at me: I'm eating in a hip hangout, I'm an artist, I give to homeless people, I recycle! What more do you want?"

"You know, the reason I didn't want to come here—I told you how the owner of this place's sister had a crush on Steiner?"

"Yes, and you blew her off and left her at a restaurant," Tawnee answered.

"Yeah, anyway, she was all into art, probably recycled and yet she drives a beemer and she thinks she's all down."

"You're just jealous 'cause they got good jobs. If you had money, the first thing you'd do is get a nice car," Roger inserted.

"Nice car is one thing, but a BMW is just showing off."

"What about where we live?" Fabrianne asked. "We're not living in some graffiti-ridden punk house in the bad part of town?"

"But that's different, we're renting."

"Big deal," Tawnee said. "To a person walking by, if they see you coming out of that house, the first thing they think of is 'look at that yuppie bitch, dying her hair orange trying to fit in.'"

"So you're saying Donna is just like us? I doubt it!"

"Why don't you ask her?" Roger asked pointing at Donna Etcheverria coming in.

Donna pulled the hood of her jacket off of her curly blonde hair and shook her umbrella dry. Following close behind was her mini entourage consisting of her male Korean friend, Kim Yi, and a redheaded female in her late 20's.

"Shit!" Erin said covering her face. *With my new hairstyle, not many people will recognize me. As long as Donna doesn't stop by the table, I'll be safe.*

"Hey! Donna!" Roger yelled. Erin punched him in the arm, really hard.

"Ow! What the fuck is your problem?"

"Why are you calling her over here?" Erin said through gritted teeth.

"She was in my class, idiot! She's my friend, too!"

Erin was about to tell him she had no interest in seeing Donna while twisting his right nipple when Donna walked over and prevented the vengeance.

"Hey Roger," she said patting him on the shoulder. "How are you doing?"

"Not bad. I got kicked out of my house so now I gotta shack up with these girls. Like Jack Tripper."

Donna scanned the table and did a double take on Erin. "Oh, my god! Erin?"

Erin turned her head and smiled, prepared for an attack. "Hi…Donna. How's it flying?"

"Oh, my god! Your hair! I didn't recognize you."

"Yeah, well…" *I have no idea what to say.*

"Where have you been? I haven't seen you in like, forever?"

I'm confused. Donna's being nice to me. Doesn't she remember the run-in at Halloween? "I was in Europe for a while."

"That's cool—oh, this is Amber Little Feather by the way." Amber smiled with a slight overbite. Everyone exchanged names and shook hands or waved hello. Amber's fingers were thin, making Erin suspect underneath the baggy rain clothes, she was very slim.

"Little Feather, is that Indian?" Erin asked.

"No, Cherokee," she responded.

"Right, Indian."

"Indians are from India."

"Oh…right. I forgot, Native American."

She pointed at Erin. "Correct-o"

"So, you and Roger are in the same house? That's so funny." Donna snickered

"Yeah…it's a scream."

"Where do you live?" Amber asked.

"Grandview."

"Well-well-well." Amber shook her head back and forth in a smug swagger. "Fancy."

At the same time, Erin and Tawnee said, "We're renting!" and then laughed.

"That's okay," Donna assured. "I just bought my first place. Matter of fact, I'm having a housewarming today." She reached into her leather purse and pulled out a pen and pad. She wrote her address and phone number on it and handed it to Erin. "That's my new address. The party starts at 4:44."

"4:44?" Fabrianne asked."

Erin showed her the address. "It's forty-four 4th Street." *Did she move there just for the cutesy address?*

"Yeah, ain't that awesome!" Donna bragged "So you guys should drop by."

"Maybe. Will Monroe and them be there?" *I have no interest in seeing a guy who I gave a hand job to.*

"Art should be there, but not Monroe. He…he has some things he needs to sort out and Peter has to work. Anyway, my table's ready. It was nice seeing you, Erin. Hope you can make it to the open house." Donna and Amber took their seat, far away from Erin's group.

Erin leaned forward and whispered. "So, what the fuck was that about?"

"What are you talking about?" Fabrianne asked.

"Obviously I didn't tell you that the last time I saw her I was so fucked up, I tried to jump in her car where I ended up getting into a fight with Peter. Before that, I ditched her at Bistro Alley to go hang out with Steiner, who she had or has a crush on!"

"So? Maybe she's a forgiving person."

Erin rolled her eyes at Roger. "I bet she's planning something. Maybe it's the wrong address. Maybe it's a crack house?"

"Or maybe you're all paranoid?"

"Whatever, Roger. You sure are gaining some eviction points."

"What are you gonna do?" Fabrianne asked.

"I don't know. I told myself, that when I came back, I wasn't gonna be afraid of people or make any more enemies. If I don't go, I'm all coward if I do go..."

"Bucket of pigs blood?"

"What"

"Carrie reference"

"Who?"

"Never mind. You should go. Especially if you're trying to smooth things over."

"I guess, you guys joining me?"

"I can't; going to paint the studio," Tawnee answered.

"I'm going to lunch with my friend Joann," Fabrianne said.

"Well, I'm going, but not with you if you're going to be acting like a spaz," Roger said.

Erin gave him a nasty look. "Right. Like you were ever an option."

After breakfast, the group split up. She chose to visit her mother at the hospital.

The rain tapered off enough for her to walk to University Circle. In the collective area of schools, she passed by the Neopolitan Academy of the Arts College. The building was large, white and plain. There were few windows and the only clue it was an art school, besides the brass sign, was a large rotating mobile in the style of artist Alexander Calder.

Erin visited the lobby. The large, echoing room gave further hints of an art school: Display cases full of various school projects, both commercial and fine, populating the area. Erin glimpsed at the 'Shoe' assignment. Various shoes, painted or torn apart and put back together, turned these ordinary objects into artistic statements. *I wonder what I would have done for that class?* In the commercial case, most of the graphic designs were lost on her as much as looking at ads in a magazine. *I'm sure the picture of the bottle of shampoo, set on top of a crop of red, glistening apples is well done and deserves to be on display, but to me, it's still just an ad.* Another display that caught her interest was the AV class video monitor showing a rock video completely made by the students and starring some local band she'd never heard of. *Now this is more like it!* The all male band, with hair in their faces, screamed and yodeled. *Those guys are cute. I wanna be in this class.* She picked up one of the 32-page brochures about the upcoming semester and departed.

After a muddy shortcut through a grassy field called Campus Greens, she arrived at the University of Neopolitan Medical School. She sat in one of the many uncomfortable fake leather chairs in the administration building, waiting for her mother to come down. During her 10 minute wait, she was able to read the entire section about the industrial artwork program. *Hey, it says even though it's important you graduate from high school, the most important thing they want is someone passionate about art. I like art and I like doing it, but I don't know if I'm passionate about it. I don't even own a sketchbook or know the name of that guy that splattered paint all over his canvas. I just want to make jewelry.*

Carolyn Callahan finally made her entrance. She did a double take after seeing her daughter. Erin laughed.

"Oh-my-lord!" her mother said, swiftly walking over. They hugged and kissed. "I didn't even recognize you!"

"That's the idea."

"Oh-oh, did you do something illegal in Europe?"

"Only in Amsterdam."

"Oh, my! So, how are you? How was your flight?"

"A nightmare, but whatever. My motto is: don't crash the plane, don't loose my luggage, everything else I can handle."

"I like your thinking. Have you had breakfast?"

"I just came from it with the gang."

"Do you mind if I grab something in the food court? I just need some coffee."

"Sure, no prob." The women started to walk to the food court. Carolyn ran her hand through Erin's hair.

"So your roommates didn't give you a hard time about running away?"

"No, everyone's been real cool. Even had a bike for me as a Christmas present."

"Shit! I forgot to bring your present to work."

"Mom! Don't sweat it. I'll get it from you later."

"Even Dan got you something."

"Dan, got me a Christmas present?"

"Hey! He likes you."

"I didn't say he didn't like me. I just think it's weird that he would get me something. I mean, he's not–you know."

"No, he's not your Father. Nor does he want to pretend to be. He already has one daughter, what does he need with two?"

"You didn't tell me he has a daughter."

"Yes, a little older than you–goes to Tech. Hey! Maybe you can talk to her about getting in there?"

"Mom! Number one: my grades couldn't get me into Tech as a janitor; number two, I have my eye set on the Academy." She handed her mom the brochure.

Her mother read through the brochure intensively, even when she was in line getting a latte at Coffee Barn. They took a seat next to the window. Eventually, Carolyn finished reading and put the brochure down.

"Well, seems right up your alley. One important question, how are you gonna pay for it?"

"Student loans. Job? I guess you're out as help."

"I wasn't giving you a hint. I'll give you what I can but I don't think I'd do your independence any good."

"I know, I know. I wasn't going to ask you for any money." *Actually, I was hoping you would at least give me enough for one semester.* "I'm gonna get a job too."

"That might work—Oh! I might have some people lined up who want to rent the cabin when it starts snowing! That should at least give you some pocket change." She sipped her coffee and smiled. "I think it's so great that you're going to school."

"I'm not going yet. I have to get a job first. You don't need any bedpan washers, do you?"

"Yuck, no! We do have an opening for a transcript assistant."

"Cool, that sounds fancy, what would I do?"

"Not as fancy as you think. You go through a stack of papers, read what the doctor has written in chicken scratch and try to translate it into English using a list of medical terms."

Erin made rapid snoring noises. "No thanks. That sounds kinda boring."

"Ooh-kay," her mother said slowly.

Oh-oh, I may have just called her own job, boring. "I just want something more challenging. Where I can do interesting things."

"Well, there is an opening for a chief radiologist, but I think you need more than the pizza place on your résumé."

"I'm not trying to be all picky, Mom. I'm sure that paper-pushing job is very interesting. But I think I need to start finding jobs related to the field I wanna go into."

"That's very astute of you. Any leads?"

"I just got back, give me at least a week."

"Right, of course." She sipped her coffee and stared outside at the rain soaked street, being used by Neopolitans, traveling to work in cars and on scooters. On the curb, medical students and patients waited to cross the street to the south campus. *Still waiting on the questions I'm sure that's on your mind: 'How was Dad and my brothers and how did the Thanksgiving meal go?'*

"Was Buster okay?"

"Huh? Uh, yeah, he was fine. Gained some weight. I think

they fed him too much."

"That's good."

There was a moment of silence. *At least show some interest in my adventures in Europe! She's being very evasive about something. Was it my leaving town without a warning? Or the time I spent in Newark? Surely she must be wondering what they all talked about. I'm not gonna help her out by bringing up the subject.*

"So, no one gave you any trouble for running off?" Carolyn said, breaking the silence.

"Not yet."

"That's good." She finished her coffee and stood up. "Whelp, I better get back to the office..." She held her hand above her head "...Got a stack of papers this high to work on."

They walked to the main lobby and hugged goodbye. *I didn't understand our conversation. I unexpectedly left town for a couple of months and the only questions are about dogs and roommates?*

#

She rode the rocking electric train back to Grandview. It seemed to purposely lunge and cause those unlucky enough to stand to almost fall. *I should visit Tawnee's studio. But, what if Lisa Ann is there? After what happened in Italy, I'm not sure if I'm brave enough to see her.* The train stopped in the tunnel near Kenwood station. This gave her the opportunity to actually study the graffiti on the concrete walls. Bold, heavy, colorful, abstract letters spelled out illegible nicknames, as figures, some realistic, others more cartoon-like, created a twentieth century Sistine Chapel.

These taggers have a better chance of getting into the Academy. They got the same amount of money as me but twice the talent. I probably can't double my talent but I can try to increase my finances. Mom's transcript job sounds boring, but it would pay a lot. Will I be working with her? That'll suck. Already feels like I'm gonna be working just to pay off Dad and Josh, is Mom gonna demand something too? She put her left foot up on her seat and rested her forehead on her knee. A wave of depression came over her. *Why do I feel so down? Perhaps it's the return to reality. Two days ago, at this time, I would be sitting in a cafe, sipping coffee and deciding if I wanted to go to the Rodin Garden or the Palace de Beau Arts. Now it's: getting into art school, paying for art school, paying Dad and Josh back…wondering why Donna was being so nice to me, and why Mom was so non confrontational.*

The train jerked forward, toward her home.

#

She didn't remember lying down on her bed wearing all of her clothes. At least she had removed her shoes before she came crashing down on her mattress. It was dark. Her lone window reflected the glow of the moon light off of the wall of the house next door. It had stopped raining and the clouds had dissipated, revealing a quarter moon. The TV in the living room was on and loud. She knew it was Roger. She skipped a confrontation with him and instead traversed the stairs to Tawnee's room. Tawnee was back from the studio. She sat on the floor of her room, rolling some clove cigarettes and listening to goth music.

"Oh, you're up," she greeted Erin.

"Yeah. I don't know what happened. I just passed out with my ass out."

"That's jet lag for ya."

"Sucks. Now I'm gonna be up 'til six in the morning."

"You need to get some wine in ya. Wine always makes me sleepy."

"We have any in the house?"

Tawnee laughed. "Booze? In this house? With the Great Unwashed living on our couch?"

Erin giggled. "You're right. So you wanna go somewhere?"

"I'll take you to my favorite place."

When Tawnee had said favorite place, Erin pictured somewhere within walking distance or at least a short train ride. Instead, it was neither close nor a short ride. After 35-minute train ride down South, they made it to The Cannery district. The Cannery was a lot different than the collection of abandoned warehouses and canning factories Erin remembered. The warehouse where she attended a rave was still unchanged, but the rest of the complex had been converted into live-work lofts containing shops, craft stores and restaurants. *I doubt the new residents will allow hundreds of people and 120-decibel house music ever again.*

In Grape Mex Texations, fake sombreros and maracas featuring corporate names, adorned the walls. They ordered an inexpensive pitcher of sangria, a bowl of avocado and vegetarian chicken soup and vegetarian molé. The soup was really good but Tawnee winced when she tasted the molé.

"Bad?" Erin asked

"I haven't had anything in my mouth that bad since a dentist drill."

"Ah, come on" Erin tasted it. "Yuck! Should we send it back?"

"Naw, I only come here for the sangrias."

Is this restaurant really any good, or is it just the closest place to eat near her studio? She felt a little down.

"What's wrong, Erin girl?"

"So many things: Gotta get a job, gotta get into school."

"You should talk to Neon; she can help you on both accounts."

"Probably."

"Speaking of art and jobs, my studio's right around the corner. You wanna check it out, later?"

"Uhh, maybe"

"Maybe?"

I don't want to say yes on the chance Lisa Ann will be there, working late. "I mean yeah…Is Lisa gonna be there?"

"On a Saturday night? Probably not. I'm sure she and Tony are out clubbing somewhere. It must have been a blast hanging out with them in Florence."

"Yeah…a real blast."

"Hmm? Did you guys get into an argument or something?"

"No, not rea…Yeah, something like that." *Saying yes is the fastest escape from her interrogation.*

"That must'a sucked. What did you fight about?"

"Oh, you know, stupid shit; the bottom line is, we shouldn't see each other so soon."

"That bites." Tawnee took a nacho chip, dipped it in a badly prepared guacamole and took a bite. "What about your friend that works at F.J. Pizza?"

"Pat?"

"I guess. The guy you hooked up with in England?"

"That's Pat. I saw him and Mimi in Manchester. I didn't stay too long though."

"Why's that?"

"Oh, I don't know..." Erin said sarcastically. "...Maybe it's because the first thing I told him was a friend of his was dead."

"Oh shit! That's right! You told me that, that must have been totally fucked up."

"It was. I mean I can understand him getting all upset that his buddy was dead and I'm telling him this right when he's on vacation. But he totally took it out on me."

"Did you tell him that you knew the guys that did it?"

"I didn't <u>know</u> the guys, Tawnee. I had run-ins with them; not like saying, some friends of mine killed a friend of yours."

"So, you told him?"

Erin looked down into her molé. "No."

"Jesus Christ Erin! Why not?"

"Because when I told him the other stuff he got all mad and the first thing he said was you came all this way to tell me this shit? Are you the Queen of Disaster? Do you get off on chaos or something?"

"That was mean."

"I know—and yeah, he was just pissed off and taking it out on me, but geez, imagine if I told him the rest?" Tawnee refilled their glasses of sangria. "I think Pat and I will patch things up, he just needs time to deal."

"And Lisa, what happened there?"

"That's—well..." She buried her head into her hands and sighed. "...Some things—I just don't want anything to get back to her."

"What did you do, sleep with Tony?"

Erin was silent.

"Oh my god! You didn't! Erin!"

"I don't want this to get back to her."

"As your house sister I can promise you it won't come out of me. But how? When? Why"

Erin gulped down some wine for courage. "How, is because of shit like this." She wiggled her glass. "The only thing I can say in Italian is un quarto litro per favore."

"What's that?"

"It's like ordering a little carafe of house wine, usually the cheap reds. Needless to say, it was cheap and I drank a lot of it."

"So you guys got drunk and had sex. Where was Lisa Ann during all this?"

"Oh, she was in the room with us."

"WHAT!" Tawnee quickly covered her mouth and looked around at the other diners staring at them. She lowered her voice to a whisper. "You had a threesome?"

"No," Erin whispered back, mocking Tawnee.

"You said she was in the room?"

"She was."

"What, was she watching you? Oh my god, is she a voyeur? I had no idea that Lisa was such a perv."

"It wasn't that organized. It all just happened and before I knew it, I'm fucked...so to speak. Or literally is the word I'm looking for."

"But why is Lisa Ann in the room? And what room?" Tawnee said, losing patience.

Erin leaned forward. "How much detail do you want?"

"You mean Ann Landers versus Penthouse Forum?"

"Exactly."

"How about edited Forum."

"Fine, instead of cock, I'll say pee-pee."

"Fine, whatever, go! Go!"

"So we're sucking down quarto litros and eating this kick-ass Italian food in a restaurant in Florence. And we're having a ball. We're like drink'n and smoke'n and eating fried stuff..." Erin waved her hands around to indicate mass consuming. "... and guys are hitting on me left and right. And there was this one guy in particular, fuck'n pulls his chair up right next to mine-talking about: 'How-ah you-ah want-ah go to party with me-ah? No?' and…"

"Sorry to interrupt, but that was the worst Italian accent—ever! Go on."

Erin paused and narrowed her eyelids "Anyway! Lisa's in the john so I can't use the old 'we're lesbians' thing 'cause if you're just by yourself, guys don't believe you."

"Right."

"So I lean over and put my arm around Tony and I say; ' I don't think my husband appreciates you talking to me like that.' And he's all: 'Husband?' So I reach over and kiss Tony and say: 'that's right.' So the guy books it out of there, and me and Tony laugh it off. But get this, Lisa saw the kiss…"

"Oh-oh!"

"Oh-oh! Is right. We both know that those two, in spite of the jabs at each other, really want to hook up with each other."

"Really?" Tawnee's face show disgust.

"Am I the only one? Come on Tawn, the name-calling is so Sam and Diane. They went to Florence together and were sharing the same hotel room?"

"Same bed?"

"Well…no, twin beds but still…"

"Sounds pretty platonic."

"Well, let me continue and we'll see. So she's all: 'What's going on you guys?' We tell her about the Italian guy and she jabs Tony with, 'He'd do anything to get a kiss.' and it didn't read like a joke. You could cut the air with a fuck'n butter knife."

"You think they made out?"

"Something must have happened between them at one point. Did they kiss, maybe? Sex? I don't know, but it was on the table."

The waitress came by and asked them if they wanted dessert or another pitcher. They refused both. "So anyway…" Erin lit up a cigarette.

"Uh, no smoking, Erin girl," Tawnee reminded her.

"Fuck! I swear every new mayor or president takes away one new right!" She snuffed out the butt and continued her story. "…So they do this back and fourth thing: 'Shut up punk rocker, die yuppie scum!' blah blah blah. We head back to the hotel; we're all buzzed. They're still doing the Sam and Dianne shit–gonna let me spend the night before I left for Siena."

"What's Siena?"

"It was this pretty little town in Italy; they had this kick-ass cathedral there—but anyway, back at the hotel room, which was small and old-looking. Kinda place you'd expect to see some Italian guy with a wife beater shirt yelling from the balcony 'Hey-ah that's-ah my-ah pizza—"

"Terrible!"

Erin laughed. "Okay, bitch, let's hear you do an Italian accent!"

Tawnee laughed. "I'm just kidding, go on."

"We're trying to figure out the sleeping arrangements. I kinda assume since I'm the guest they'll let me take one bed and they'll share the other–because they're roommates."

"Of course."

"But noo, more back and fourth."

"Sam and Dianne?"

"More harsh this time."

"Peg and Al Bundy?"

"I have no idea what show they're in but I'll take your word for it. This time it was: 'I'm not sleeping in a bed with him, he masturbates too much. And he was like: She's just mad 'cause I think about her face to <u>keep</u> from masturbating."

"Harsh…and a little funny."

"Major. So I get sick of them arguing and I just went to the bathroom, changed into my sweats and got into the bed away from the window. They see that, and she's all: 'Well, she choose your bed, you better get in there and fuck her.' I was like: 'Hey! Don't drag me into this!'"

"That was totally uncalled for."

"Yeah, so they call a truce–actually they just shut up. She gets into her bed, he gets into mine, er-ah his bed–we go to sleep."

The waitress gave the girls their bill; Erin used her nearly maxed credit card and took cash from Tawnee. "Now, at about 3 o'clock, she gets up and goes to the john. Tony reaches over and spoons me. I don't know if it's just to piss her off or what."

"Did you elbow him?"

"No, I guess I should have, but here's the thing. I don't know if I told you this but I've sorta known Tony since I started working at F.J. Pizza. He use to come in and we'd chat a little—nothing serious. We didn't even know each other's names. But still, back then I thought he was kinda cute."

"Ah, so you were enjoying it."

"Of course. The wine, food, Florence a cute guy spooning you."

"Did he let go when Lisa went back to bed?"

"He did, sorta. I had my hand on his and he was touching my bare belly. He did a slight pull away but I sorta kept his hand against me. But that's all I wanted! At this point, in America, I had lost my job, two relationships with two guys were game over, I was in a car accident and arrested, I got slammed by Pat in England; but here I was, in a romantic city, full of good-ass food and wine and being cuddled by a cute guy. That was enough right there. I was happy with that....And then came the hard-on."

"Oh, no."

"Oh, yes, he apparently was enjoying the cuddle a little too much. So it's against me and I don't know what to do. I'm not going to turn around and go at it. Lisa's fuck'n right there! I just sort of freeze. Time passes and it's still there and he's starting to slowly move his hand down into the pubes area."

"Did you let him?"

"Thing is, when I grab his hand, he moves his hard-on into my butt. When I move my butt, he takes the opportunity to move his hand down."

"How awful, why didn't you just clock him?"

"Did I ever tell you about the time I gave guys hand-jobs instead of fucking them?"

"You didn't!"

"No, but that's the state I'm in. When I drink, it's like, if I can get this guy off, then he'll leave me alone. I'm like the perfect model for why guys like getting a girl drunk."

"So you jacked him off?"

"No, he did a pretty good job himself."

"Eww!" Tawnee's face grimaced.

"He's using one hand trying to finger me while the others on his hard dick, rubbing on my lower back trying to lower my sweats down."

"Gross!"

"It wasn't as gross as you think. It was a little sexy…in a high school, juvenile, virgin boy kinda way."

"What's Lisa doing during this?"

"She's pretending to be asleep. I mean, our backs were turned to her but I could feel her eyes on us. And even though we kept it quiet as hell, she had to have been wondering: 'why do they keep moving around?'"

"How long did this go on?"

"Eventually he realized that his dick was not strong enough to lower my sweat pants and he moved his hand up to my tits and started squeezing while his other hand waggled his cock–er–ah, I mean pee-pee—on my lower back."

"Did he cum?"

"Yep, all on my lower back and sweat pants."

"Barf!"

"Yeah, very porno. So I got up, went to the bathroom, threw away the sweat pants, took a bird bath, came back and got into bed with Lisa Ann."

"What? Why did you do that?"

"I don't know. Tony's bed was all nasty, now. I had no interest in cuddling him anymore. I guess I was feeling kinda used."

"What did Lisa do?"

"She just kept her back to me all night, which was fine. I was not in the mood for anything but sleeping."

The bill was returned and signed. "In the morning, I got up really early, packed my bags and got the hell out of there. Tony was like: 'Where are you going?' I said my train was leaving at six, which was a lie; I was wandering the streets for three hours. Lisa didn't say anything, guess she was pissed at me. And I left. There you have it. From hand jobs to whatever fetish guys like coming on girls' lower back is called"

"Back jacking?"

"Oh–my-god! Really?"

"No, I just made it up."

Erin giggled.

The girls went outside into the cold misty air. It was a short walk to Tawnee's studio. The area used to be for cleaning and housing boats. Many identical storage garages with rusty roll up doors, had huge numbers painted on them. Tawnee's and Lisa Ann's was number 37. "I thought about calling it studio 37 but Lisa says it's too much like studio 54," Tawnee informed, jiggling her key in the lock until it opened. "You know, Erin…"

"What?"

"You have a real good memory."

"Sh-yeah right."

"You do, you <u>should</u> go to school."

"If I had a good memory, I wouldn't keep getting into fucked up sexual situations."

Tawnee rolled up the doors to reveal a 1000 square foot, freshly painted, masonite bricked room with a high ceiling. Various arts supplies, hardware, sculptures, paintings and other objects to be displayed, lay strewn about. Erin was in awe and envy. *To hear Tawnee talk about it, I never really expected it to be so artsy and…real.* "Wow! This is an awesome space!"

"Thanks. And check this out." Tawnee rolled down the metal door and walked over to a light panel. She flipped a switch. The room was illuminated with dots from a spotlight and a shimmering, spinning disco sphere.

"Whoa! That's awesome!" Erin spun around. "This will be great for parties!"

"We're gonna have an open house, sometime next month. Puff n' Stuff said he'd DJ"

Erin kept spinning around until she got a little dizzy and nauseous. "Oh-oh, better cut that out." She ended up on the opposite side of the room from Tawnee. In the corner, an area was separated by a large chain linked fence. She went to see the fenced in area. "What's this for?"

"I think it was some kind of storage thing. When we got here, there was all these old nets and fishing rods in there. We're thinking of using them as decorations at the opening."

"You could put naked guys in here and they could dance at the party."

"I like that; putting their asses and dicks against the fence."

"I'd show up for that," Erin giggled and studied the boxes of art. She couldn't really see anything in the flickering light. "Knowing men, they'll probably want to jack off on me."

"That's gross. Don't be so hard on yourself."

"I must have a sign that says act weird around me." Erin tried to climb the chain-linked fence. The openings were too small for her shoes. "You know, my ex-roommate Mary Jo had a studio in this complex too. I think she subsidized it with all that pot she sold." The thought of drugs gave Erin an idea. "Hey! Do you have any acid?"

"What? I thought you were all jet lag and shit? Why do you want that?"

"It's this room, all the lights and art. This would be the perfect place to drop a tab."

"I wish, but no. I haven't had acid since high school."

"Hey! We're near the Acid Pit! We can go there!"

"You mean they actually sell acid there? I thought it was just a name."

"It is. But it's a club–club equals drug dealers–drug dealers equal acid."

"I like your thinking Miss Pierce. Unfortunately, Acid Pit equals place you got fired from and said you'd never step foot into again."

"They hang out in the parking lot...I think. C'mon, let's go."

"Are you sure? What happen to your dry spell?"

"Who cares? Lot good it did me. Still fucked up without alcohol or drugs."

"How did you fuck up?"

"I should have never told Pat about his friend, I should never have got in bed with Tony and there's some other stuff in France."

"Other stuff?"

"Later—my point is, shit just follows me around."

"Maybe you're putting off some freaky vibes that attracts freaky guys."

Erin grabbed the fence. "Whatever. Maybe I should just be a lesbian."

Tawnee laughed. "You? A lesbian?"

"What? I could be."

"I don't think so."

"And what, are you an expert now? Oh, that's right, you said you use be one."

"I didn't say I <u>was</u> one. I said I thought I was one...You see, you remember everything."

"Stop trying to change the subject. Are you gay or not?"

Before Tawnee could open her mouth and explain, the metal roll-up door started to rise. Erin's immediate response was: *police! They know we're thinking about buying drugs!* She ran to the back area and hid behind a large metal utility shelf. The door raised just enough for two silhouetted figures to walk underneath it. Erin craned her neck around to see who it was. Their voices were a better identifier.

"Tawnee? What are you doing here? And in the dark?" Said the voice of Lisa Ann.

"Just checking on things? What are you doing here?"

"I wanted to show Steiner the space before we see The Angry Hand Job show at the Pit."

I could tell that was him even before she said 'Steiner'. There's only a few idiots who'd be wearing shorts in the winter.

"Hey, you! Haven't seen you since the party," he said to Tawnee, giving her a hug. Tawnee half hugged him. And looked back at where Erin was hiding.

Lisa walked over to the light panel and cut on the rest of the lights. "Oh cool, you finished painting!"

"What is that, fire truck red?" Steiner asked.

"Something like that," Tawnee answered looking back at Erin again."I'll be back, I gotta dump something." Tawnee walked towards the hidden Erin.

Erin searched for an exit. *Can't say I like being referred to as something to dump..*

Tawnee guided Erin away from prying eyes, to a back exit to the outside.

"Oh-my-god! I don't believe–the two fucking people I want to avoid in the whole city and they show up at the same time!" Erin loudly whispered.

"What about Kevin?"

"Kevin? He better be the one watching out for me—tell me to fuck off? Bastard! But for real, why are those two hanging out together?"

"They know each other. Why wouldn't they?"

"Are they dating or something?"

"What does it matter? Not like you're gonna be hanging out with one of them and then the other shows up."

"Oh my god! They are dating! Why didn't you tell me?"

"I don't know if they're dating. I've never seen them make out or anything. And again, what does it matter? This is one of the people that made you run away to Europe and a girl you want to avoid!"

"Yes, and now they've teamed up like the Legion of Doom, out to get me."

"Don't be so paranoid. They probably don't even talk about you."

"Tawnee?" Lisa Ann yelled. "Where's the fucking extension cord?"

"I'll be back in a minute!" she yelled back. She turned to Erin and talked in a quieter voice: "So, you want to wait around for me to slip away?"

"I don't know, I was really looking forward to the taking acid thing."

"We can still do that, just not here."

"I know. I think I'll just head on home."

"Are you sure? I just have to blow these guys off."

"No, you stay. You can spy on them and see what's up."

"Ahh, espionage. Okay." The girls hugged. "Are you going straight home?"

"I don't know, I might call Lashell since I'm down here."

Lisa Ann called for Tawnee again; Tawnee rolled her eyes in displeasure, waved to Erin and went back inside.

Erin was unable to find a pay phone anywhere in the complex to call Lashell. *Either the redevelopers hadn't yet reached that state or figured anyone who would patronize Grape Mex Texations or Das Haus Contemporary Furniture would have their own cell phone. I should have asked to use Tawnee's.*

The trip to visit Lashell aborted, Erin chose to go home and perhaps read until she fell asleep. During her journey to the NRT station she intersected the road that would take her to the Acid Pit. *I have no interest in dropping acid. But a part of me wants to see how things are at my old job.* She detoured toward the club. *I need to see it. It's not like I have any interest in seeing anyone I used to work with or any desire to go inside, but, unlike my living situation, local laws or the Cannery, I need to see if something I have a memory of is unchanged.*

The industrial warehouse looked the same. What was different, the marquee advertising the band: 'The Angry Hand Job', also Informed: 'Last Live Band Room Show Tonight'. *I'm confused. Surely with such a crowd lining up outside, they wouldn't have a need to close the band room?*

She got closer to the club, but not close enough to be recognized by the doorman, whom she recognized as Maxx from the boarding house she used to stay in. She asked a pale-faced blonde in the long line about the band room situation.

"They closed the upper rooms 'cause it was too expensive paying bands. Now they just use DJs," The girl informed.

I can't believe my ears. The Acid Pit was always the place bands strived for playing one day. The first stepping stone for a record contract. Now, it's gonna be a bunch of guys spinning records? Even this girl in line, wearing light blue jeans, is a sign of the Acid Pit's death. Anyone that would show up at the Pit, dressed like her, would usually be verbally assaulted by the staff and sent packing. What about the other clubs—

Gothica or Club foot? I feel like my mom complaining about how cheap ticket prices for concerts used to be.

#

Arriving home, she found Roger on their couch watching some political program on war atrocities. *If I had even a remote interest in watching TV, I know it'd be something light and entertaining.* She retreated to her room and checked her e-mails. There was one from Paul, her friend she visited in Amsterdam. He asked if she had made it home safely. *Shit, I forgot to tell him and Mr. Humphrey I'm back.* She wrote him and Mr. Humphrey. She added an apology to Mr. Humphrey for not staying as long as she wanted and for arguing with Pat.

It was 11:03 PM. In spite of three glasses of weak sangria, Erin didn't feel sleepy. She got dressed and went to the back patio. The sky was clear, aiding the brightness of the moon. She set a towel on one of the wet, white plastic patio chairs, sat down and lit up a cigarette. Grandview was quiet. Every now and then, she would hear a car honk or a large truck pass. The sounds were so faint she knew they were actually blocks away, closer to the train station. She inhaled a therapeutic lung full of smoke and glanced at her new bike, parked under the awning near the patio doors, covered by a blue, plastic tarp. "Why not," she said getting up.

After a wobbly start, she was able to get back in the groove of riding. *This thing only has three speeds and its weight feels like a small car; definitely not made for racing, traffic weaving or mountain biking. Guess my friends know I won't be doing any of those things. I haven't rode a bike in over five years. 'It's just like riding a bike,' is a crap saying. If things were really as easy to do as getting on a bike after years, then why did coming back home feel more like getting on a 10-foot tall unicycle?*

She pedaled around the Grand View neighborhood and cut over to Central City Park. As far as she could tell, the park was abandoned. The blue streetlights guided her safely through its tree-lined paths. *Probably hundreds of robber-rapists hiding in the bushes, ready to take my emergency burrito money. How many times did I walk to work through this park? How many times did I goof off? There's the spot where Kevin confirmed his gayness. For some reason, I feel like I should see a statue there. Like they would build a shrine that indicated: 'Here, on this spot, Erin Pierce began her downward spiral into the fiery dating pits of hell.'* She looked at the city lights reflecting off the duck pond. *Everything is the same and everything is different.*

She took another lap around the pond and rode on until she was in the parking lot of Central City Plaza, location of her old job. The lights were off at F.J. pizza parlor but next door at Café Olé, still on. Inside the cafe, her old supervisor, Tracy Kessler, drank a cup of coffee and, in spite of the new city ordinance, smoked a cigarette. *This is not a happy sight. She looks like she's sulking. Tracy's one of my heroines, always causing trouble if you screw her over. Maybe she had had a hard day at work? But a bad day for Tracy would be a rude customer that leaves before she has a chance to put a tampon in their calzone.* Erin walked her bike into the café.

Behind the counter, a dark haired girl with glasses looked at Erin and stopped carving some words into the wooden stool she was sitting on using a ball point pen.

"Can I park this in here?" Erin asked.

She looked at the bike, shrugged and said: "What-ever," before starting to write on her arm with the pen. Erin leaned the bike next to a rack of alternative newspapers.

Like the others, it took Tracy a few seconds to recognize Erin. "Holy Fucking shit!" she yelled. She arose from her seat and almost tripped over her table trying to hug Erin. "Your hair! Oh my god! Where have you been? We were so worried about you after Ed fired you!" Like the others, Tracy felt Erin's orange hair. *Hmm, Tracy's hair has some dark roots growing in.* "Wow, what did you do? Join a punk monastery?"

"I don't think they'd have me."

"Ho-ho! Up to no good on your sabbatical, huh?"

"Sometimes."

"So tell me about it. You sent us that creepy postcard from—where was it?"

"Musée Dupuytren in Paris."

"Yeah, whatever that is. Soo, in England, did you hang out with Pat?"

"A little...He didn't mention me when he came back?"

"He didn't talk much about anything when he came back. I guess it's because of Ned's death and he missed the funeral and all."

"How was it?"

"The funeral? Oh, the family had their own thing but the rest of us got together at the Oi bar and had our own gig. Sort of a wake. It was a blast...or as much fun as it could be."

"Right, right. How are you doing? Heard Barbara's the new Ass Manager."

"Oh, god! Let's just say that getting fired is the best thing to happen to you!"

"Nothing's changed, huh?"

"Got'n worst! Jeannie's a total pussy fart! I almost got physical with Barbara-Beyatch; even people under me are get'n on my fuck'n nerves. They're all these fuck'n teenagers who call anyone over 21 sir or ma'am."

"I guess the glory days are over."

"I'll say: No you, no Mary Jo, no Robert, no Lashell, no Doug, no Pat..."

"Wh-what? What do you mean, no Pat?"

"Oh, he didn't tell you? That's strange. Pat quit today, you didn't know?"

Erin's face turned pale. "What! Why?"

"Jeannie, believe it or not. She told him he couldn't wear a shirt that said: 'Xit Happens.'"

"Shit happens? That's kinda bold to wear, even in front of her."

"No, no. Shit was spelled 'X-I-T' and had a picture of some native guy on it."

"I don't get it."

"Me neither, but he told me that the 'X' was pronounced like S-H. So if we couldn't figure it out, how would a customer?"

"Is that what happened, a customer?"

"No, what happened was, he was explaining it to me and Jeff and she overheard him."

"And she fired him?"

"No, she was trying to be cool about it. She was gonna write him up for inappropriate or offensive attire. I mean, come on! Mary Jo, fuck'n wore tutus and fishnets to work and you used to wear that David Koresh shirt—what happened to that shirt?"

"Got burned up in a fire."

"Ironic."

"Very." Erin looked at a vagrant coming out of the men's room. He sat at a table, far behind Tracy, and started counting a huge wad of one-dollar bills. "Sounds like Jeannie was out to get Pat. That's odd, 'cause she used to be kinda cool…until she wrote me up and kept me from being supervisor—I take it back, that bitch was out to get me!"

"Out to get us all."

"So Pat quit 'cause she was gonna write him up?"

"After they argued a bit. But it was such a little thing, not worth get'n fired or quit'n over. I guess he'd just had enough."

Erin ran her right hand over her bristly hair. "That sucks."

"Yeah…but how about you, how was Europe?"

"I had a blast, I'm sorry to come back."

"Why did you?"

"Ran out of money, plus I was thinking of going to art school."

"Oh, cool! I didn't know you did art."

"Just some jewelry-making. I'm not interested in the other stuff."

Tracy took a drag on her cigarette and looked at Erin's bike. "It's cool that you have plans." She took a man's watch out of her patch-covered backpack, checked the time and put it back. "Did you get laid?"

"Gaah! You and Lashell."

Tracy laughed. "Well, did you?"

"What about you? When are you escaping from pizza hell?"

"Ha!" Tracy mocked laughed. "Where am I gonna go?"

"What do you mean? Before I left, you called and told me how J.J. and them could get me a job where they worked."

"Getting another job is no problem my dear, but where J.J., April and Spike work, they all have their own version of Ed. The only place I know with cool bosses, they don't pay enough."

"F.J.P. doesn't pay anything, either..." Tracy gave Erin a sinister look. "...Unless you're shaving off the top." Tracy guiltily looked away. "Oh my god Tracy, you're not!"

"Not exactly."

Erin raised an eyebrow. "Tracy?"

"I just lie about the price of the food to some customers I don't like. Add a nickel or a quarter to the total, if they're drunk, a dollar. End of the day when I do the register, anything over goes right in my pocket as hazard pay."

"Oh-my-god! That is so wrong...and yet brilliant–I'm torn."

"Me too, I'm addicted to it now. Always trying to see how much shit I can get away with."

"What's your usual haul?"

"Average day, about $10–record was $20. Lotta ripped off fuckers that day."

"Man, Trace. How long can you keep this up? If Jeannie catches you..."

"Whatever. She wants to fire the survivors anyway."

Erin was in a daze. *Ex-boyfriends, club closings, Pat freaking out and now a person I've always considered a rebel, now, just a common thief. I want to return to Europe. Money or not, why the hell did I come back?* Tracy talked some more about work. *Sure, I had trouble in Europe, but at least there I could be anyone. Here, I might as well be that stupid girl with the blonde dreads again. Nothing has changed. If not gotten worst. I feel depressed. I want to get away from Tracy but I don't want to be rude.* Tracy wrapped up the conversation and headed out. Erin followed.

At the register Tracy stopped and talked to the girl behind the counter. "Shawn, you didn't hear what we were talking about, did you?"

"Sure did. I'm tell'n," Shawn answered sarcastically. She continued filling in the graffiti she had carved into the stool, with the ink pen. *I wonder if Tracy would do something horrible to her to keep her secrets?*

Tracy laughed. "I already know what you guys do over here..." She turned to Erin. "...They fuck'n void shit out of the register."

"Only when they don't give us raises," she answered in a coquettish manner, still looking down at her artwork.

"Their boss is a total cheap-ass." *She's making an excuse for Shawn in a way to make an excuse for her own stealing.*

The girls went their own paths. Erin rode her bike South towards the river. *I never noticed how the streets on the North Side have a slight hill to them. I feel like the city is pulling me along, all I have to do is occasionally rotate the pedals.*

It was cold. The windchill factor of the ride was making her fingers feel a little numb. When she put her hands in her armpits the bike started to sway toward the curb. She quickly grabbed the handlebars and alternated her hands between armpit and steering.

The old Victorian houses became less renovated the further she got from Central City and toward East River Valley. Although the projects were long gone, some blight still remained: Abandoned furniture, cars, shopping carts and articles of clothing littered some areas. The closer she got to the alternate shopping area, things became a little cleaner. A Moose Juice smoothie bar, a Coffee Barn cafe and a deli she'd never heard of all announced their future intentions of being built by spring. *Odd, a mainstream café like Coffee Barn would even consider setting up shop at such an early stage; guess they know something I don't. Wait a sec, I know where I am...*There, rising like a big grey monolith, the Forty-four 4th Street lofts, and the home of Donna Etcheverria.

Erin looked up to the huge windows of the gray cube. None of the residents had curtains or blinds. *Do they want people to see all their stuff?* There was music coming from one of the four units. *By my guess it's at least 1 AM. Donna's party has been going on for eight hours, fifteen minutes! I'm sorry I missed something that can last that long.* A figure came out on to the balcony and looked down; it was Donna, holding a glass of something. Erin was about to scurry before Donna had a chance to recognize her; it was too late. Donna leaned over the balcony and zoomed in on Erin's identity. "Erin?" she called out. Erin took her foot off of the pedal.

"Er-hi, Donna," she said sheepishly.

"What are you doing down there?"

Crap! She saw me. "Uh-er, I just got out of something. I thought I'd come by and see if your party was still going."

"It's just a few of us left right now. Earlier, there were like 50 people here."

"Wow, I'm sorry I missed it. Oh well, I guess I better head ou—"

"You don't have to go, we still have drinks and some snacks."

"Oh no, I wouldn't want to..."

"Don't worry about it. Come on up, I'll buzz you in." Donna left the balcony. Erin looked around. *Is there an escape route around here? What is she up to?* "Bucket of pig blood," she muttered, finally understanding Fabrianne's Carrie joke.

She carried the 50-ton antique bike up two flights of stairs. *For the amount of money they pay, you'd expect the tenants to have an elevator—screw the handicapped! What were the architects thinking?*

Donna was waiting at the top flight. *Hmm, no weapons.* Donna looked at Erin's bike as if it were a large muddy horse. She promptly instructed her to leave it in the hallway.

After an awkward hug, Donna gave Erin the 50-cent tour. The inside looked like a modern museum, furnished by Ikea. It had two levels. The upper level bedroom loft was over the dinning room and living room.

Through the large windows, Erin could see the lights of South Neopolitan and imagined that during the day one could see the river. *I like this! If I had this view, I would spend half of my time staring out and thinking. That black bathroom was large enough to swing a broom in. But the kitchen is smaller than the one in my house. Without any walls, I can't tell one section from another. I'll take Donna's word for it when she pointed out the office and dining room.* Ending the tour in the conversation area, she was introduced to the leftovers of the larger party. One, she already knew, Quincy Zeitheit, the 40-years-old, longhaired music critic. She didn't know him through acquaintance but by his column in the alternative newspaper: What Weekly. *I heard he still lives with his mom.* The second and third guests she had seen this morning: Amber Little Feather, and Kim Yi.

At the same time Amber said, "Well, hello," the CD player started playing a down tempo rap song a lot louder than Erin would ever dare to torment her next door neighbors with. "You're the late bird."

"What?"

"As in early bird?"

"Oh, yes. I just got out of something."

"Like what?"

"Huh?" She looked at the tiny silver speakers on the bookshelf. *How can such a loud sound come out of those tiny little speakers?*

"What did you just get out of?"

None of your damn business? Kim was looking at her as well, waiting for an answer. "Funeral." *Maybe that'll shut her up.*

"Oh, I'm sorry. Who died?"

"My innocence." *Why did I say that?* For a second, Amber and Kim stared at her, and then each other. Amber broke out laughing. Erin fake laughed to play it off.

After an hour of drinking a glass of Cabernet, Erin felt warm and a little relaxed. *I have no idea how much Donna paid for this couch, but it's not resistant to red wine stains.* Before Donna could notice the small red dot, Erin had placed a pillow over it. Amber finished talking about the discovery of her Cherokee heritage. Apparently she'd had no idea she was a Cherokee until last year, when a long lost relative came to visit. *Amber is as much Native American as I am Irish. Her last name is Schulman.* Every paragraph of Amber's cultural exodus was interrupted by Zeitheit, who would either make an inappropriate joke or try to connect the subject back to his own life. *Donna and Kim have their own conversation going. Kim never joins in the group conversations and they never include him. As far as I'm concerned,*

Donna's the only one that speaks to him. I've never sensed any romantic connection between those two. If anything, he's a celibate asexual or a closeted gay nerd.

At 1:58AM she felt a little sleepy. *I'm finally getting tired. Is it the wine, like Tawnee said, or is it the endless bragging of Zeitheit? No one asked me about my life or what I did for a living. This takes away any guilt for leaving.* She interrupted Donna's story about a fashion show for cats she wanted to go to.

"You're leaving?" Donna asked.

She acts like I was supposed to spend the night. "Yeah, I have to ride up that big ass hill."

"I'll take you."

"What?"

"I'll take you. You live in Grandview, right?"

"Uhh, yeah."

"Then I'll take you."

"You don't have to do that."

"I've been inside for a million hours, I need to stretch my legs."

"In your tiny beemer?"

"I traded it for an SUV…Probably should get some plastic bags to cover your tires though…"

Heaven forbid if you get mud on a Jeep.

"If you're heading, maybe we should head out too?" said Quincy.

"That doesn't make any sense. I'm coming back–this is my house," Donna complained.

"Well, it is pretty late, and I'm having breakfast with E.F. Laura," Quincy further informed.

He was looking for any excuse to leave.

"Yeah, I gotta be at work by 11."

"Oh…okay," Donna said sadly.

Donna looks like a stink bomb had been lit and thrown onto her wine stained couch. Hope she doesn't blame me for sucking the life out of the room.

Kim asked Amber if he could get a lift. *Yep, they've all been waiting on a smoke screen.*

On the descent down to the garage, Erin realized she hadn't bought Donna a gift. She lost all guilt when Donna asked: "Is it true you slapped Steiner?"

"What?" Erin played dumb.

"At his birthday party? I heard that you slapped him."

"That was his birthday party? Oh shit! I feel guilty."

"So, it's true?"

"Yeah, but I slapped him 'cause he called me up and said he was gonna kill himself. I drove all over town only to find him throwing a party."

"So it wasn't because he was cheating on you or anything?"

"Oh, I'm sure he was cheating on me. But we were never really dating, so I can't get mad about that."

"Oh…"

Did she invite me up just to ask me about Steiner? "Why? Did he say I slapped him in a jealous rage?"

"Oh, I didn't talk to him. I heard it from someone else."

Erin returned home at 2:21AM. The living room was dark, except the glow of a TV. She knew Roger was in there; no one else would be viewing a program featuring an Asian woman wearing a black, strap-on dildo, performing anal sex on a pigtailed blonde woman in a farm dress. Erin entered the darkened living room, walked in front of him and made a bee-line to the kitchen. *Why didn't I go into my bedroom? I must be in shock and not thinking straight. Not sure if it was the sight of Roger wrestling with his pants or that jingling belt, zipper sound that spooked me. Now I'm trapped in the kitchen. Okay, I need a knife to kill him or gouge my eyes out!* She came to the decision that anything involving a knife would be a bad idea. She choose to sit down at the kitchen table and think. *Okay, what to do? Maybe he wasn't doing what I thought he was doing. Yeah, right, then why were his pants down? Maybe he was getting ready for bed, or peeing on the carpet. Possible, but not while watching a porno!* She shivered in disgust. *Okay, this is what guys do, being the disgusting pigs that they are! It's no big deal. He won't do it again and we won't ever talk about it! How do I get back to my room without walking past him?* There was only one exit, which led back into the living room. *I should crawl through the window onto the patio, hop over the neighbors fence, go through their yard to Walnut Street, walk a block back around to Chestnut Street and re-enter through the front door. Hmm, dirty dishes in the sink. I'd have to step on, move or wash those to open the window, fuck that!*

The problem of escape solved itself. The front door opened and closed. *He left. That saves us both embarrassment.* She remained at the table, unable to move. *I've had fantasies where a bunch of oily muscled guys are masturbating in front of me, but like most fantasies, if you bring it into reality and use stand-ins, it throws a bucket of ice water on it.*

As if she were checking for wolves in the living room, Erin slowly crept out of the kitchen. The TV was off as was the empty VCR. *Whatever cinematic masterpiece Roger was watching is now with him.* She ran into her bedroom and slammed the door. She caught her breath and lay down in hope the night of excitement had exhausted her and would cause an end to the insomnia. It was true she was tired, but she felt too tired to sleep. She tried an assured cure, reading. After cutting on the radio, she settled down with a book about the history of jewelry-making. In the section about Mexico and the Mayans, they mentioned words like Xel-Há and the pronunciation of 'X' pronounced as 'Sh.' "Ah-ha," she said. *I knew I'd seen that before. Pat must have been wearing a Cancun T-shirt.* She turned the page to the section about India. "Poor Pat..." she sighed. "... Poor Tracy..." She closed the book and lay it on her chest. "... Fuck 'em...Poor me." She yawned and shortly fell asleep.

Part Two
The Friend Zone

If she folded the wings a little bit more, Erin might be able to get the paper airplane to make it all the way to the wall. When she tossed it, it nosed dived like the other two and landed two feet to the right of the metal garbage can. Erin sighed. It wasn't a sigh in response to her failure, it was from boredom in its purest form. She spun her chair around and looked at the bulletin board. If she had any interest in anything remotely medical, she was sure the note announcing a seminar on geriatric calcium degeneration would hold her interest, but it only made her feel a little dumb and more isolated.

She would sacrifice half of her pay to have a window in place of the cork scenery. This gave her the idea to take a break and look for an actual window. She had to find out if the weatherman had been wrong again. *But, what does it matter if it snowed or not? If the roads get really bad, they'll probably cancel classes for the day-but so what, I'm not a medical student. What did they call me at orientation? 'The Administrative Support Team.'*

On her desk was a stack of papers. *If I were doing my job right, there wouldn't be any papers there at all.*

She looked at the stack she was supposed to sort through. It was a simple task. The work didn't require too much brainpower: Read the doctor's handwriting in the patient diagnosis lines, look in a big book to see if she could find a symptom which came close to looking like the doctor's chicken-scratch handwriting; enter the ailment into a computer spreadsheet program which she had no idea how to use, repeat. *If I make it through the probation period, I can toss paper airplanes all day and it'll be a lot harder to get me fired, than F.J. Pizza.*

The work was tedious, boring and lacked human contact, with the exception of seeing Agnew once or twice per week. To compensate, she had befriended another building hermit. Pamela Barlow worked down the hallway in Reproductive Sciences. Her job was just as tedious as Erin's and involved looking at pictures of cells on a computer screen, putting red dots on each cell and then exporting the dots into a program that counted the dots.

As far as she could tell, their jobs were part of their bosses' research or doctoral studies. One day, she imagined, their hard work would lead to a cure for a horrible disease of some sort. At which point, their bosses would receive huge awards while the temps would get laid off because the research was finished. Erin walked down the hallway to visit Pam. She passed an elderly Black nurse who nodded hello to Erin after taking a glimpse of her security badge. *If it wasn't for this badge, I'm pretty sure my orange hair and 'Hot Rod God' T-shirt would alert the insecure security guards.* She peeked into the Reproductive Sciences lab. Test tubes, Bunsen burners, centrifuges and computers created a lab which would impress Dr. Frankenstein.

I can't see Pam. I know she's in here somewhere, surfing the web or playing a video game of some sort. "Pam?" she called out. There was no response. She called out again. There was a rustle as if Pam were getting up fast. She appeared over a chicken egg incubator machine and had a very surprised look on her face. Pam had a tough-girl appearance, which even she described as a 'Robert Crumb' type, after the style of the underground cartoonist who loved to draw tall, thick Amazon-like girls. She wasn't that much taller than Erin but she was built in a broad, borderline plump way and always sported big clopping motorcycle boots. When she discovered the visitor was Erin, her faced relaxed. "Hey!" she said.

"What are you doing?"

She walked over to Erin. "I was catching some Z's I fuck'n didn't sleep at all last night. My fuck'n neighbor was having a fuck'n orgy or something.

I like the way she uses 'fuck' for everything. "Sup, man?" she asked Erin.

"Not much, just taking a break. Wanna see if it's snowing?"

"That's cool. I love when it snows, cars skidding out and shit. Last year, saw this guy fuck'n mosh <u>right</u> into this homeless motherfucker."

"Oh my god! Was he all right?"

"The guy or the hobo?"

"Hobo."

"I don't know, maybe. He got up and kept on—whatever."

"When I was growing up in Jersey, when it snowed, it was always a big deal–school closed, accidents–shit like that. Here, people don't even slow down."

"People in Neo are always in denial, like those fuckers you see wearing shorts n' shit–what's up with that?"

"Sounds like my ex boyfriend, Steiner. You know him?"

"No. Hey! Lets go to the eighth floor. Bet you can get a good view from there."

The girls left the lab and took the elevator to the top floor of the East building. As Pam had predicted, looking through the hallway window, though slightly blocked by a soda machine, was an exceptional viewpoint. The sight offered a twinkling show of multicolored city lights and flowing fireflies of cars moving along the streets. A small part of Downtown North could be seen. The clock tower's glow was like a giant orange beacon whose purpose was to attract the tourists to the shopping district like moths to a light bulb, or a lighthouse repelling the poor from the rocky shores of its high priced stores.

"Rad," Erin said, summing up her opinion of the view.

"Yeah," Pam agreed. "Too bad you can't open this window. Some fucker probably flew out of here one time."

"Probably."

"You ever try?"

"Try what?"

"Bailing?"

"You mean suicide? No. I mean, I thought about it but never came close." *Except that one time on the bridge.*

"One time, I stole my moms Valiums and took some and they caught me, so instead of saying I took them to get fucked up, I said I was trying to kill myself, so they sent me to one of those troubled teen rehab camps."

"Oh, my god! That's awful."

"Yeah, I ended up running away with this guy. Lived on the streets for a summer before the fucker got himself busted for selling weed."

"So you got picked up, too?"

"No, I moved back home."

"Parents must'a been hell'a pissed, huh?"

"Naw, naw. They were glad to see me. That was one fucked-up summer."

"Sounds like it. Man, I thought my life was messed up, yours is like sucks-on-5th-gear."

Pam laughed. "Can be, can be."

They stared outside for a few minutes. Erin could see all the way to the hills; the air was very clear and crisp. Nothing indicated a coming snowstorm.

"So, what are your plans after work?" Pam asked.

"Not much. Me and my friend Lashell are gonna meet with some girl that has a room for rent in North Depot."

"Hey! That's my 'hood!"

"Really? It's not <u>you</u> is it?"

Pam laughed." No! My roommate's great, he's a trip."

"Boyfriend?"

"Who? Allen? No, I love him too much to date him, you know what I mean?"

"Definitely." *Sorta like me and Pat. Been months since I last talked to him. Without him, I officially have no guy friends.*

"Why? Are you looking for a place? Roommates driving you 'nanas?"

"It's not for me, it's for Lashell. She's still living at home."

"Fuck that! Hey, you guys should drop by afterwards."

"We might. I'm not sure about Lashell, but I'll try. Where do you live?"

"Here..." Pam took a business card out of her fake leopard fur wallet, wrote her address on the back and handed it to Erin. Erin looked at the card. On the front, a cartoon of a red devil girl in a bathing suit typed away on an enflamed computer.

Above it, the words 'NaughtyLittleDevilGirl/Designs.com' also in red flaming letters.

"What's this? Are you an artist?"

"Sorta. I do web pages and shit like that."

"Well, what are you doing here?"

"Freelance shit's too sporadic—I gotta pay rent!" Pam looked behind Erin at the clock on the wall. "Hey, look! 6 o'clock. We-is-out of here!"

They said their goodbyes. Erin returned to her windowless office, retrieved her things and went to the Administration Building to meet Lashell.

Lashell was engaged in a lengthy conversation with one of her co-workers. *Hello, ready to go, Lashell?* After picking up on Erin's subtle clues such as rapping her fingers on the countertop, they were off.

As they had done every day in Erin's two weeks of working, Lashell would give her a ride before heading across the bridge. Today, they drove a little north to the suburban-like urban neighborhood. Erin read the roommate-wanted ad in the back of the free independent newspaper, What? Weekly. "Hey, Shell. It doesn't say anything about non-smoker in here."

Lashell furrowed her eyebrows. "You mean wanting one or being one?"

"Both."

Lashell let out a disapproving groan. "If she smokes, it's going to be strike one."

"You can't be too picky. This is the first apartment I've seen in your price range that ain't in the South or all ghetto"

"Ghetto or not, I'm not settling."

"Will you be okay if you have to stay with your mom?"

"Hey-ell no. I need a place of my own. You go to our house and it's all her: Her chairs, her TV. I opened the refrigerator and it's all shit she eats! Plus I can't bring a boy home. When me and P.J. were dating, we had to do it in his car!"

"Romantic," Erin said sarcastically.

"Plus, her hints that I should pay more money since I got a new job have been get'n more frequent. I mean, shit, if I have to pay more rent, shouldn't I at least be able to bring boys home?"

"Of course."

They rode past University Circle. Erin saw a brief glimpse of The Art Academy. *Can't wait to see the admissions lady tomorrow. Probably too late for spring semester. Not enough money, anyway. If I stick with this boring job, maybe I'll have enough by summer.*

After the university area, there was much change in the architecture from Victorians, hip cafes and coffee houses to stucco houses with patios on top of their garages, as well as auto fix-it shops and other car-related business. *Ugh, hate these garage houses. Looks like a lot of yuppies are starting to move out here— don't remember seeing the decks tricked out with sculptures and greenhouses.*

Lashell made a right off Orange Avenue onto Apple Road. "This where Steiner lives?" Lashell asked.

"He lives off Pear," she corrected. She looked back at Pear Street, as if she could see around the corner, down two blocks to his house. *And then what would I do with those super powers? What advantage would I get from observing him? So what if I could confirm that he and Lisa Ann are really dating?* She rolled her eyes at the thought that perhaps she was jealous.

"What's that address again?" Lashell asked.

Erin read the newspaper. "5124."

"Day-ng! Waaay the fuck out here!"

"Not too bad. I think you're still on the train line."

"She-it. I'm not rid'n that troop carrier to work. That's why I got Betsey." She tapped the dashboard of her Mustang.

"I miss having a car. So fucking cold I can't ride that bike anymore."

They passed a couple of liquor stores and check cashing places. "Oh-oh! B.L.O.W.U.P alert!" Lashell said.

"What's that?" Erin asked being shaken out of deep thought about finances.

"You don't read E.F. Laura?"

"Is that <u>that</u> drag queen writer in the Weekly?"

"Yeah, she...he's a trip. Talk'n about, you can always tell a bad neighborhood from the B.L.O.W.U.P. Factor: Bars on windows, Liquor store, Old folk's homes, White flight, Urban, Projects."

"Old folks' homes?"

"He's not saying they're bad, just that they always put them in poor neighborhoods. Probably because it's cheap to build in them."

There's like a liquor store on every corner. In Grandview, a liquor store would be an over-priced wine shop.

"I don't know...this is strike two," Lashell complained, looking at yet another check cashing store. "How many mother fuck'n check cash'n places do you need when ain't nobody got no job?"

"Give it a chance, Shell. Even the bad part of Kenwood is across the streets from lofts."

"You can talk, Miss Grandview. You already live in the perfect 'hood...'cept Roger."

"That's the story of my life, everything would be perfect, except whatever."

"You tell Fabrianne about him masta-bate'n?"

"No, not yet"

"What about Tawnee?"

"Yeah, she just laughed it off like it's no big deal. I mean, I can't go home unless I'm sure he's out or asleep; a prisoner in my own home."

"A prisoner in your own home would be an opposite problem. Is he pay'n rent?"

"No. I think he bought some groceries, but it's always shit I won't eat."

"Why are you put'n up with that shit? Show his ass the door!"

"Not that simple. Tawnee and Fabe feel all sorry for him. But, like, why should we have to suffer just 'cause he only wants to live in the North Side and can't afford it?"

"What about get'n his ass a roommate?"

"What? Like you?"

"Hell naw! Someone who already has a place."

"That's just it. Rogers such an asshole that he claims the people he's answered ads for were all hippies, yuppies, posers or whatever–always an excuse. I honestly don't believe he's answered more than two ads."

Lashell spotted the apartment complex address and pulled into the parking lot in front. The architecture appeared rather box-like and sported a red and yellow, 1960's style façade. "If this had a gate around it or bars on the windows, it could be housing projects—strike three," Lashell complained.

"Maybe it looks better on the inside."

"Look at that," Lashell gestured with a jut of her head in the direction of two Latino teenagers working on a Buick's engine.

"What? Those guys? I've seen worse. You've seen worse, in your own neighborhood. Long as they're working on that car, they ain't doing drive-bys."

"I was meaning that the one with the white shirt's pants are so low you can see his boxer bottoms, but I see where your mind is at, Miss Grandview."

"Stop calling me that! You know you were thinking the same thing!"

"Oh, just 'cause they ain't White they gotta be all Boyz in D Hood?"

"Don't start with me, you know that's not how I am!"

"We're all like that. It's just the level. I mean, you're cool with stuff and shit. But you ain't above being a little prejudiced."

"Bullshit! I'm the least prejudiced person I know!"

Lashell laughed while getting out of the car.

"What? I am!"

"C'mon, Erin, everybody's got something."

"Whatever! I'm the least racist person you know!"

"I didn't say you were a racist, just you make assumptions about people based on their appearance."

"Whatever—this conversation is over!"

"Ho ho, getting all testy eh? I hit a nerve?"

"What—ever!" *Cram it up your ass, Shell!*

#

Erin knocked for the second time on the door of apartment #301. She knocked extra hard, hoping this time the renter would hear them over the loud music. She looked at Lashell. *She looks like she wants to say 'strike four.'* Lashell twisted her mouth. *A part of me is totally enjoying her having to look for a place to live like I did last year. I don't want her to spend the night in a car or have run-ins with skinheads, but maybe it'll make her more sympathetic.* On the seventh knock, the music was turned off. There was a long pause. The peephole went dark and the door opened. A White female, in her late twenties, sporting a bleached, blonde, spiky hairdo, appeared. *She looks surprised. Is this the right address?*

"Oh, shit! You're here," the tenant said. She put a broom and dust pan down and opened the door a little more. "When you left a message, I thought It'd take at least an hour to get here." She reached out her hand to Erin. "Lashell?"

Erin felt like laughing. *Do I look like a Lashell? If I said that, would Lashell make a racial issue out of that?* "No, Erin. This is Lashell." Lashell stepped forward and shook the woman's hand without smiling.

"Oops, I'm sorry. I'm Christine Richards. You can call me Chris. Nice to meet you, Lashell. I was trying to clean up before you came."

" 'S okay, least I can see how you really live."

"Oh, no-no! I was working on a project last night."

The living room was littered with cardboard boxes, spread newspapers, rolls of seamless paper, a lamp minus a shade and a large 4x5 camera with a flash box. *This room smells like beer, cigarettes, pot, and a hamster cage, covered by an outdated air freshener.*

"What project?" Lashell asked.

"I'm a photographer. See, that's my work." She pointed to the large, 30x40 black and white photo on the wall, dry-mounted on foam board. It was a gray cat nuzzled against a bare breast.

"Cool! Is that you?" Erin asked. "I recognize that from the Screw the NEA show last Halloween."

"Yeah—Hey! You guys want anything to drink? I got beer, wine, water…vodka?" Chris asked

"I don't drink," Lashell said rather coolly. Chris had a look of concern, as if she had insulted Lashell.

"Mix 'em together for me," Erin joked. Chris paused and then laughed. Lashell shot Erin an embarrassed look. Erin widened her eyes back at her. *Loosen up!*

After Chris had retrieved a beer for herself and Erin, they all sat down. Erin took a swig of her beer and looked around. Lashell sat next to Erin and crossed her arms. Chris turned the volume up on the stereo.

"Where are you from?" Chris asked Lashell

"South Neo."

"Really? Born and raised?"

"Uh-huh."

"Whoa, I think you're like the second native I've met since I've moved here. Seems like everybody's from someplace else. You too, Erin?"

"Me? Naw, I'm a Jersey girl."

"Been here long?"

"About seven years. You?"

"About three. Moved here from Atlanta."

"Oh! That's where Mary Jo was from, or was it Seattle?" Erin asked a bored looking Lashell.

"Oh, my God! You know Mary Jo Reece?"

"Sure, she was my ex-roommate."

"Right on, I love her! I haven't seen her in forever."

"That's 'cause she moved to Tibet."

"Tibet?" Chris broke out in a raucous laugh. "That's just like her! Crazy ol' Mary Jo. What did she do with that big bag of pot?"

"Oh, you know about that, huh?"

"You kidding? That shit was gold! We started calling her the Bag Lady!"

Erin laughed. Lashell's mouth corners stretched toward her jaw in disapproval. Sensing her boredom, Erin tried to steer the conversation back towards the roommate quest. "So, you need a roommate?"

"Oh, yeah, I forgot. Yes, let me show you the room." They all stood up. Chris led them down a carpeted hallway to a dark back bedroom. It was 144 square feet and had a huge, mirrored sliding closet door. It smelled of photo chemicals. There was one small window, too high to look out of.

"Me and my boyfriend used this as a studio."

"Oh? Someone else is still living here?" Lashell asked.

"Oh, no. He moved out a year ago. There's nobody here now. What do you think?"

"It's...nice."

Even my room has more light than this cave.

"Whelp, I guess I'll have to think about it," Lashell said cheerfully.

"Oh, is the price okay for you? You don't like the room?" Chris asked, acting worried.

"Oh, no, don't worry about it. I just need to check things out with my finances and stuff."

"Oh...okay."

She knows Lashell is lying

Chris lit up a cigarette to completely unseal the deal. "Oh, do you mind if I smoke?"

"Naw, it's yo house," Lashell said.

"So, boyfriend moved out huh? That sucks," Erin said looking at a black and white photo on the wall of a lily.

"Yeah."

"He a photographer too?"

"Naw. He was an artist."

"Bad breakup?"

"Dang, Erin! All up in her business," Lashell complained.

"I'm sorry. I'm just curious. I'm going to go to the Academy in the spring, wanna take their jewelry-making class. I just wanna know if two creative people can get along without ego clash," Erin apologized.

"No, it's okay. Things were great. We fed off of each other's creativity. We broke up for other reasons, but I have nothing against him."

"That's cool. It would be nice if I could be friends with my exes, but they're all assholes." *I'm feeling a little too open to Chris—*

I blame it on the beer. We should leave before I ask Chris about her sex life. "So, you ready to hit the road?" she asked Lashell.

Lashell acted caught off guard. "Uhh, sure."

Chris walked them to the door. They said their goodbyes and Erin thanked her for the beer. On the walk down the stairs, Erin started to talk about the visit, but Lashell shushed her quiet. Inside the Mustang, after the doors were closed, Erin started to speak again but Lashell interrupted.

"Oh-my-god! That bitch is so high!"

That's not what I expected to hear. "Wha-what? What are you talk'n about?"

"I thought for sure a crackhead like you could sense another drug head."

"Hey! Fuck you, I've never done crack!"

"I don't know if it's crack or whatever—all I know is that girl's on something."

"She seemed okay to me."

"That's what I'm talk'n 'bout. You smoke so much shit and hang out with people that take shit, you get used to it."

"So, I guess you're gonna keep on looking?"

"Oh, fuck'n please! Even without her strung-out ass, I ain't stay'n in that bat cave!"

They left the complex and started on their journey home.

Was Chris on something? How could I have missed it? True, her place was a mess and she seemed a little confused at times, but people say the same things about me. The car turned onto University Avenue. *Oh! Pam's address is near there.* "Oh! Drop me off here!"

"What? What are you talking about?"

"My friend from work lives near here. I said I would visit her."

Lashell pulled the car over, next to a bus stop. "How you gonna get home?"

"Well, they obviously have a bus here, or I'll take the train."

"Girl, the buses out here stop at 10 and that train must be a mile away."

"Well, you can come with me."

"No way! I've had enough socializing with pot heads for today!"

"Okay—bye!" Erin quickly got out of the car and started walking. Lashell pulled away and continued on home. Erin was a little angry. *She's so judgmental! Not everyone who drinks is a drug addict and just 'cause I'm afraid of gangs of boys with baggy pants, doesn't make me a racist!* She walked by a lube shop and then a gas station. *"I mean, I would be just as afraid of White boys in cowboy hats —whatever, Shell! Why do I always have to defend myself in front of her? It's like I can't tell her shit without her thinking I'm a slut or a crack whore. Glad I didn't tell her about Europe. Can't talk to Shell; can't talk to Mom; can't talk to Fabrianne—this sucks.*

When Erin reached a cross street, she realized she was in the 1500 block of addresses and Pam lived in the 100 area.

"Goddamn it! Pam must be 20 blocks from here!" She looked around, it was unclear for what. As luck would have it this road had a bus heading in the right direction. She ran to the metal sign with the blue letter 'B' for bus on it and caught the #77. *The driver looks disappointed that I made it, like the highlight of his night is leaving people who lose the race to the B sign—asshole!*

The bus lumbered south. The houses slowly lost their suburban look and the area became more and more like the University Circle area. At every stop, students clustered to board the bus. By the time Erin got off, she could see Neo Tech's campanile.

"Walking distance my ass!" she complained, back-tracking a block to Fig Street. The houses and apartments here were mostly from the 20's and 30's and some had columns. *This place would be more to Lashell's liking. Not only is there no B.L.O.W.U.P. factor, but the low pants youth are young academic types.* She stared into Trotsky's Cafe. "This is not North Depot. What was that bitch thinking?"

Pam's building was a three-level Latin Quarter style. It looked like it'd be more at home in New Orleans.

Erin pressed the downstairs door buzzer. Pam immediately responded. "Hello?" Pam said over the intercom before laughing.

"Pam? It's Erin."

"Far out! Hold on, let me buzz you in." There was more giggling and a guy's voice in the background. *Is this a bad time to visit? She having sex?* The door beeped and Erin went through an iron gate and climbed the stairs. She forgot to ask which apartment to go to. Each floor had only two doors so she assumed the open one would be Pam's. The gamble didn't pay off. As she entered the first open door, there was neither Pam nor a guy, but a frizzy haired woman who had just put a guitar case down and was returning to close the door. "Oh shit! I'm sorry," Erin apologized, more startled than the woman who remained calm.

"No prob," she said, slowly closing the door.

Erin quickly continued climbing the stairs. *Well, that was embarrassing.* There was another open door. This one she cautiously examined. "Hello?" she announced, slowly peeking inside. When she looked to the right she screamed. Her scream came before confirmation or identity of any threat. She saw a large white thing near her. A nanosecond later, midway through the scream, her mind reacted by jerking her body away from the object. At the end of the second, she identified the white as the head of a rabbit, an Easter bunny style with a smile and large cartoon-like eyes. It was a mask, which didn't make her feel any safer. "Oh shit!" she yelled. When she saw Pam appear from the other side of the door, she relaxed a small amount.

The rabbit laughed and apologized: "I'm sorry," it said, in between giggles. Erin realized she had been the victim of some sort of practical joke. She'd never liked practical jokes, because she was so gullible. Everything from whoopee cushions to a fly-in-a-plastic-ice-cube had bested her more than once.

"We're sorry, we couldn't resist," Pam apologized.

"It was her idea," the rabbit said, removing its head to reveal the human inside. It was a light-skinned Black guy. He wore small round eyeglasses, a 5 o'clock shadow of facial hair, and the hair on his head was in tiny braids. He reminded Erin of Donna's friend Duncan, whom she had suspected of being prepped to date Lashell.

"You scared the shit out of me!" Erin complained, holding her heart like it was going to stop.

"I'm sorry," he apologized again.

From Pam's laughter, she had obviously put him up to the prank. "What is that?"

"It's a prop for a movie we're making. It's sort of like the Easter Bunny goes ape shit and starts offing other holiday icons: Santa, Saint Paddy, etcetera."

Erin laughed at the concept. "Rad! I didn't know you guys made movies. *Actually I don't know what you do, considering I don't know you.*"

"Yeah, we were going to film some scenes tomorrow but the weather man said it might snow."

"I think if it snows, you should film anyway," Pam interrupted. "When you kill Monroe, all that blood on the snow—fuck'n kick-ass!"

"Monroe?"Erin asked. "Is he a blond-haired guy that wears glasses?"

The guy looked puzzled. "Er-yeah?"

"Oh, my God, I know him!"

"Really? Cool."

"Well… not so cool. Not on good terms."

"Really? What, did you guys date or something?"

"Is that what he said? What else did he say about me?"

"I'm not sure, considering I have absolutely no idea who you are."

Pam laughed. "I'm sorry. Erin, this is Allen. Allen, Erin"

They shook hands. *His hands are softer than most men's hands I've shook. He ain't no construction worker.*

"So, how did that thing go with your friend?" Pam changed the Monroe subject.

"Oh! You rat!"

"What? What did I do?"

"You told me that you lived in North Depot."

"I do."

"No you don't. This is University Circle. That girl's house was fuck'n 90 miles from here, past the patio houses."

"But this is <u>still</u> North Depot."

"I don't think so. I saw students, coffee houses and shit."

"But it's still North D! Am I nuts?" Pam asked Allen.

"Yes, yes you are nuts. And you are both wrong." Allen put on a fake British accent: "This is the up and come'n University North or South Depot, luv. Depending on which real estate agent you listen to, eh?"

"Man, I go away for a couple of months and they create two new neighborhoods," Erin said setting her backpack onto the floor.

"Really? Where'd you go?"

Pam spoke with her own fake British accent: "Erin's been across the pond. Liv'n the 'igh life, guv'na"

"Really? Did you go to Paris?"

"Sure. I love Paris."

Allen excitedly grabbed her arm. "Me too! You see, <u>Erin</u> liked Paris," he said to Pam.

Were they talking about this earlier?

"Hey! The people were fuck'n rude and smelly," Pam complained.

"She went in the summer, as a kid, when the local's are on vacation and it's full of sweaty fat tourists," Allen informed Erin.

"I've only been in spring and winter," said Erin. "The people were about as nice or smelly as they are here."

"That's not saying much," Pam complained. "Anyway, getting to my original question, how did that thing go with your friend?"

"What friend?" Allen interrupted.

Pam did a mock scream of frustration.

"What?"

"Fuck'n stop interrupting!" Pam complained.

"Hey! I'm more curious about her dating Monroe."

"Gad! "Erin expressed shock at Allen's gall.

"You'd have to excuse him, Erin, he was born without a tact gland," Pam said putting her hand on Allen's shoulder.

"Hey, it's not like I have a job interview with her tomorrow," he countered.

"So, what if she were someone you were try'n to pick up?"

"Anyway!" Erin jumped in, "...the room was too dark and only had one window. I thought the girl was cool, but Lashell didn't like that she smoked and thought she was on crack."

"Lashell? Is she a Black girl?" Allen asked

"And what makes you think she's a Black girl?" Erin raised an eyebrow.

"I don't know, same reason you don't see White girls named Mai Wong?"

"But your name's not Tyrone or Leroy?" Pam injected.

"True, what's in a name? It is not hand nor foot..." Allen got on one knee and grabbed Erin's hand. "Am I not a Capulet and you a Montague?"

Erin looked at Pam. "Is he always like this?"

The threesome departed to get some beverages at The Cafe Across the Street, which actually was its name. Erin learned a little more about Allen: He had graduated from the Art Academy, worked at Van Go's Art Supplies, made his own home movies and self-published his own comic called XampireX Mutants of the Apocalypse. Although he had gone to the Academy, he didn't know any of Erin's roommates or ex boyfriends.

"Different world," he explained to Erin.

"I can't believe you don't know Steiner. I thought everybody would know him."

"He doesn't know who Allen Montgomery is, why the hell should I know him?" Allen said.

"That's the second time I've heard you mention him, tonight..." Pam said to Erin. "...Are you like totally obsess-o over that guy or something?"

"No! It was just one of those things—it's a long story,.Maybe over tea instead of coffee." She sipped her latte.

"Must'a been a real ass-kicking. I can relate," Allen said.

"It was." *The tone in his voice hinted of actual sympathy. It's been a while since a guy was nice to me without trying to trick me into sex.*

"So you guys broke up and now you're looking for a place to live?"

Pam tapped Allen on the back of the head. "No, dildo! The apartment is for her friend...Laqueeda?"

Erin laughed. "No! Lashell!"

"Who apparently is White," Allen said, after sipping a watery Italian soda.

"No, she's Black."

"Is she cute?"

"Ah, you're into Black girls now," Pam teased.

"What's that supposed to mean?"

"I thought you didn't like Black girls?"

"I've never said that. I'm very open to all races!" Allen appeared insulted.

"Then why don't I ever see you chase after Black girls?"

"First of all, you've only seen me chase after Madam X and that girl that works at Last Chance Records, and second, I've never tried anything with you."

"That's 'cause I wouldn't let you."

This conversation has taken on a harsh tone. Before Allen could retort, Erin cut him off. "Who's Madam X?"

"That's what we call his ex girlfriend—can't say her name," Pam answered.

"Really? Was she your total obsess-o?" Erin asked Allen.

"It was the best of times and it was the worst of times. Then it just got worse and worser and worst."

Pam put her hand on his shoulder for emotional support. "Poor sweetie, that was a bad year."

"Like Erin said, over tea not coffee," he said tapping Pam's mocha.

Allen and Pam started to talk to each other about the movie they were making. It wasn't being made for money or to enter into a contest, they were just doing it because they wanted to. *I liked that, doing art for the sake of art.* When they discussed if they were going to film tomorrow, it reminded her of an earlier subject.

"So, how do you know Monroe?" she asked

"He works at Van Go's and he was my roommate right after my ex cheated on me."

"Oh, my God! She cheated on you? ...It is a she, right?"

"Good lord! Why does everybody think I'm gay?"

Pam laughed, put her arm around his shoulder again and kissed him on the cheek: "It's because you're so cute."

"Yeah, right," he said sarcastically. "It's because I'm not all abusive and Neanderthal-like. Maybe that's it? If I slapped Chris around a bit, maybe she'd stayed faithful."

"Naw, she would've totally kicked your ass," Pam informed.

A bell went off in Erin's memory. "Did you say, Chris?"

"Yeah...that's her. Why? Do you know her too?"

"I'm not sure. Does she have wild, spiky, white hair? Live in North Depot?"

"Well, I don't know where she lives, but I guess she could have dyed her hair. Was her last name Richards?"

"Yeah, that's her!" Erin said slapping the tabletop.

"Holy—fuck'n—shit!" Pam exclaimed, half laughing. "She knows your ex! And you know hers!"

"Monroe's not an ex! And I don't know your ex, she was the girl looking for a roommate."

"Holy shit—again! What are the odds?" Pam said to a stunned Allen. "How did you contact her?" she asked Erin.

"What Weekly."

"Ahh," Allen complained." Leave it to her to advertise in the most popular alt rag in town. Guess she's not too picky about who she gets."

"So, how's she doing? Did she look okay? How did her place look?" Pam asked.

"Hey!" Allen interrupted Pam's barrage of questions. "I have absolutely no interest in her life. You two talk when I'm not around!"

"Dude, you need to do an Evel Knievel and get over it."

"What the fuck ever," he said, crossing his arms.

Pam is being insensitive. She seems to always take Allen to the brink of anger and then pull back into kindness.

Pam put her hand on his back and gave a comforting rub. "Poor baby," she cooed.

"So, you work with Monroe?" Erin asked.

The trio returned to the apartment to watch one of Allen's films. It was a music video which had been shown on the local public access channel, consisting of black and white images of Allen, Monroe and a familiar, skinny, blonde goth girl, running around an old abandoned factory located west of the city. Not only was he an amateur filmmaker, but also a very amateur industrial musician. The soundtrack was a cheap Casio synthesizer, banging railroad spikes and a pounding drum machine recorded with a screaming baby backbeat. Although it was not Erin's type of music, she at least understood and therefore could appreciate the message in the videos. After that they watched a video which starred Pam and again the girl Erin recognized. In the science fiction story, Pam played a robot that could turn into furniture on cue, usually at the most inappropriate times, the funniest part being when she tried to disguise herself as a toilet.

"Who is that girl?" Erin asked Allen, while he bought freshly popped popcorn from the kitchen.

"Her? That's Sal. She also works at the store. She's actually my supervisor."

Erin didn't know anyone named Sal—or Sally, which she assumed it was short for. "She looks so familiar."

Erin laughed at the angry Pam on the screen, after transforming herself back from a litter box.

"I know, it's a little lowbrow, but we had to do it," Allen apologized.

"No, it's funny. I like your films."

"You should show her your porno movie," Pam suggested.

"Wha-what?" Erin said, raising the pitch in her voice.

"It's not my porno movie. I just took some scenes from a bunch of them and spliced them together. I noticed that they were all the same. All of the sex positions were always in the same order." He was getting more and more embarrassed. "Believe me, it's an art thing—with quick cuts and shit! Like a remix of porn—I'm not like some pervert or..."

"Chill," Erin said, cutting off his defense. "I don't mind porn, as long as it's done right." *He apologizes a lot.*

"M-me too. I mean I don't like to see women slapped around and stuff."

"I had an ex boyfriend who use to try to choke me during sex," Pam said to a stunned Erin and Allen.

"Uhh, you never told me that," Allen said.

"Like how would that come up? Oh, Allen, if ever we are having sex, could you please, oh so kindly, try not to choke me to death?"

Erin laughed. "I think the weirdest thing Steiner wanted to do, was anal. I mean, really, do I look like I'm into that?"

"It's not so bad," Pam confessed. Erin and Allen looked at her in shock.

"Eww! Really? Did you use lube?" Erin asked.

Allen put his hands over his ears and started saying: "La-la-la, I hear nothing!"

"Oh, Allen, you're such a good little Catholic boy," Pam said, getting a handful of popcorn.

"Hey! I'm Catholic too," Erin announced.

"That explains why you won't do anal," Pam jabbed.

"Hey! I can get pretty freaky in bed, don't you worry, missy," Erin said. "There's other things: Spanking, biting, name-calling." Allen looked embarrassed. "...Back me up, Allen, am I right?"

"Don't ask him," Pam jumped in. "Him and Chris were the super-freak couple; like fuck'n rabbits."

Allen smiled and was silent.

He looks embarrassed but proud. "Was she a nympho? Is that why she cheated?"

"Tea, not coffee," he repeated.

I feel conflicted about Allen. The minute I peg him one way, he turns out to be the opposite: Good Catholic or porno watching perv? Comedy filmmaker or industrial musician? She looked at his face while he told Pam how he had put garlic salt on the popcorn. *He has very attractive eyes, perhaps equal to Kevin's and the rests of his features are within my standards of date material. But, there's like a big wall between us with a red sign on it that says: Do not date! I don't know why I feel this way.*

"Holy shit!" Pam said looking in the direction of the window.

"What?" Erin said, expecting to see something horrible outside. Instead, she saw massive white, fluttering movement. She got up and walked over to observe. Pam and Allen followed. There was fluttering white everywhere. The ground below was mostly hidden by it. The cars collected it like spoons and the streets were graphite lines slowly being erased by powdered sugar.

"Holy shit, indeed," Allen added. "The weatherman was actually right?"

"Well, one outta five ain't bad," Pam said, pressing her hands on the cold glass. She breathed hot breath on it and made a cloudy patch. She then used her finger to write 'fuck' in the space. Allen reached over and used his finger to write 'You' underneath.

"You wish," Pam said.

"Man, it must be at least five inches out there." Erin marveled at the speed the storm was operating. "Shit! NRT's going to be operating at a snail's pace. Maybe I should head."

"Out in this?" Allen looked worried. "Your orange hair will turn white."

"Don't worry about it. In Jersey, this is jack! I walked to school in shit like this."

"You're from Jersey?" Allen asked.

"Ahh! Come on, you should stay. We can go get coco and play in the snow," Pam suggested.

"And sleep where?" Erin asked gesturing to the couch.

"That's actually a sofa bed," Allen informed. "You can have my bed and I'll sleep there."

"Oh, no, you shouldn't give up your bed. I should just go."

"Don't be crazy. It's dangerous out there."

This exchange of offer, refusal, offer, went on for two more turns. Pam, sick of the dance, laid down the final solution: "Erin! Fuck'n sleep on the sofa bed! Allen, get Erin one of your coats and hats so we can fuck'n go shopping!"

"Fine, whatever," he sarcastically agreed.

Erin borrowed a brown fedora and a brown coat with wool trim from Allen. "You look cute," he complimented. They all stepped outside into the winter blizzard. The snow was coming down fast. *I like stepping outside when it first starts to snow. With all these layers of clothes, it's like being an astronaut leaving a moon lander.*

Is this suit going to protect me from the elements of this new world? Where am I? Am I alone on this planet or are there other brave souls, stepping out of their space ships to explore?

"Listen," Allen said.

"What?" Pam said loudly.

"Shh! Listen!"

They were all quiet and listened to the silent shock from snowfall, when the city is first paralyzed into a standstill. Cars were off most of the roads, people and animals had run inside for warmth and the snow flakes dampened all sounds to create a temporary pause in the urban chaos of the city. Erin smiled and sighed. Pam, who didn't know what was going on, said: "What are we being quiet for?"

"Geez!" he yelled.

I like that Allen understands that quietness from snowfall. Finally, a man that understands me. Wonder what he would be like as a boyfriend? Pam said: 'I love him too much to date.' What does that mean? I know what it's like to have a platonic male friend. But me and Pat were never single at the same time. But Allen and Pam are both single, surely the idea has entered their heads. Pam ran off to the side and started gathering snow. Both Allen and Erin knew what she was doing. They also started gathering snow for the impending fight. Allen got the first salvo of attack, with a snowball to the knee. He countered and missed. Pam was aiming for Erin, but Erin was able to hit her in the sternum, even before Pam could cock her arm back.

"You bitch!" Pam complained. Allen laughed until realizing he was next. He managed to throw one near her right butt cheek, after she had got his left arm. Both Allen and Pam teamed up on Erin and started chasing her, wildly throwing snowballs and laughing the entire time. Near an area, which used to be park benches, now white dunes, they finally scored two points on her, one on her back, the other on her right leg.

"Okay, stop! She laughed. Allen tossed one more and missed her head by inches; she returned fire and hit him in the face, sending his glasses flying. "Oh my god! I'm so sorry she said, half giggling. He was pissed. Erin ran over to help him look in the snow for his eyesight and his pride. Pam laughed, hard.

"Watch where you step!" he hissed.

"Sorry, I didn't mean it," Erin apologized.

"Whatever!"

"Now that was funny!" Pam complimented. "Where'd you learn to throw like that?"

"Two brothers and softball."

"Awesome."

Allen and Erin looked for his glasses. They found them near a covered cardboard box. "Oh, look! A sled!" he said.

The biggest nearby hill they could find was further into the University of Neopolitan area and part of some kind of athletics field. At first, the box didn't work at all. Whoever would get in it would stand still on top of the hill or if trying to force the box down, would go tumbling, to much laughter and ridicule. Allen opened the box to make it flat and then slowly went down the hill, stepping on it to pack all of the snow and created a clear-cut sledding trail. This was much better. Now, anyone taking that route were treated to a fast and sometimes harrowing slew at high speeds, usually ending in a wipeout when it evened out at the bottom. They were having a ball taking turns going down, sometimes in pairs or, once, as a threesome. It never occurred to Erin that, even though she had just met Allen, she was comfortable with letting him wrap his legs around her and grab her waist for support.

Eventually students and others venturing out after midnight showed up at the slope and also started laughing and sliding down on various contraptions, from garbage bags to a stolen stop sign. It was fun at first, everyone was sharing in the revelry of wintertime. But then came a group of frat boys. About four large guys, who were not only loud but perhaps drunk. They yelled, jumped down the hill without sleds, tackled each other and called each other pussies or fags. When one of them, trying to slide down on his rear almost ran into Erin's head, the trio had enough and continued on their journey to the store. "Fuck'n frat boys always gotta ruin everything," Pam complained, loud enough to be heard by them. There was no retort. Erin was glad. She didn't want their evening ruined by some kind of physical violence.

After picking up some coco powder, Kahlúa and whiskey for what Pam called an Irish Black man, they trudged back to the apartment. Erin liked the Kahlua and coco but felt the added whiskey was a little gross. It wasn't long before they had made Erin's sofa bed and all three lay on it, watching a local music video show on cable access. It reminded Erin of Donna Etcheverria and a show on the channel called 'Shut Up America!' Erin asked the other two they knew about the show or the person, both denied knowledge.

"Man! I thought everyone knew who the Etcheverrias were; you guys are out of the loop."

"Fuck the loop!" Pam yelled, a little louder than she wanted.

"Shh!" Allen exclaimed.

"Oh, fuck off! Like the neighbors care," she said and then took a sip of her concoction. "That bitch downstairs, always fuck'n playing her bass and shit--at 2 AM. last week."

"Ooh! Ooh-ooh!" Erin yelled. "I accidentally walked in on her on the way up here."

"Dang, you know everybody, Erin!" Allen said. "You're like the Rod Serling of Neopolitan!"

"Who?"

"Twilight Zone?"

"Come again?"

"You know, Twilight Zone?" He started doing the theme song to the TV show.

"I know the Twilight Zone; what does that have to do with me?"

"He's the host of the show?"

"Annd, you're losing me."

"He always shows up and something happens, and yet nobody can see him? Like, if you see him you're screwed, but he's everywhere and nobody notices?"

"I have <u>no</u> idea what you're talk'n about."

"Yeah Allen, what the fuck are you going on about? Fuck'n Twilight Zone?" Pam drunkenly laughed. Allen looked insulted and became quiet. "But seriously, your ass does seem to know a lot of people. What's up with that?" she asked Erin.

"I used to work at F.J. Pizza. You meet everybody through there."

"Really? I never saw you there."

"I used to have blonde dread locks?"

"Hmmm, no."

"I think I remember you," Allen said.

"Ahh, how sweet. You see, <u>Allen</u> remembers me." Erin elbowed Pam.

"Course he remembers you. Probably looking at your tits or something."

"Again, just 'cause I don't want to see <u>yours</u>, no reason to be insulted," he said back.

Pam turned to him and lifted up her shirt, exposing her 32D breast. Allen turned his head in embarrassment. Erin thought it was funny but rude. It could have been the spiked coffee but the next thing she knew, she had lifted up her shirt and flashed her breast at him also. Pam and her broke out in laughter, Allen put his hands on the side of his head, like horse blinders.

"He loves it," Pam said rubbing his head. Erin continued to laugh. *My brain's editor is telling me to take this joke no further. I can imagine exposing more than my boobs. I can see Pam matching me, skin for skin. And then off would come clothes and then Allen's pants. Then, a threesome. Allen would be a bad person to do that with. He seems kinda fragile and burned. If he was a heartless barbarian like Steiner, it would be easier. Yes, Steiner is rude and a pig, but he wouldn't expect anything else after it was over. Allen would want a relationship or to do it more than once. Things would get messy.* Erin rubbed his head also to indicate: 'No hard feelings, right?'

#

The sunshine surprised Erin. She had expected it to still be snowing. She guessed the time to be around 8 or 9 AM. She lifted herself off of the sofa bed and peeked through the window. The yellow sun lay on a turquoise sky. The winter storm had passed and now the city was getting back to it's noisy pace. A salt truck drove by, uncovering the streets and taking away anyone's excuse for not going to work or school. She didn't have to be at work until noon so she had time to make it back to her own house to eat and clean up. Allen came from his bedroom, wearing red plaid pajamas. *I wonder what he would be wearing if he didn't have company?*

"Good morning," he said cheerfully.

"Morning," she said. "What time is it?"

"Around 9. Do you want some breakfast?"

"N-no you don't have to make anything. I was gonna grab something at home."

"No problem. I was gonna cook anyway."

"Uh, okay. But nothing fancy."

"Right-o," he said heading into the kitchen.

Allen ignored her recommendation for nothing fancy and made crepes with fruit and whipped cream. She had never had breakfast in bed before. When he bought it out to her on a tray with a glass of orange juice she felt like a princess. "Oh, my God! I told you not to go all out."

"Believe me, this is normal. If I have time, I usually make breakfast; ask Pam...if Miss Lazybones gets out of bed."

Erin took a bite of a strawberry. "Thanks, you're so sweet." He winced when she said 'sweet'. "Oh! But I don't like juice in the morning. You have any coffee?"

"Uhh... okay. I could make..."

"No-no-no! Don't worry about it. If you don't have any, I'll get some later—this is great," Erin apologized for sounding demanding.

She laid out her napkin on her lap, took her fork and started eating a crêpe. "Oh my God, this is so good! I loved these things in Paris! They had them in those booths at

Tuileries gardens…" There was a sausage link on the plate; she winced.

"I know what you mean, near the Louvre…What?"

"…Is that a veggie sausage?"

Allen had a worried look on his face. "Are you a vegetarian?"

"Sorta. I mean, I ate meat in Europe, but I promised myself I'd switch back when I came home." He took the link and put it on his plate. "I'm so sorry. I'm being a bitch, ain't I?"

"No…it's fine…I should have asked. Believe me, you have nothing on Madam X."

"Yeah, what about her? Nasty break up, huh?" *Gotta change the subject.*

"What's there to say? We dated for about five years and then she cheated on me."

"Five years? Wow! You were practically married! But why did she cheat on you?"

"You know, some shit came up. I guess I was in school, not paying enough attention to her or something."

"That's no excuse."

"What about you and that Steiner dude?"

"He really wasn't a boyfriend. I mean, we dated but there was really no talk of an actual relationship."

"So it was open?"

"Yeah, but mostly on his end!" Allen laughed. Erin punched his arm. "That's not funny," she joked.

"I'm sorry."

"Don't be so sorry." She punched his arm again. "You apologized too much, have confidence in yourself." *Maybe I said too much.*

"I know, I should be more like Steiner."

"God, no! You don't want to be like him. He was an asshole."

"But you dated him?"

"I know. And that was stupid of me. But you're so sweet and talented and…"

"Sweet?" He shivered in disgust.

"What?"

"You said sweet, again."

"What? What's wrong with sweet?"

"You might as well have called me gay."

"What! I don't think you're gay?"

"But you wouldn't date a guy who's sweet?"

"Sure, I would."

"But you dated Steiner."

"I've dated sweet guys before." *Mmm, not really.*

"Then why did you break up with them?"

Erin was getting a little angry. "Why does anyone break up?"

"Don't get all huffy, Erin. I'm just saying that guys don't like being called sweet."

"What's wrong with sweet? What should I say? Cock-master? Allen, what a cock-master you are!"

Allen laughed. "It's not the word, it's the implication."

"I don't think you're gay. I've chased after a gay guy before. He wasn't sweet at all."

"Case and point—girls don't date sweet."

"That's not true!"

"Would you date me?"

So, that's what this is about. "…In a different situation."

"Ah-ha!" he said claiming victory.

"Ah-ha what?"

"Nice guys finish last."

She realized she was going to have to put a lid on this conversation and Allen's intentions before things got out of hand. "Allen, You're a very nice guy and…"

"Please don't say sweet," he begged.

"I was going to say 'talented and all'. But…"

"Here comes the but."

"Can I finish?" she said, peeved. "I just got through some crazy ass things. I went to Europe to get away from most of them. I'm not in any position to be dating anyone right now."

"Ah, speech number 29."

"Wha-what are you talking about?"

"What you said is sorta like the 'It's me not you speech.'"

"What? That wasn't a speech—Fuck you! I'm not like that! Don't pretend like you know me!" Erin got out of bed and started to get dressed. She had forgotten she had taken her pants off, giving Allen a panties show. She didn't care. She quickly put her pants on. "I had some real problems with guys, here and in Europe. I'm surprised that you didn't say I don't date Black guys or call me a lesbian! And how do you even know if I wasn't already dating?" Erin grabbed her backpack and opened the door. Allen was silent which she knew was for the better. If he said one more accusatory thing, she wasn't sure what she would do. "Thanks for breakfast," she said, closing the door behind her.

It was very bright outside. The sun reflected off of the snow. The streets had been cleared, cars and trucks sloshed about their daily business, ignoring the five inches of snow on either side of them. People were going to work, with the exception of the kids taking advantage of the snow day. Erin knew she was going in to work later. She was an adult and adults went to work. Her confrontation with Allen made her feel very childish. She felt she was in the right and he had no business accusing her of anything, but running away from someone who bought you breakfast in bed and let you stay the night reminded her of what she wanted to change about herself when she came back from Europe.

After taking the #77 bus, the West-East train and a walk from Grandview station, she was home. Before she opened the door, she took a breath. *If Roger is here I'll have to go to my room until he leaves. I feel like I'm running away, from my problems again.* She swung the door open with a vengeance, this time prepared to confront Roger face to face. *This is my house and I'm not gonna be afraid of coming into it, but I really don't want to see him masturbating again!* Her courageousness was wasted. Roger was gone. Instead, she came face to face with Tawnee, eating a bowl of oatmeal and looking through the window. Buster jumped off of the couch, A.K.A., Roger's bed, where he had been told a million times not to be.

"Hey! Erin girl," Tawnee said.

"Hey T., you just get up?"

"No, I haven't been to bed yet."

"Holy shit! What did you do last night, or who?"

"I wish. No, I was hanging out with Lisa and Annette, planning our opening tomorrow."

"That took all night?"

"Well…we did that and then had some wine…took some Ecstasy and played out in the snow. Lisa actually ran outside naked and made a snow angel."

"Hey! I played in the snow too…minus the Ecstasy naked thing."

"It was fun. Where were you playing?"

"Up in U. Circle or South Depot—whatever it's called. Shit, I just remembered I have to go back to that part of town to talk to the admissions officer at the Academy! Hope they're open on a snow day."

"Someone should be there. I was just getting ready for work. You wanna commute together?"

"Definitely."

#

On the train, Tawnee read the sex adds in the back pages of What? Weekly.

"This Asian woman only dates White guys and this White guy only wants an Asian woman." She took a red magic marker and like some other couples in the section, matched them together with a red line. "Ain't that weird, they're attracted only to each other's race, but hate their own." Erin, leaning on Tawnee's shoulder, studied the red links she was creating on paper.

"Speaking of guys that only date one race…"

"What?"

"Well, not really, that's what Pam accused her roommate of." Erin sighed, thinking about the fight with Allen.

"Who?"

"I was hanging out with Pam from work and her roommate who was a really cool Black guy…until he hit on me."

"What did he do?"

"It wasn't like: 'Yo, baby!' or anything like that. It was more like—he's a really great guy, sweet, smart but you know…"

"Really a woman in disguise?"

"No!" Erin laughed. "He's just not my type."

"Cause he's sweet or Black, or is it sweet and black? Is he made of chocolate?"

"No!" Erin laughed. "Not because he's Black. I've dated Black guys before…Well, guy. I didn't want to tell him, but I just didn't get that vibe. He thinks it's because he's nice—like I only like assholes or face boys; makes me sound shallow."

"Don't get offended, Erin. I understand the appeal of face boys and that type. Hell, as we know I've slept with them, so I can totally relate, but you need to be honest about it."

"Hey! I was…well, I guess I did tell him I didn't want to date <u>anybody</u> right now."

"Yikes! Not that old excuse."

Erin gritted her teeth. "I'm afraid so. He left me no choice, Tawnee. I want to keep him as a friend but I don't want to lead him on. I mean, how do you do it? You're friends with all of your ex's? How do you keep guy friends from trying to fuck you?"

"I guess I'm just up front with them."

"But I <u>was</u> up front with him and he got pissed."

"No, You gave him the 'it's not you, it's me' speech. They don't want to hear that shit. They recognize that."

"So what do you say?"

"Something like: I like you a lot, but I'm not going to fuck you. We can hang out and have fun, but if you want anything else, I can't give it to you and we should just go our separate ways."

"And that works?"

"Mostly. There have been some guys that wanted more, but they give up."

"And the rest never try to get into your pants?"

"Oh, of course. Men are horn dogs. But I expect it. And I repeat: I like you a lot, but I don't want to fuck you. If you want to be friends, yadda yadda yadda."

"He'd never go for it."

"Erin, if he really wants to be your friend, he will."

"But what if some guy just wants to fuck you, he'd pretend to go along with it?"

"Like Steiner?"

"What?"

"I like him, I like his company and he's a lot of fun. But there's no way I'll be alone with him while I was drunk."

"But what good is that? What kind of friend should you have that you can't trust while you're drunk?"

"Do you think Roger will try to jump you?"

"Eww! You know how I feel about him right now."

"Whacking off story aside, do you think he has a chance of hitting on you? If you were drunk?"

"God no! I'd clock him."

"Exactly my point. You can defend yourself from Roger who's your friend and yet that other guy has what? Some kind of magic whammy penis of seduction?"

Erin laughed. "No, I just don't want to hurt his feelings."

"Whatever, you can't save everybody, Super Girl." Tawnee patted Erin's leg. "Here's my stop. Tell me how the thing goes." Tawnee kissed Erin on the cheek and departed.

She'd be a better match for Allen.

#

Betty adjusted her glasses and studied Erin's application. Erin had yet to figure out her accent. At first she thought British? But it was a little rough around the edges. Then the poster on the wall of the Sydney Opera House firmly placed her in Australia. *Until not too long ago, I mixed up Australia and Austria. It always confused me how Hitler could invade a place so far from Germany.* With such feeble thoughts, she worried about her chances of getting into school.

"Oh, yes, yes, I talked to Neon," Betty said. "She says you're very talented at doing jewelry, like her."

"Well, I'm not as good as her," Erin said modestly.

"Yes, and you are interested in industrial arts as well."

"That's right."

"Well then..." Betty tapped on a computer keyboard. "...
I've been looking over your high school transcripts..."

Uh-oh. And my arrest record and bad grades

"...And although you didn't do too well in New Jersey, you
were able to bring your grades up, once you went to school in
South Neo...especially your math scores."

I had such a crush on my math teacher. "Yeah, They're good
enough to take at least one class, right?"

"One class?"

"Yeah, I was just going to take Jewelry Making."

"Really? What I was going to tell you is, although you have
some rocky spots on your grades, if you took like a make up
math class, in geometry, and a basic drawing class, you could
actually qualify for our Associates program."

"Say what?"

"Yes. That's what I thought Neon was trying to get you
into."

"Wait. You mean I could get into the regular program and
get a degree?"

"Well...not the Masters or B.A. program, but yes, an
Associates."

"Me...in college? But, my grades?"

"That's why you would have to take a geometry class. It's a
prerequisite for some of our classes. And a life drawing class
was Neon's idea."

Erin was speechless.

"But if you just want the one class that's..."

"No! Wait. I have to think. I didn't think I had a chance to
get into the regular program."

"You want to think it over? If you want to get in, you
missed the spring deadline but we could start you off in
summer."

"I'll have to get back to you."

"All right dear, you have my number."

The conversation over, Erin needed to go someplace and
think. She barely had enough money to take the night classes.

Now she could go beyond her original goal and achieve something better.

She walked a few more blocks to the food court at her work. She sat at a table near a window, drinking coffee and eating a cold, flakey, raspberry croissant. Her job wouldn't start for a few more minutes. She was uncertain whether or not her boss would make an appearance. He *rarely shows up on a clear days, so a snow day is a gamble.* She saw a girl outside who may or may not be Lashell trying to step over a three-foot snowdrift. She had no motivation to find out who the girl really was. *I'm not so much pissed at Lashell, as much as I'm burned out by her constant harping. It's like Lashell has a loaded gun of insults, cocked and ready to go, waiting for me to do or say something stupid. That woman could be another 20-something-year-old Black girl with dyed hair and a cell phone.* Erin never found out. She took her coffee and croissant and hastily exited.

The office would be her sanctuary. She spent her hours searching the porn sites on the internet. She never had a fear of being caught by some kind of magical website tracking program, sniffing out goof-off perverts for termination. If anyone ever made the browsers visits to 'Lick 'em Harder Big Boy.com' an issue, she would ask them to prove it wasn't her boss, or a pervert janitor walking the hallway, looking for free internet access.

As exciting as the shot of the two guy's double tongue cunnilingus on the blonde nurse was, after a few hours she slipped into her usual boredom. *As expected, Agnew never showed up. I have no idea what he does. Perhaps he works at home.* Her concern for his attendance was far out-prioritized by the game of solitaire she had started on the PC.

At 5:15 her day became interesting. Allen appeared at the doorway with a shy knock of apprehensiveness. Erin scrambled and fuddled around, not because of his unexpected presence, but because the window for 'Women biting mens' asses.com' was still up on her computer screen. She closed the window, only to be assaulted by numerous pop-up ads, each advertising other porn sites or pills for a larger penis. Allen caught a glimpse of oral sex before Erin gave up and completely cut the machine off.

"Working hard?" he joked.

"What do you want?" she responded, angry and embarrassed.

He laughed a little. "I came to pick up Pam-Pam. We're going to see Big Black Cock a Doodle Doo at Club Foot. Thought I'd pop by and see how you're doing."

"I'm doing great," she said coldly.

"Really? You sound pissed."

"Of course I'm pissed. You accused me of lying just 'cause I won't go out with you."

"Not exactly what happened, but I didn't mean to piss you off."

"Is that an apology?"

"As much as I can muster."

"Really? You can do better than that."

"Uh, okay." Allen got down on one knee, as if proposing marriage or begging. "Please forgive me! My mouth has no safety valve! It say-ith what it wants!"

"You're such a goof ball." Erin prevented herself from smiling as best as she could. She still let a half smile slip through.

"That mean you forgive me?"

"Forgive you? It's not like we're dating or anything."

"What? Dating? Where did that come from?"

Why did I say that? "You know what I mean."

"No. Why do you keep bringing up dating?"

"What I mean is, it should be no big deal. We should have like an understanding if we're going to hang out."

"Like what? No anal?"

She laughed. "Shut up, I'm serious. You have to accept that there can't be anything between us."

"You've already made it clear about that. I'm just here to smooth things over."

"Good...So we're cool then?"

"I am, are you?"

"I told you my dating situation."

"Yes, not dating anyone, got it."

I'm not entirely convinced. "Right, and as long as you're okay with that—Can you get off the ground? Very distracting." They laughed. Allen stood up a second before Pam entered the room.

"So, you kids make up?" she asked.

Did they talk about this earlier? Maybe Pam talked him into apologizing.

"We're cool," he answered. "You ready?"

"Damn right. Allen tell you we're going to Club Foot?"

"Yes, Big Clock something."

Allen laughed. "Close enough."

"You wanna go? Gonna met some buds, drink some Buds, smoke some buds?"

" I wish, but I'm not a big fan of Club Foot."

"I'm actually gonna skip out on the last part," Allen announced.

"Allen doesn't do drugs; such a good boy." Pam pinched his cheek.

"Really? Maybe I should hook you up with Lashell," Erin said.

"Ahh, the infamous Lashell. As long as she's cute and not all hootie hoo, reel her in."

"And fuck'n has big tits," Pam added.

"Hootie hoo?" Erin asked.

"Doesn't hurt," Allen responded to Pam.

"Allen likes big tits. Have you seen his comics?"

"What's a hootie hoo?" Erin asked.

"Hey that girl that works at Last Chance Records had small ones," Allen defended.

"But they still pop out like oranges. Hell, even I wanna feel 'em..."

"What the fuck is a hootie hoo!" Erin yelled

"Oh!" Pam answered. "They're fuck'n like, you know, the girls that wear leopard print pants, leather jackets and big hoop earrings."

"Home girls?"

"...Sure, if this were the fuck'n 80's." Pam laughed.

"Hootie hoo? Sounds racist."

"Helloo, special license exempt from racist label," Allen said raising his hand.

"Bullshit! I've seen plenty of racist Black people–I worked with one at F.J. Pizza."

"Au contraire, orange hair, it's imp—"

"Blah blah blah, Malcolm X!" Pam interrupted. "It's fuck'n after six. I need a beer. You can tell her your theory later." She started pushing them out the door.

"Okay, well discuss it later," he suggested.

"Why don't you two hook up when I go to Sal's? Train goes by your hood, right Erin?"

"Uhh-er." Erin fuddled around.

"I think Erin is afraid if we get together, It'd be a date or something," Allen informed.

"I never said that," she retorted.

"I am right, though?"

"It ain't a fuck'n date unless <u>you</u> suck his cock...and <u>you</u> get fucked!" Pam crudely said, pointing at each one of them. "Now, do you two plan on <u>any</u> of that happening if you meet later?"

Both Allen and Erin yelled 'NO!' at the same time.

"All right then, it ain't no fuck'n date," she concluded.

"Gee. What kinda dates does she go on?" Erin asked.

"Tell me about it," Allen added.

In the downstairs lobby, Lashell was gossiping to two women behind the desk. Erin waved goodbye, knowing Lashell rarely stopped mid sentence to return a parting remark. This time, when she looked over, she not only cut her gossip-gathering off, but she walked over to Erin and her group.

"Heey girl! What's up?" she greeted exuberantly.

" Shell? Just heading out."

"Really, going club'n huh?"

Clubbing? Not me, these two." Erin gestured to the others. Pam waved hi. Lashell introduced herself to Allen. Lashell shook his hand but didn't bother to make as much effort with

Pam. Allen volunteered he knew Lashell had met with his ex, yesterday.

"Oh, she was your ex?" Lashell asked, a little apprehensive.

"Yep."

"Well, you're better off without her, that girl looked like she was on crack!"

Allen had a cringed expression on his face. Erin knew it to mean: *Don't tell me about her! I have no interest in her life.*

"She was tow up from the flow up!" Lashell laughed and touched Allen's arm. *Wait, is she flirting with him?* Allen remained neutral to her advances. *Maybe he <u>doesn't</u> like Black girls.*

"My beer goal is getting further and further away!" Pam interrupted. "You guys ready?"

"I am," Erin said.

"How come you ain't going club'n?" Lashell asked Erin.

" 'Cause, in spite of what you think, I'm not some al-key party girl."

Lashell tried to laugh off the old insult: "I never said that. I said I can pick out that type, better than you can."

"Like his ex?" Erin said, setting her up.

"Oh yeah, girl. Allen, you are so lucky to be outta that house; smell like Cheech and Chong's house!" She laughed and grabbed Allen's arm again. Allen's eyes widened and he grinned, to hint of escape from this girl. Erin picked up on the cue and put her hand on his back. "We better go, you guys don't wanna miss your band."

"Really? Who y'all gonna go see?" Lashell asked, further delaying them.

"Believe me, you don't wanna see them," Erin informed.

"How do you know?" Lashell acted insulted. "I might."

When Pam said it was Big Black Cock a Doodle Doo, Lashell's face looked stressed for a split second and then turned into the same grinning expression Allen had, when he was covering his true feelings. "Oh, okay. Well, I'll skip out on that one. I'll talk to you later, call me when you get home," she said to Erin.

"We'll see, I may be out all night. You know how us clubbing crack heads like to stay out."

Lashell gave the fakest laugh of her non-acting career. "You're such a trip. Later."

Erin was waiting to get outside before commenting on Lashell's actions, but not being one for tact or protocol, Pam spoke before they had reached the door. "Oh-my-God."

"Yeah, I know," Erin responded.

"Yeah," Allen said. "Sucks about Chris."

Erin gave him a double take. "Wha-what?" Pam gave him a similar reaction.

"What?" he asked.

"What do you mean, what?"asked Pam

"Huh?"

"That girl!"

"What about her? Not my type."

"Not your type? She practically had her knee pads on!"

"Knee pads?" Erin asked

"Our little code for blow jobs," Allen answered.

Erin laughed. "I swear, I've never seen Lashell flirt like that."

Pam put her arm around Allen. "He didn't notice 'cause she's Black."

He removed her arm. "Again, not true."

"Then why don't you pursue Miss Thang back there? Do you think she's all hootie hoo?"

"No, because I'm not in any position to be dating <u>anyone</u> right now."

Erin was speechless. *Allen's words matched mine, the 'It's me not you' excuse. I can't challenge it. If I disagree with him, I would be calling myself a liar. Did Allen know this, was that a dig? Pam also didn't challenge. At one point, had the same excuse come from her?*

Pam and Allen separated from Erin to go to Club Foot. Erin told Allen to call her when he was free. She remembered Pam saying: "I love him too much to date him." And she had agreed with her. *How can I not be romantically interested in someone that would make Lashell act like a giggling school girl? And why not Pam? Surely someone who would date a homeless drug dealer should date higher on the social chain?*

When she opened the door to her home, she once again caught Roger in the middle of something. She didn't see any pants coming on but she did see him: eject a tape, shut the TV off really fast, and hurry pass her and out the front door. He ignored Erin's presence as well as the chilly air outside. She went inside and slammed the door shut. "What—the—fuck?" she asked. "That's fucking IT! Once, I can slide, but now, you're turning our house into a jack shack!" In anger and disgust, she stomped up the stairs and searched out Fabrianne. She was in her room, talking on the phone and sorting laundry. Erin waved hi and was going to return to the downstairs but Fabrianne waved her in.

"Erin just walked in...Yeah...I do, I don't know about her.Erin, do you have anything red?"

"What? Maybe, I don't know—who is that?"

"Tawnee. She's trying to get people to wear red for a theme, tomorrow."

Erin recalled the name for the studio Tawnee, Lisa Ann and Annette had chosen was Red Life Gallery. "I'll have to look."

"She's gonna look.....Don't stay too late, 'bye bitch!'" She laughed at Tawnee's response. The conversation ended, Erin immediately started to inform Fabrianne about Roger. "So, I came home—"

"Hold that thought." Fabrianne held up her hand and started to put her coat on. "You gotta come check out my baby!"

"Huh? Baby? What? Did you get a dog or something?" Erin followed her downstairs and outside.

"Speaking of dogs, Buster peed on the rug."

"Goddamn it! I forgot to take him out this morning!"

Fabrianne walked around a yellow SUV, parallel parked in front of their house and stopped.

"Well?" she said holding out her hand to present the surprise.

"Well what?" Erin looked around.

"My car?"

"Your Nova? Where is it?"

"Not the Nova, knucklehead. I traded that piece of shit in."

Erin's eyes widened. *I would be less shocked if she had just announced she was actually a man.* "An SUV? You bought...an SUV!"

"Yes, ain't it cute?"

"Cute? Fabe! It's an SUV! It's the car of the enemy!"

"Oh, fuck the enemy, they can't tell me what to drive."

"But, those things pollute the environment and suck up gas!"

"I know, I thought about that and then I thought, there are more pick-up trucks in Neo than anything and yet nobody rags on them, and it's the same vehicle with back seats."

Erin buried her face in her hands and moaned out of frustration. "But it's still the enemy's car."

"Well, if Yuppies can build lofts in the ghetto, we can invade their world. C'mon, let's go for a ride."

"No way, man, I had to ride in one of those with Donna Etcheverria and I was looking over my shoulder the whole time."

"Don't be such a snob, Erin." Fabrianne was a little angry.

"Rebel to the end, baby!"

Fabrianne rolled her eyes. "Okay, rebel. I was going to treat you to dinner, but if you don't want your friends to see you..."

"Fine!" Erin said sarcastically. "But if my friends see me, I'm duck'n!"

#

Erin liked Fabrianne's baby. She liked being up high, the feeling of power compensation, the yellow color—like her brother's Tonka trucks they never let her play with—and she liked the plastic bobble-headed Jesus figurine on the dashboard, establishing a rebellion in the belly of the yuppie beast.

In the restaurant, after their food had arrived, Erin debated if she should praise Fabrianne's career success. To do so would approve of Fabrianne's lifestyle change. Instead, she said, "I guess your job is working out for you."

"I like it, so far," she answered, stirring her Mango Lasi.

Erin added more chutney to her plate. She'd never had chutney before, and she wondered how she had eaten so many times at Dr. Bombay's Indian Restaurant and skipped it.

"So what were you gonna tell me about coming home?" Fabrianne asked, breaking off some currant naan bread.

"What?"

"You were gonna tell me something before we left and I cut you off."

It took Erin a few seconds to remember. *How could I forget catching Roger again?* "Oh, oh-oh! That's right!" she said excitedly. She calmed down and took a breath. Like a doctor preparing to tell someone they're dying. "It's Roger..."

"I know, I know," Fabrianne said, running her fingers through her hair. "I know he's supposed to be out by now. The rental market is really insane. You wouldn't believe what a piece of shit apartment in Kenwood is going for."

"Actually that's not...Kenwood? Really? Who wants to live there?"

"Apparently everybody! There's even a Coffee Barn there."

"Wow...Anyway it's not just him staying, I think his lack of companionship has gotten the best of him."

"What? Did you catch him masturbating or something?" Fabrianne laughed and sipped her lasi. Erin's deadpanned expression hinted she had guessed correctly. "What?" Fabrianne almost yelled.

"Yep. Caught him twice."

"Oh, my God! Oh, my God! Where? When?"

"A while ago when I got back and today, in front of the TV."

"Oh, my God! I knew he would do something like this."

"Huh? What? You know he's a perv?"

"No, I don't mean <u>like this</u>..." Fabrianne shook her hands down, like banging on piano keys. "I knew he'd do something stupid to sabotage everything."

"Well, that's Roger."

"No, you don't understand. He's acting out because I have a date."

"Whoa! You have a date?" Erin yelled.

Fabrianne shushed her. "It's no big deal, just this guy from work, I'm taking him to the opening."

"I <u>bet</u> you are." Erin laughed at her own dirty joke.

Fabrianne chuckled a second later. "But I think he's acting up. Whenever he's all stressed he does something crazy."

"Like what?"

"Like masturbating out in the open...He was out in the open, right? You didn't catch him in your room did you?"

"No, on the couch."

"But when we broke up, he was all 'I'm gonna kill myself and shit.'"

"Oh, my God, really?"

"Yes, that's why I'm afraid to just kick him out."

"What? You feel responsible? You guys broke up because he's a dick, and you know he wouldn't kill himself."

"Probably not that, but something else, stupid. He put my T-square in the wall after I left; totally killed our security deposit."

What the hell is a tea square? "Then why tell him you're dating?"

"I'm not dating."

"Whatever. You have him in the house? In your life?"

"Because I still love him, Erin."

"If you love someone, set them free."

"Don't quote Sting on me. It's not that easy."

"Easy or not, we can't have him sleeping on our couch."

"I know." Fabrianne put her face in her right hand. "I'll figure out something."

Erin put some sag paneer on her plate. *If the situation was reversed, could I toss a suicidal ex out on his butt?* "Maybe he's not acting out. I mean, you didn't have a date a month ago."

"You're just saying that because you want him to be kicked out on his own merits."

"Sure, why not?" Erin agreed, without guilt. "Whatever it takes."

"You should cut him some slack. You seem to forget that he kept you from getting raped that time."

"I didn't forget." *I have. How could I forget Lars, pointing a gun at me? Roger showed some courage that day. Now he's just a homeless pervert.* As Erin pondered the fate of Roger, Fabrianne checked her voicemail. "Oh yeah," Erin said reaching for the phone. "I need to check my messages. This guy's supposed to call me, may I?"

"Aren't you afraid one of your <u>cool</u> friends will see you?" Fabrianne said, wiggling the phone back and forth.

"You're the only <u>cool</u> friend in here." She took the phone.

After getting another lesson in cell phone use, she checked the voice mail. There were three messages.

The first was from Lashell: "Hey girl. Who that boy I saw you with? Call me." Erin laughed at Lashell's desperation. Out of cruelty, she would not call her back.

Message number two was from Allen: "Hey Erin. I'm going to skip the band after Big Black Cockadoodle Doo, because they suck hard and long. I'm going to be hanging out at The Cafe Across The Street until about midnight if you want to hang out. Hope to see you there...and no, this is not a date! Ciao."

The third message was from Mimi Garrett. *I never expected to hear from her until things were clear with Pat:* "Hey Erin, it's Mimi, your long lost friend. Just call'n to see how you're doing. Haven't heard how the rest of your trip went....hopefully better than ours...Any-who, I'll try to call you later. Pat's still upset, so bad idea to call here, he lost his job in case you didn't know... Anyway, T.M.I., I'm rambling...call you letter, I mean later...Damn beer!"

Sounds like a drunk call. Poor Mimi.

She handed the phone back to Fabrianne.

"So, Erin, guys calling you? Romance on the horizon, Miss Pierce?"

"No, just friends." Erin drank some of her Indian beer.

"Why? Is he ugly?"

"Gawl! You guys! You must think I'm so shallow."

Fabrianne had a sly look on her face. "Well?"

"He looks fine. I just don't want to date him."

"Gay?"

"Oh, for fuck's sake!" Erin looked up at the ceiling. "No, he's straight, single, smart and funny and yet I don't want him. Is that so wrong?"

"No, as long as he knows that."

"I told him."

"Good job."

Erin finished her Indian beer and nibbled on some papadums.

#

An hour after parting ways with Fabrianne, Erin sat across from Allen while he finished his rant about Blacks and racism. Unlike her brief talk with Cliff at her old job, there was no accusations, condescension, or patronizing from him. Erin's opinion seemed to mean something. Even if he debated some of her beliefs, he listened without interruption.

Allen concluded his point: "...So you see, Blacks can't be racist but can be prejudiced or bigoted. Because they are not the power in charge and therefore cannot use policies to discriminate or hold someone back of a different race."

"But what about reverse discrimination?"

"Reverse discrimination is an oxymoron because the opposite of discrimination is not to discriminate. Yes, Blacks can be prejudiced, but by creating another word for what Blacks do, they are then assumed to be of a special case or capable of a different form of discrimination or scenario which means they are not equal to Whites and affirmative action is therefore proved to be needed."

"Huh?"

"In other words, I believe that there have been cases where a Black was hired over a White because they were just better at that job. But if you got hired at a company over a White guy because say, they really did want a more diverse staff, regardless of your skill level, then that same White guy crying boo hoo over me taking his job wouldn't say shit about you. You never see 'reverse discrimination' cases with two White people. So why do these assholes get so mad if you're Black?"

"Wow." *This feels like my brain has been unclogged, like the first intelligent conversation I've had with a guy.* "You want to split a dessert?" she asked.

"Sure. I recommend the banana cheesecake. And I even <u>hate</u> bananas."

"It must be good."

"It is. Took me forever to order it again because Madam X always did."

"Ahh," Erin whined, feeling a bit patronizing. "It must be officially over."

"If I asked you out, then it's over."

"I thought you said this wasn't a date?" She was a little nervous she had been misled.

"I meant earlier this isn't going to be a date unless you say it is."

"What do you mean me?"

"You're the woman."

"What the hell are you talking about?"

"As the woman. You're usually the one to decide if there will be kissing or otherwise later. Men, we have no idea what to expect. We're hopeful but clueless."

"That's a load of crap. We can be just as clueless."

"But c'mon. If you decided at this moment that yes, this is a date and wanted to make out, do you think I'd resist?"

"No, because you're a pig."

"Pig or not, if you reversed the situation and I made a play for you, do you think it'll be a date?"

"No, because I'd clock you."

"Exactly. You have a choice. Mine is about avoiding violence."

"Jesus, Allen! She really kicked your ego's ass." He didn't respond. "It's not so easy for us either, you know."

"It has to be a bit easier."

"Bah!" she guffawed. "Get the cheesecake and I'll tell you about last year."

The delicious banana cheesecake led to more talking, this time from Erin. She briefed him on the events of last year, hoping perhaps they would explain why she didn't want to date anyone at this time. He laughed at things she'd never found funny until now, be they slapping Steiner at his party or leaving Kevin at Hell Burger.

"That place burned down," Allen interrupted.

"Good. Not that I'd ever go there again."

"Wow, Erin, you should write a book about your life."

"Yeah right, how does it end?"

"It's up to you I guess."

"So, what about you? We're sorta having tea, not coffee, what's the story with you and X?"

"What's there to tell? Five years, cheats, the end."

"But there has to be more; you guys couldn't go from hot and heavy to cheating in one day. Did she get all drugged out? Go psycho?"

"I like both of those answers, lets go with that."

Erin started to put her jacket on and prepared her backpack. "Ooo-kay, I guess I better head off then."

"What? Why? Where are you going?"

"If you're gonna be all secretive after I just spilled my guts to you, then why bother hanging out?"

"Okay, okay. Geez! Do you always bolt at the first sign of trouble?"

"Only when someone's not being straight-up with me." She clasped her hands together, sat back and looked at Allen, waiting on him to start his own story.

He took a deep breath and leaned back in his chair. "You know what I want?"

"What?" She raised an eyebrow and expected him to say: 'You'. She mentally prepared a speech for not dating.

"A dessert wine."

The closest place they could find serving good dessert wines and open at 12:35 AM was halfway to Erin's house in Grandview. Yogi's was a yuppie eatery which bragged of a highly rated sea bass and a six-page wine list. Its round, frosted green glass bistro tables, downtempo techno music, glowing, colored bar and a long line of loud, black-clad, cell phone talkers coming out the door didn't exactly make Erin think this was a good place to talk privately. She made a suggestion she might have some plum wine left over from her homecoming and they should go to her place and talk. As a warning shot to his hope of getting lucky, she added information about the train running until 4, so he should have no problem making it back. When she said: "No funny stuff." It resulted in an eye rolling reaction from him.

Suffering from Roger shell shock, Erin slowly opened the door and peered in. This time there was no Roger or masturbating, but it was still an alarming and unnerving sight to see Steiner descending the stairs.

"There she is!" he said proudly and slightly smiling. Erin was flabbergasted. Before she could say, "What the hell are you doing here?" he interrupted.

"Don't worry, we were only dropping Tawnee off."

"We?" Erin furrowed her brow.

Annette Dean came down the stairs, followed by Tawnee. When Tawnee saw Erin, her expression went from happy to worried and a little nervous.

"Oh, shit! You're home!" Tawnee said.

"Yes, imagine that, coming back to your own home," Erin said sarcastically.

"Hi, Erin," Annette said. "I love your hair."

"Thanks... Tawnee what's..."

"I know. They were just giving me a ride. Fabe said you were out on a date."

"A date?" Allen said.

Erin grabbed his arm before he could say any more. "Let me show you that thing I was telling you about." She pulled him into her bedroom and closed the door halfway. Allen sat on her bed.

"A date?" he repeated.

"Shush! You wish!" she snapped, putting her head close to the open door to hear Steiner talking.

"That her new guy?" Steiner asked.

"I guess," Tawnee answered. "You better go before she comes back."

"What's up with you two?" Annette asked.

"Nothing on my end," Steiner answered, opening the door. "So I guess we'll see you tomorrow," he said to Tawnee.

"You better come—free box wine!"

"All right! Box wine!" he yelled and complained.

Tawnee laughed. "Bye, Nettle. See you at noon."

There was a pause, possibly for hugs, then the sound of the door shutting.

"Tawnee!" Erin yelled.

Tawnee slowly entered the room with a guilty grin on her face.

"What the fuck was he doing in our house?" Erin yelled, pointing at the front door.

"I'm sorry, I really thought you were out on a date."

"That's no excuse for him being in my house!"

"I know. But he really wants to make amends."

"He can make amends with my Doc Martins!"

"Ouch!" Allen commented.

"But you can't be sneaking out of places whenever he shows up. How were you going to go to the thing tomorrow?" Tawnee asked.

"I hadn't thought about it. And what, is he dating Annette now?"

"He's not dating anyone."

"Not even Lisa?"

"Nope. I actually think he's still hot for you. But I'm just guessing."

"What? Is he on crack? Why would I go back to him after what he did?"

"Oh, my God! Is that Steiner?" Allen asked

"You catch on fast," Erin remarked.

"Hey, don't take it out on..." Tawnee gestured at Allen.

"Allen," he answered.

"Hi, Allen, Tawnee." They shook hands.

"I'm Erin's date," he joked.

"We were not on a date!" Erin yelled.

"Then why did you invite me back here to show me a thing? I thought for sure I was gonna get lucky."

Tawnee laughed. "He's funny."

"I didn't want Steiner to think I was all pining over him and stuff...and get off my bed!"

He stood up. "Man, worst—date—ev-vuh!" Tawnee laughed.

"It's not a..." Erin buried her face in her hands. "Every time I come home, there's someone I don't want to see. Did Fabe tell you I saw Roger again?"

"No way! Wait, you told Fabrianne? What did she say?" Tawnee informed Allen: "Fabrianne's our third roommate; her ex is crashing on our couch."

"I don't want to think about fucking Roger, I have to figure out what to do with Steiner," Erin complained.

"Fucking Roger?" Allen asked. "Is there a comma in there somewhere?"

"He's funny!" Tawnee laughed. "...You're funny," she said to him.

"Yeah, funny," Erin complained. "I mean, seriously, why the fuck would Steiner want to get back together with me? After I slapped him?"

"He thought it was funny," Tawnee answered.

"What?"

"Yeah, you know Steiner, anything that happens is interesting."

Erin groaned. "Auggh! What does it take to get even with that guy?"

"Why do you have to get even? I thought you wanted to know how to be friends with your ex's?"

"Only if they deserve it."

"Nobody deserves forgiveness Erin, it's something you have to earn," Allen stated

"That's deep," Tawnee complimented Allen and smiled.

"Earned, deserved, whatever. I want him to learn a lesson, and <u>earn</u> an ass kicking! I should show up at the thing tomorrow with Allen."

"Yes...God knows how horrible <u>that</u> would be," Allen said rolling his eyes.

"Stop rolling your eyes! No, you'll be my date and he'll know that I've moved on and he can't have me."

"And if he punches me out? The last time I was in a fight was with customer service at the mall."

Tawnee laughed. "I wouldn't worry about that, he's a Buddhist."

"I didn't know that," Erin said, taking off her shoes.

"You never asked him. This is what you learn from being friends."

"And not having sex with them," Allen added.

"Shut up, Allen. Buddha schmuddha, he's gonna need him after I get through with him."

"You need to rub your hands together and laugh maniacally when you say that," Allen suggested.

Tawnee laughed. "You're so funny."

Allen asked Tawnee what the 'thing tomorrow' was, while Erin searched the fridge for plum wine. There weren't any alcoholic drinks available. Erin suggested they postpone Allen's life story for now.

"Ooh-kay. Back to North Depot for me." He headed to the door.

"You have to go all the way over there? In the cold?" Tawnee asked. "Why don't you let him spend the night?"

Erin gave her an angry look. "Because the evening is shot. And plus, where would he sleep? Not on the couch, thanks to fucking Roger—Don't start!" Erin interrupted Allen, who started to comment on her words.

"He could sleep in your bed."

Erin laughed. "Sh-yeah right!"

"Well, you could share my bed."

She laughed again. "Oh, no, and leave him alone in my room? God knows what things a guy would do in a girl's room."

"Trust issues. Major trust issues," Allen said.

"Well, he can't stay with me," Tawnee said sadly.

Allen's eyes lit up. "Why not? I like that idea." He laughed.

"I know you do, sweetie, but we just met and sometimes I wake up horny."

"Wow! I like her!" Allen pointed at Tawnee.

"Be that as it may, horn dog, there's no place for you to stay," Erin said, about to open the front door.

"Unless we all share a bed," he suggested.

"Oh, you'd like that. Every man's fantasy comes true." She poked Allen's shoulder.

"No, wait. That'd work," Tawnee said. "That way, he won't be left alone in your room to do things guys would do in a girl's room and I won't have to sleep with him."

"E-gads. That last part makes me feel like a hassle," he said.

"Get over it," Erin said. "You aren't getting lucky tonight. The last time I stayed with two people, one asshole tried to have sex with me all night. If you stay, your first move will be your last!"

Allen gestured to Erin. "She's really good with the threats."

Erin kicked Allen out of the bedroom and put on some sweats. *I hope he ain't gonna try anything like Tony. I wondered if Tony is gonna show up at the opening? He is, after all, Lisa's roommate.* When Tawnee came into the bedroom wearing a black sleeper shirt, Erin asked about Tony.

"He might be there. I'm not so sure he and Lisa are talking," Tawnee answered.

"Great, more people to avoid. Are you sure I have to go?"

"You better." She hopped in bed. "Okay, who sleeps where?"

"Well, I don't want Allen rubbing his dick on me."

"Ewww! Dude! What the fuck's up with that?" Allen's face scowled.

"So, I'll sleep in the middle." Tawnee scooted to the middle of the bed.

"But what if you wake up all horny? You'll jump on him and go at it, in my bed!"

"I love your planet," Allen said to Erin.

"Kinda unrealistic. So you go in the middle." Tawnee moved to her left.

"Hell-lo! Horny poking guy next to me," Erin complained.

"Oh for crap's sake!" Allen complained. He took an extra blanket and a pillow and lay on the floor next to Tawnee.

"Problem solved! Erin can have the <u>whole</u> bed, Tawnee can go back to her room."

"Ahh," Tawnee whined. "I like sleeping with people...In the nonsexual way."

Erin felt guilty. *If Allen was willing to give up the girl sandwich fantasy, then perhaps he isn't as much of a horn dog as I thought.*

"Tawnee put a pillow next to him. I'll sleep on the floor too," Tawnee said. "That way we can still be together, like a slumber party."

"Don't be stupid, you guys!" Erin complained. She walked over, picked up their pillows and put them back in the bed. "We'll <u>all</u> take the bed."

"Are you sure?" Allen said standing up. "I <u>am</u> a horny poking guy who apparently jumps on women in the morning?"

"Yes, it's fine as long as Tawnee hits the middle."

Tawnee took her original position in bed. The other two crawled in on her sides and Erin cut off her light with a warning of: "No funny stuff!"

Six minutes after they had settled in. Tawnee broke the silence by asking Allen where he had come from.

"Atlanta," he answered.

"Really? I can't hear your accent."

"Three years in Neo will do that to you."

"Why did you come here?"

"Ex girlfriend. She wanted to be part of the scene."

"Oh, you moved here during all <u>that</u>."

"Yep, and then the scene was over and we were left in an overpriced apartment spending all of our money on rent."

"And then she cheated on you?" Erin inserted.

"What?" Tawnee asked

"Erin is getting a little ahead of the story. No, that happened when I went back to school...yours as a matter of fact."

"Ooh-ooh!" Erin yelled. "I forgot to tell you, I might be going to your school!"

"That's great! You got in?" Tawnee gave Erin a shoulder hug.

"Pretty much. I have to take a math and drawing class at Community first. That, and get some money."

"What are you gonna take?"

"Get this, I'm thinking of the Associates in Industrial Arts!"

"That's so fucking cool! That's what Lisa has. I wish you could talk to her."

"Well, that's what I get."

"Bitch'n! Is your mom or dad gonna pay for any of that?"

"Naw, I wanna leave them out of it. 'Cept I need to talk to my mom about our cabin's rental."

"You own a cabin?" Allen asked.

"Yeah, three bed-roomer, up in Mountain Springs."

"Near Étoile?"

"About 20 or 30 minutes south. We go there to use their hot springs. Why? You wanna rent it?"

"That's where Madam X took me for my birthday one year. That was the most relaxing time I've ever had."

"Wow! That place is expensive. She must'a really been loaded."

"She was, had a job as a photographer's assistant for F Word! magazine."

"We should all go up there sometime, like early March, before it gets expensive," Tawnee suggested. "Get liquored up and then hop on over to the springs."

"Uhh, the springs are clothing non-optional, you know," Erin groaned

"I know. You have a problem with that?"

"Not with you and me."

"She doesn't want me to see her naked, especially liquored up," Allen explained.

"She's having some trouble trusting men right now," Tawnee explained.

"Especially one," Erin added.

"What? What did I do?" Allen said in defense.

"Not you, butt nugget! Steiner."

"Oh yes, the man women would rather go out with instead of me."

"Geez, Allen, this is that confidence thing I was talking about."

Before Allen countered, Tawnee interjected: "Well, I think we've all had our heart's asses kicked. Ya just have to learn to roll with the punches."

At around three AM, Erin heard someone speak. She opened her eyes expecting to see Allen and Tawnee having sex or some other disturbing activity. Instead she only saw Tawnee, looking up at the ceiling. Allen asked her again if she was awake.

"I can't sleep; got the opening to worry about," she explained.

"Are you guys ready?"

"We have all of the side stuff like snacks, booze and a DJ, but I still don't feel ready."

"It's pretty cool that you get your own gallery, at what, what are you—23, 24?"

"26."

"Really? You look so young."

"Thanks, I drink blood."

Allen laughed. "But seriously, I mean I'm 28 and I'm still working at an art supply store. I'm very jealous."

He's 28! No wonder I'm not into him. He's hella old.

Allen and Tawnee started discussing what it was like working crappy jobs while trying to work on your artwork. Erin lost interest in the subject and dozed off. When she awoke, they were discussing Tawnee's brother. He was also an artist, but he lived as a farmer in the country. Erin nodded off again. When she awoke, they were talking about God and religion. Allen believed we were like amoebas in a jar, trying to tell people what the being outside looks like and acts like, although we have neither the intelligence nor comprehension to prove its motivations. Erin drifted off. Next subjects: pain threshold, if you could get plastic surgery for free, which body part would you change, hair care for dreads and braids and finally relationships. Erin wished she could have been awake to eavesdrop on the last subject because Allen must have given a full answer for why he broke it off from his Ex.

"...Wow, that's terrible," Tawnee responded sadly. "I can't believe she did that."

"I know. I mean, if she told me first..."

"Exactly! Wow, that's so wrong!"

Erin wanted to yell. "What? What?" But feared losing out on any future revealing information, to come.

"Dude, no wonder you can't trust anyone," Tawnee said.

"I still trust people, I'm just very choosey who I expose my belly to," he answered. "Maybe that's why I can identify with Erin and her need for revenge on that Steiner guy. Thing is, I don't even want to be around her enough to take revenge, you know what I mean?"

Erin's gamble was a loss. They switched subjects and began discussing anger management. Erin slept again and didn't wake up until morning. She looked over and viewed Tawnee sleeping in Allen's arms. It wasn't a cuddle one does after sex. It was more innocent like a cat on a lap or a welcomed stranger on an airplane who has fallen asleep on your shoulder. She didn't know how to respond. *One part of me is glad two people I like like each other, but on the other hand I feel a little left out. Tawnee learned Allen's story. That was what I was supposed to learn. He owes it to me! That was my property!* Ignoring the danger of Tawnee's 'horny in the morning' warning, Erin risked a trip to the bathroom. After she finished and flushed, she could already hear them talking some more.

They had moved to the kitchen. Allen was preparing something.

"Allen's making crepes," Tawnee informed.

"Huh, really?" Erin was taken aback. *How can he prepare crepes for her too?* She felt a little angry. *Was that just a pick-up device?*

"I'm also making egg custards, poached in the shell," he added.

"What the hell is that?"

"It's like a poached egg thing with cream and butter, served in the shell. I usually use truffle oil, but I didn't see any in your cabinets."

"Good luck in finding salt," Tawnee joked.

"Why didn't you make this for me?" Erin said scornfully.

"I would have, but you stormed off." Allen's retort was a little bitter.

Erin had nothing to say. She went to get some coffee beans out of the cabinet. Allen continued to work.

The crepes Allen made tasted better than the batch he had made for Erin. The egg custard was a little too rich for her. But, good or bad, their serving made her feel under-serviced at his house.

He and Erin made a plan for meeting. The opening started at 7:30. She expected in no uncertain terms he would look nice and play his role of fake boyfriend

Before he left, he gave Erin a polite little hug but the one he gave Tawnee was everything short of a goodbye kiss.

"It was great talking to you," Tawnee said.

"You too," he added.

After the door was shut, Tawnee picked up her cell and started checking her voice mail.

"So…" Erin said, "you guys seem chummy."

"Yeah, he's so sweet." She held the phone up to her ear.

"He tell you why he broke up with his ex?"

"Yeah, were you awake for that? It was so wrong."

"And?"

"And what?"

"What was it?"

"Oh, you didn't hear—hold on." Tawnee listened to one message intensely. "Goddamn it, Annette!"

"What, what?"

"She forgot the code and set the alarm off. I gotta go." She ran upstairs. Erin followed.

"What did he say? Was it drugs?"

"Hold on…" Another message was checked. "…Oh, cool. Terry's' coming."

"Who?"

"School friend—Drugs? What?"

"His ex, was it drugs?"

"No. Did you guys talk about it?"

"No, that's why I'm asking you."

"Uh-oh, are you interested in him? Oh Shit! Did I screw things up by staying in the room?"

"No to all questions. I'm just curious about what makes him tick."

"You should give him a shot, he's nice."

"If he's so nice, why don't you date him?"

"Sounds like some kind of slam: 'If he's so nice, why don't you date him?'" Tawnee repeated in a whinny voice.

"That's not what I mean."

"Then what do you mean? He's a nice guy."

"That's why I won't date him."

"Oh, this is that guy. I didn't realize. He's cute, you should give him a shot."

"But you wouldn't date him, right?"

"I'm interested in someone else right now. I never go after two people at the same time…anymore"

"Who?"

"This guy that works at that new bookstore on 10th—hopefully he'll show up.Anyway, if he was out of the picture, I'd totally go out with Allen."

"And his lack of confidence and sweetness doesn't bother you?"

"Lack o' confidence is because of that bitch whats-her-face. And I've never had any guy make me breakfast. What's wrong with that?'"

"Nothing, I guess."

"If I can put on Freud's glasses for a sec, I'd say the problem isn't Allen, it's you, dearie."

"I know, Steiner, blah-blah-blah."

"Steiner my ass, this is going waaaay back."

"Please don't tell me I'm in love with my father."

"I was thinking more of Peter Fisher. But your dad thing is good enough."

"Peter? What does he…"

Tawnee received a call on her cell. "Hello? Hi…Have you tried the password…Well go tell the security guard…I don't know, I'm sure with all that ringing, someone should show up —Nettle! Don't spaz out—I'm on my way! Try to find a security guard—I'm on my way, bye!" Tawnee put her phone away, put on some black motorcycle boots and almost ran down the stairs. "I'll talk to you later Erin girl, Net's freak'n out."

Erin sat on Tawnee's bed for a few minutes and thought about what was said. *Is it true? Are my problems with Peter, not Steiner, dragging me down? Maybe it's time for me to take a leap of faith? Give in without worrying about someone's past relationship. So what if something bad happened to him; it's unimportant. Tonight I'll take a chance. I won't dwell on anyone's past. Today I'll shop for a sexy red outfit, something that says: open for business. I'll give Allen every chance to make a move. Unknown to him, he'll be the one to choose if he gets lucky. Yes, tonight's your chance Allen Montgomery. You wanna date? You're gonna get one! Tonight, I throw my heart into the dating ring. Caution be damned!*

#

The current population of Northern Neopolitan hovers at around 1,344,000. Of this, more than half are women. If you subtract how many are White photographers between the ages of 21-32, live in the North Side, in North Depot and have dated Allen, you'd have a very small chance of meeting them somewhere on the street. Erin therefore would increase her chances by going directly to Chris Richard's house.

She knew it was a bad thing to do, but she refused to get screwed over by another boy. She had to find out why Chris and Allen broke up. If she asked Allen, he'd tell her. But she wanted both sides of the story. She wanted to make a decision based on a full report, not the words of a wounded, bitter ex-hating male. Pam would probably be able to give more of a balanced perspective, but her crass comments and teasing, wouldn't be worth exposing Erin's intentions to date her friend.

She knocked on the door and tried to come up with an excuse for being there. Perhaps she came to look at the room for rent again.

Chris answered the door. She wasn't wearing shoes or socks and her overalls had nothing underneath. She took a second to think and then recognized Erin. "Oh, hi again...Wait, not Lashell...Ariel?"

"Close enough. Erin, hi again," Erin waved.

"That's right, your friend with the major 'tude is Lashell."

"Yeah, sorry about that. She's usually less stiff. She's just under stress looking for a rental and all."

"Right, right. So what's up?"

"Oh...well, uh, I was wondering if you've come across an earring. I might have lost it here."

"I haven't seen anything, but you're welcome to come look around."

"No, that's cool. I probably left it at my friend Allen's house." Erin dropped her bait.

"Allen?"

"Yeah. He's a friend of mine. Lives near here."

"Allen Montgomery?"

"Y-yeah?" Erin acted surprised.

"How weird, I know him."

Erin reacted unaware and happy: "Get the fuck outta here! No wait...Chris? You're Chris, his ex?"

"That's right." Chris didn't act surprised.

"Wow! What a coincidence."

"Yep." Chris looked suspicious.

"So, you're the Chris. Wow. Far out. So Allen was the guy that moved out?"

"No, that was someone else."

"Oh, okay. So that was like the in-between guy?"

"What?" Chris was a little miffed.

"Oh sorry, I'm all up in your business. I'm usually not all nosey," she lied.

"I don't believe in rebound boyfriends or—hey, you wanna come in? I don't like talking out in the open." Chris gestured to the inside.

"Sure." Erin stepped inside. The living room was cleaned and organized, in contrast to Erin's last visit. She looked around. *Chris has a lot of cool, hip furniture.* She especially liked the wine rack mounted on the wall, an old traffic light. Where the red, green and yellow lights would be, instead, illuminated bottles of wine. Chris sat on a cupcake-shaped Ottoman and lit up a cigarette. Erin sat on the plush purple couch. It was the most comfortable couch she'd ever sat on.

"Wow, this place looks different," Erin said squeezing the arm rest.

"Yeah I know. It's all clean and shit. You guys came over at a bad time. I had this job I was cramming on."

"Oh believe me, I've seen worse...I've done worse—anyway, you were saying?"

"Oh, right. So, if the rebound guy weren't the real thing, then Allen and me wouldn't have been together so long."

"He was the rebound?"

"Oh, big time, the guy before him raped me, so Allen was a big improvement."

"Oh, my god! Really?" *She shared that info easily.*

"It was back in high school, the son of my churches pastor —preacher's sons are the worst. He got away with it too, nobody wanted to prosecute, my parents didn't believe me."

"Oh my god. How did you get over it?"

"I never got over it. You never do. But, I learned to live in spite of it. Allen was helpful with that."

"You didn't date since high school?"

"I've been out on plenty of dates. But I didn't have an actual relationship until Allen; same with him, I was actually his first real girlfriend."

"You mean as opposed to a blow-up doll?"

Chris laughed very hard. It was like she hadn't laughed in weeks. "No, as in relationship, headed for marriage, the works."

"You guys were <u>that</u> serious?"

"Are you like interested in him or something?"

"Oh, no! I'm just curious. He told me what happened between you two. I was just curious to hear your side."

Chris took a drag on her cigarette. "Really? What did he say?"

"He said that you cheated."

There was a very long pause. Chris shook her head and sarcastically mumbled: "I cheated?" over and over. She blew through her lips in disagreement, ran her free hand through her hair and took a deep drag on her cigarette.

"I'm sorry, did he say too much?"

"A very simple explanation if any."

"So, it's bullshit?"

"Yeah, I cheated all right."

"Oh."

"But that's 'cause he didn't touch me for months."

"Holy shit! Months?"

"Yep. I did something he hated and he got mad at me and refused to even touch me. When I cheated, he wasn't even speaking to me, 'cept to say rent is due or shit like that. I mean I know I could have tried harder to smooth things over but he was in school and we didn't see each other enough to get that quality time thing." She snubbed out her cigarette. "But, you know, he didn't take any initiatives either."

"And you cheated?"

"It wasn't cheating as far as I felt. It was over between us." She looked down at the floor and moved her feet around. "It was more like publishing the obituary. Doesn't make the person any more dead, just official."

"Still sucks, though."

"It did…It does. I shouldn't have done it…But you know what?"

"What's that?"

"I think it was for the better."

"Huh?"

"Well, you know, I thought we had this nice stable relationship and shit, and I do one stupid thing and he just tosses the relationship out the window—like seven years meant nothing. I think I freed him. He apparently didn't really want to be with me. I gave him a good reason to take the moral high ground and get out."

"Uhh, what did you—"

"How's he doing?" Chris interrupted Erin's question.

"He seems cool. I just met him so I have nothing to compare it to."

"He still lives with Pam Barlow?"

"Yeah, I work in the same building as her."

"I like Pam, we've been through some of the same shit."

"I like her too."

"He dating?"

"Who? Allen? Not that I know of."

"What about you?"

"What about me?"

"Are you interested?"

"I thought about it."

"I guess I scared you off, huh?" Chris laughed.

"No, it's all good. I need to know what to expect before I jump in the pool again."

"Right on, right on. You and me both—Hey! I was about to have lunch. You want to go to Yogi's?"

#

Erin never thought she would be back at the trendy eatery again. It was a lot more tolerable in the afternoon: It was quieter, the patrons were more relaxed and less coked up and the lunch menu was at least $20 cheaper.

From the cheap bottle of an Australian Chardonnay the girls had purchased, Erin consumed three glasses. With each glass, she felt more relaxed and talkative around Chris. She asked her if she had a drug or alcohol problem, as Lashell suspected. Apparently she was indulging too much a couple of months ago but had managed to get it under control by throwing herself into her photography. The way she talked about photography, it was like a replacement drug.

Erin liked Chris. Sure, she had cheated on another person she liked, but was still interesting. In her former life in Atlanta, she drove a pink hearse, was in a band called Festering Uncle

Fester and had a one-woman art show. Her and Allen's luck seemed to end when they moved to Neopolitan. Being labeled a freak in Atlanta was a lot easier than being one in Neopolitan, where even your mailman dyed his hair purple.

"I know what you mean," Erin said between bites of her Waldorf salad. "I use to have blonde dreadlocks and no one ever gave me a second look."

"When did you change?"

"When I was in Paris."

"I was there with Allen a few years back."

"Yeah, he told me…" *Oops, I shouldn't have said that.* "…I'm sorry, you probably didn't want to hear that."

"That's okay, that was a good week."

Erin's 4th glass caused her inebriated brain to ask Chris if she wanted to go to her roommate's art show, completely forgetting about Allen's opinion on such a scenario. *I figure if I can hang around Steiner, then Allen can be around Chris. It'd be good for us.*

\#

After dinner, Chris tempted a DUI and drove Erin to Ripped to Threads. The hip used clothing store was one of the few original venues in the 10th Street Area. Erin waved bye to Chris and watched her pull away. While entering the shop, Erin held the door for five teenage girls to exit the store. None of them looked at her or said thank you. "It's okay It's my job," she said. Tawnee was behind the counter, helping ring up a blue-haired, 40-year-old woman's stack of clothes. Erin waved and started looking at items on the sale table. *These prices aren't aimed at anyone who's really punk.*

When Tawnee finished, she walked over to Erin. "I have the perfect dress for you for tonight, sugar," she said flipping though the costume rack. She pulled out what appeared to be a red, 1920s flapper dress with shimmering tassels.

"Me? In that?" Erin asked.

"Sure. It'll look cute."

Erin checked the price. It was twice as much as she was willing to pay. "I don't know, T, with my pale hairy legs and fat ass?" Erin spoke a little loud, causing a Black woman to look at Erin's butt.

"Shave, and Allen probably likes big asses."

"Oh really?" Erin lowered her eyebrows. "Just because he's Black?"

"No, 'cause he told me—goofball!"

"You guys sure did talk a lot."

"It was fun, he's nice."

"Well, guess who I had lunch with?"

"Allen?"

"Close, Madam X!"

"Get the fuck outta here! No way!" Tawnee grabbed Erin's arm.

"Yep and I got the other side of the story."

"Really? Is she a ho?"

"No, that's just it, she's totally cool! He totally deserved what happened."

"What?" Tawnee looked skeptical.

"Yeah, I mean, what she did sucks, but he totally acted like a jerk before she did it."

"Jerk? Of course he's gonna act all weird. She aborted his kid!"

Erin felt a thousand butterflies lay a thousand eggs in her stomach. "Wha-what?" she said in disbelief

"Yeah–oh, shit! You didn't know that? Damnit! I shouldn't have said anything."

The Black woman had been listening to their conversation. She curled her lips and then walked to another part of the coat rack.

Erin sat on a chair used for trying on shoes. "No, it's fine. He was gonna tell me but I thought it was gonna be the usual break up stuff. Not that!"

"Pretty heavy, huh?"

"So, what, is Allen that Catholic? I mean I'm not that fond of abortion either, but I'll fight to the death for the right to get one."

"No, no, he's like you. She got one when he was out of town."

Erin covered her mouth with her hand. "Without telling him?" she mumbled.

"Didn't even know she was pregnant!"

"Good Lord! That's horrible! No wonder he didn't speak to her." She shook her head. "I feel like such a dumb-ass. That poor guy, how could I have lunch with her?"

"You didn't know. Maybe there's even more to the story."

"What more? She's a cheater and an abortionist—is that right? Abortionist?"

"I don't know."

"And! I had lunch with her and took her fucking side!"

Tawnee started organizing some leather belts. "Two sides to every coin, Erin."

"What two sides? How can you defend her?"

"I'm not defending her. You yourself said she's a pretty rock 'n chick."

"And I invited her to your show."

"You what?" Tawnee laughed. "Oh-my-god, you didn't! Why? Allen's going to kill you!" She continued laughing.

"I know. I'm so stupid."

"Man! This is going to be a helluva bash."

Erin put her head on her knees. "Do you guys sell axes?" She pointed to her neck. "Just chop along the dotted line."

#

The more her buzz wore off, the more the desire to be executed subsided. After spending a couple of hours at home, she felt less guilty and blamed everything on the wine, including buying the flapper dress.

No one on the NRT train saw her dress because of the heavy coat she was wearing to protect her from the cold and the snow flurries, which had begun.

The weather made the walk from the stop to the Cannery extra slippery. When she arrived at the gallery, she saw Lisa

Ann outside, smoking a cigarette. She at least had managed to match her red pants with a long red coat.

"Oh, shit, here we go," Erin muttered.

"Hey!" Lisa said.

This threw Erin completely off guard. "Uh, hi. Lisa. What's up?"

"Nothing much, you're the second one here...well, second that doesn't work here."

"Really? What time is it?"

" 'Bout 8:30"

"Wow, that sucks. Where is everybody?"

"Annette says it's the weather, but I think it's the Red Level show at the Roxy."

"Oh, my god I love them! I would love—but this is good too."

Lisa scowled. "There's food and shit in there if you want." She gestured to the entrance. *The way she said that, sounded like she was cutting the conversation short.*

Erin took the opportunity to escape. "Right on, I'll go check it out. I'll see you later." She left Lisa and went toward the sound of the dance music. For all its bass and volume, Erin expected to see wall-to-wall dancers and other festivities. Instead, she saw a mostly empty studio decorated with art on the walls and on pedestals. A DJ stood in the caged-in area near the snack table spinning records for the only attendees: Tawnee, Annette and Allen.

"There she is!" Annette said. She was dressed like the traditional Little Red Riding Hood with red cloak and basket. Erin took off her coat and waved to Allen and Annette.

Tawnee gave a catcall whistle. "That dress really likes you," she said. Her own outfit looked like some sort of red rubber latex fetish-wear leftover from a Halloween devil costume, minus the horns and tail.

Erin danced over to the table. Tawnee danced a little with her. "Are we it?" she asked Tawnee.

"Steiner said he'd come, but you know him."

"At least I don't have to worry about running into anyone I don't want to see." Erin twirled Tawnee around. She was happy. *The only thorn will be Lisa, and she seems content not to talk about Florence.*

"Have some wine," Tawnee suggested.

"Don't mind if I do." She danced over to Allen and the table. Everything on it was red: the wine, cherry tomatoes, smoked salmon, licorice and countless other items, laid out before her. "Neat—Hey, Allen!" She hugged him.

"You look nice." Allen mostly wore all black but had a long red scarf.

"Thanks. Nice scarf."

"It's Pam's. I didn't have anything red."

"Goth to the end, eh?"

"Darn straight. So I guess your ass is off the hook."

"Hell yeah, baby! I mean I'm sad of course that their gallery show is a bust, but it's so much easier not having to hide from Steiner or anyone else."

"Well, on the other side, you don't get to rub your devilishly handsome boyfriend in their face."

Erin laughed. "Maybe next time. I think Steiner already figured out that you weren't my boyfriend. You know he's still pining for me?"

"Cool. I wish I could crush someone who was pining for me."

"Well, maybe we'll parade me in front of your ex one day."

"Nah. I have no interest in seeing her, even for revenge."

"But, what if she like ran into you, what would you do?"

"I've seen her a couple of times: book stores, concerts, one time at my work. We usually just nod hello; it's no big deal."

"Oh, good."

"What do you mean?"

"Nothing–I mean it's good that you can be civil." *I hope.*

Lisa Ann came inside. "What were we thinking having an opening during that concert?"

"Big deal. If nobody comes, we'll just drink all the wine and eat all the snacks," Tawnee said

"Yeah, think of it as a private party," Allen added.

"Yeah, really…" Tawnee picked up a plastic wine glass, put some red box wine into it and lifted it up. "A toast…" The rest of the group grabbed similar glasses and filled them with wine. "…to the important people showing up." They clicked plastic and drank.

Erin danced to the remixed version of *Lady in Red*. Allen joined her and then the rest. She took turns with each person, including Lisa. *Lisa seems to have forgiven me, if not put things aside. Maybe I should ask her about it.* "So…what did you and Tony do after I left for Siena?"

"We went to Lugano, hung out there for a couple of days and, then came back."

"You didn't fight any more?"

"Not really, we sorta went our separate ways during the rest of the trip. I moved out a week later."

"Shit. I'm sorry to hear that."

"No biggie."

"I hope I had nothing to do with it."

"How would you? You just spent the night."

"Yeah, but Tony was…you know?"

"An asshole? Yes, yes he is."

"But you were all upset and sarcastic and stuff."

"That started waaay before you showed up. It was all building since Venice. We just had enough of each other."

"So, I guess there was no romance thing going on."

Lisa started laughing so hard there were tears in her eyes. "Oh man! That's <u>too</u> fucking funny! No way! Tony's a yuppie asshole, I'd never date him!" She continued laughing. "Excuse me, I need some water before I choke." She laughed on her way to the refreshment table.

I'm confused. Did I misread them as a couple? What other misjudgments have I made? She danced over to Allen. He was trying to dance with Tawnee, but she kept moving from person to person. *I feel a little put off. Here I am, prepared to give Allen a chance, and he seems like he'd rather dance. I'll up the ante a little and dance directly with him.* She touched his waist. Instead of grabbing her or some other physical contact, he started acting goofy and dancing like John Travolta in Saturday Night Fever.

"All right, old school!" Tawnee yelled and laughed.

Rejected, Erin went over to the snack table. The lack of insulation in the building was making her a little chilly. She shivered and rubbed her arms. Allen walked over in order to pour another glass of wine. By her arm rubbing, she expected him to at least put his arm around her to warm her up. He ignored the bait and stuffed a cherry tomato in his mouth.

"You must be cold," e mumbled, looking at her legs.

"Little quoto litro will take care of that."

"Huh?"

"It's Italian. When I was in Italy, they had—"

"Not you," Allen interrupted and pointed at the door.

Erin turned around to see what was going on. If you gathered everyone in the world whom Erin wanted to avoid, added some strangers to the mix, put them all on the same bus and then unload them in front of her, you would see what she was experiencing at that moment. One by one, sometimes in pairs or groups, people started filing into the gallery. Among the crowd, she saw: Steiner with Peter and Debbie Chan; Kevin with Graham and Kathy; Pepe and Chelsea; Donna with Kim; J.J. with Tracy; and Fabrianne with her date, whom Erin realized she knew.

"Shit-fuck! Shit-fuck! Shit-fuck! Shit-fuck!" She walked to a far corner and turned her back to everyone. "Shit-fuck! What the hell is going on?" she pondered. "Why is everyone here at once? What about the concert? And why are Peter and Steiner together?" Someone tapped her back. It startled her and she turned round, ready to hit them. It was Allen.

"Hey, your ex boyfriend is here."

"More like boyfriends!"

"What?"

"Steiner's with my earlier boyfriend! Remember the one who stood me up for Europe?"

"Oh, yeah—whoa!"

"Also, that gay guy I chased after, and this guy who tried to fuck me in Italy!"

"Wow! You want to sneak out the back door?"

"Been there—did that. Besides, looks like Tawnee and them have some boxes and shit blocking it now." She pointed to the obstacles. "Haven't they heard of a fire code? You must think I'm a total wad now."

"Right now? No," Allen joked.

"Fuck'n ha ha. I'm serious. I'm totally screwed. There ain't a person in here who I want to see."

"Gee, thanks."

"You know what I mean."

"Well, you said the reason you wanted to go with me was to make your ex boyfriend jealous. Now you can stick it to three other guys at once." As Allen was speaking, he was looking at Tawnee talking to some guy Erin hadn't seen before. He was tall and skinny, wearing all black leather, including a coat, and had dyed, oily black hair.

Must be the guy Tawnee wanted to show up. Looks like he just gotten out of a goth shower. "Jealous?"

"What?" Allen said being shaken out of a hypnotic stare.

"That's some guy that works at a bookstore on 5th Tawnee invited."

"Whatever."

Erin poked him in the stomach. "You're jealous, aren't ya?"

"What are you talking about? Whatever! Just because I'm not chasing after you doesn't mean I can't go after anyone else."

"Whoa! Where did that come from?"

"No-where—you said you wanna be friends, so don't rag on me if I look at other women!"

"Whatever to you, Allen! You're all mad 'cause her ass ain't into you!"

"Oh Really?" he responded sarcastically. "Is that what she said? Oh-Great-Expert-On-Dating? Miss Three Boyfriends in one place!"

"Fuck you! I won't be the only one!"

"What are you talking about?"

Erin was about to reveal that Chris had been invited but dismissed her statement with another "Whatever" and departed. She had no idea where she was going. Every direction had a person she had no interest in seeing. She remembered Fabrianne and her date and walked over to them.

Her date was a long-jawed 20-something year-old with hair like Andy Warhol, but brunette. He was wearing a white dress shirt with tie and red suspenders.

Fabrianne waved to Erin, "Erin this is Bob Upton."

"I know…" Erin said. "…I know you!"

Fabrianne and Bob looked confused. He squinted his eyes, trying to think. "Really?"

"Think of me with long red hair…"

"Uhh, no, can't think I remember you."

"…Plane to Europe? …You were biking around with Salome and Larry?"

"Oh, my god!" he yelled before hugging her. "Holy crap! I remember you! You had no place to stay!"

"Yes, and you guys told me about your friends, Mr. Humphrey and Marie Callier…"

"And Suzette and Paul! Yeah-yeah! How'd that work out?"

Erin briefly filled him in on her adventures in Europe. Bob gave his tales of biking the continent, filled with friendly villages, dangerous close encounters with mountains and cars and a quest to go to a dance club in each city they spent the night.

Fabrianne's trying not to look left out and bored.

Erin cut Bob off as he talking about a club he found in Germany that had martini glasses with glow sticks in the stems. "So, how do you guys know each other?"

"We both work in the same office," he answered.

"That sports stuff place?"

"It's not a sports stuff place!" Fabrianne corrected. "They design memorabilia for sports stadiums!"

"Well… sports stuff," Bob said shrugging.

"That's cool. Fabe's my roommate."

"Far out! She told me. Small, small world," Bob said before taking a swig off a beer bottle "So, you see the other guys yet?"

"No, you're the first. Erin looked at Fabrianne. *Her expression is definitely a 'wish we would somehow include her in the conversation'.* "So, Fabe…Is <u>Roger</u> coming?" *Shit, that was stupid! Why did I bring up her ex boyfriend?"*

"No idea, who cares?" Fabrianne said, narrowing her eyelids.

Erin wanted to make an escape before she ruined Fabrianne's first date. She looked around for another safe target.

"Who's Roger?" Bob asked.

"Oops! I see my friend J.J., I'll be back, I gotta say hello!" Erin interrupted.

"Oh, Ok," Bob said. "We should get together sometime and trade travel stories. You know about that art show in Amsterdam where a guy pees in another guy's mouth?"

"I do…" Erin said unfazed.

"Fuck'n hilarious!" he laughed.

Fabrianne looked perturbed and disgusted.

Bob is not gonna score tonight. "…Yeah, I gotta go see J.J." Erin left as quickly as possible, before causing any more damage.

She quickly crossed the floor to prevent eye contact with anyone she didn't want to see. Jira (J.J.) Jamshidi leaned on Tracy and almost stumbled. It wasn't the kind of stumble one does when tripped, it was one laced with drugs or alcohol. She looked the same as Erin had last seen her: Long, tightly braided dreadlocks, olive skin and even while wearing a coat to stay warm, a presence of willing sexuality. "Er-hi, J.J.?" Erin said with a bit of apprehensiveness. J.J. Seem to have a hard time focusing on Erin and speaking.

"Sorry, Erin," Tracy apologized. "She just took some crazy shit 30 minutes ago for the Red Level show and what happens? They postponed the show; fuck'n snowed in Texas. Band's stuck, or some shit like that."

"How'd you end up here?"

"J.J. works with your roommate, what's her name?"

"Tawnee?"

Tracy snapped her fingers and pointed at Erin. "Right, right —Theodore!" It was now apparent to Erin that Tracy had also taken some 'crazy shit'.

"You-you guys need any help?"

J.J. laughed. "Your hair looks orange!"

"It is orange."

"It is orange... It is orange... It is orange" J.J. said like an echo"

"No, April's gonna be here soon, she'll take care of us," Tracy said. "She always takes care of us."

"I love April," J.J. said "We should fuck her." The two girls burst into laughter.

"Ohhh-kay. I'll check in on you guys later. Don't take any more of whatever you have."

"Thanks mommy," Tracy said in a funny voice. Erin slipped away.

"I love Erin. We should fuck her too." J.J.'s repeat joke caused the same howls of laughter.

Once again, Erin was escaping from another awkward conversation. Like a ship trying to find a beacon of hope, she scanned the room for another safe harbor to go to. She was out of options. She wanted to find Tawnee, but she was nowhere to be seen, as was the guy with the oily black hair. Allen was standing near the DJ cage, bobbing his head and drinking. *He's pretending to have a good time in spite of being alone and looking like he wants to leave.*

The music boomed and thumped. People drank and talked loudly about the art on the walls: Tawnee's art, mostly pen and ink drawings of junk yards, factories and industrial scenery; Annette's mostly weird ceramic vases and pots, so abstract in shape there would be no way most of them could actually hold water or flowers, and Lisa's work. Erin's always admired her jewelry, made of old watch and machine parts. Lisa had moved on to making large humanoid sculptures out of discarded bicycles. Erin retreated to a far corner near some unpacked boxes camouflaged by a red sheet over them. From her vantage point, she was able to spy on all of her old nemeses: Steiner, Peter and Lisa hung together and appeared to be enjoying themselves. Peter had dyed his hair blonder. *I just realize from his distance and my short, orange hair, he probably doesn't recognize me. It doesn't matter; I wasn't going to confront him or Kevin anyway, not on Tawnee's big day.*

Kevin Goldberg hadn't modified his look in any way: same Beatle cut hairstyle with sideburns, and an outfit that looked like a brown, silk suit. By some unwritten rule, the two groups never mixed—it was the Grimes versus the Clubbers. The Grimes clowned around, drank their free beer and took cheap drugs, while the Clubbers, sauntered around, sipped their wine and took designer drugs. *Wonder which group I'm in?*

Allen still stood by himself. *Perhaps I was a little mean to him just for staring at Tawnee. Of course he would be interested in Tawnee. Tawnee's pretty, tall, skinny and has tattoos and piercings in odd places. Of course he would pursue her over me, even if I were willing and able.* She considered going over and apologizing.

Pam and Chris had entered. Erin watched the drama. The girls walked over to Allen. They spoke to each other. There was no yelling. Pam laughed. Chris kindly touched Allen's Arm. They looked around. Allen spotted Erin and pointed at her. Embarrassed, she waved hello.

"Fuck!" she muttered, *Why are they looking at me?* Pam walked over. Allen and Chris looked like they were having an awkward conversation.

"Mrs. Mother-Fucker!" Pam joked.

"What? What did I do?"

"You didn't tell me you invited Chris to the Gallery."

"Like a dumb wad, I invited her to a place where the person who wants to see her the least is."

Pam looked back at Allen and Chris. They rocked back and fourth, pretending to dance a little. "Well, they seem to be okay. I thought he'd be all Kruger if he saw her."

"What are you doing here?"

"Fuck'n Red Level show got cancelled. Chris goes, 'Well, I know where there's a gallery thing across the bridge."

"I thought you guys didn't hang out anymore?"

"I tried not to tell Allen about it—I guess we're both busted, huh?"

"I won't tell if you won't."

"But hey, maybe it's for the better. They can make up, be friends again."

"Doubtful, not after what she did to him."

"The cheating thing?"

"No, the abortion thing!"

"That? He has no right to be mad at her about that."

"Are you nuts? She had it without even telling him she was pregnant?"

"Of course she didn't want to tell him. Allen was such a total cock wad back then. I mean, I love him and he's a little better now, but he was sooo insecure and always accusing her of wanting to cheat with her hip new friends, especially this guy named Kurt who made porno movies."

"P-porn, what?"

"Yeah he actually makes amateur porno. He's pretty cool; he never hit on us. But Allen <u>hated</u> him. Thinking he was getting Chris in the business or some shit. When she found out she was pregnant, she asked Allen, point blank, 'What would you do if I got pregnant?' You know, like a test, and he says: 'Ask you to get an abortion, we can't afford it!'"

"Good, Lord! Was that a joke?"

"I guess. Not very fuck'n funny."

Erin grabbed the sides of her head. "Ah, man! I can't take it! One minute Allen's cool and the next he's an A-hole. I can't trust any men anymore. Have I told you all of my ex-boyfriends are in this room right now?"

"Far out. You gonna kick their ass?"

"No...I want to just run, but that's what I used to do. I have to stay and fight it out. No matter that I've ruined Fabrianne's date, Kevin doesn't even seem to recognize me and Steiner's wearing shorts, even though it's snowing." She gestured to the different scenes taking place.

Chris and Allen joined Erin and Pam.

"Hi Erin." Chris hugged her.

"So...Erin. I didn't know you and Chris knew each other so well," Allen said with deep suspicion in his tone.

"Yeah, I told you I hung out with her before I met you." *I hope Chris didn't tell him about the lunch date.* He raised an eyebrow.

"Hey-ey! Erin!" Steiner said patting her on the back.

"Steiner," she said coldly.

He looked at the other girls, waiting on an introduction. Not depending on Erin, he introduced himself and they all shook hands. He turned his attention to Chris, mostly, and asked her what she did for a living.

"This is my ex boyfriend who faked a suicide in order to get me to come to his birthday party," Erin said to Pam but loud enough for Chris.

Instead of being embarrassed, Steiner embraced the story and bragged about it. "Yeah, it was the only way to make sure everybody came. I mean, who's gonna come to your house for cake and ice cream?" Chris and Pam laughed. Erin and Allen sneered.

"So, where's your girlfriend, Debbie Chan? Or is it Lisa?" Erin tried again to embarrass him away.

"Lisa? I haven't had a girlfriend since you dumped me for that gay guy. Hard to get over that kind of rejection."

"Ahh," Pam and Chris pined.

Steiner's turned my words back on me, making him the victim and me the cold-hearted bitch that dumped him. Erin gritted her teeth and was about to tell him to beat it.

Tawnee's voice could be heard over the stereo speakers. "Hello, everyone and welcome to our opening night." People cheered and hooted. She went into a round of thanks, including the DJ whom Erin really hadn't been listening to. *Didn't I work with that guy at the Acid Pit?* Tawnee turned the mike over to Lisa and Annette who encouraged people to buy their art and recycle their bottles and cans in the blue bins. During all this, Steiner was still making small talk with Pam and Chris. Erin inched over to Allen to see if the sight of Steiner talking to Chris had somehow formed a temporary truce of mutual hate. It had, he had narrowed his eyes and crossed his arms in anger.

"Nice night, eh?" Erin said sarcastically.

"Lovely," he responded in kind. "It couldn't be any better unless my hair was on fire."

"Or his hair."

"That'll work—got a match?"

"I'd pay to see that." They both laughed at their sadistic wishes.

Erin wanted a cigarette. Unsure if Tawnee and the girls complied with the new non-smoking ordinance, Erin went outside to smoke. Next to the building were some other smokers: Chelsea, Kevin and Tracy. Kevin looked at her, the look on his face registered he knew who she was. She snubbed him with her best sneer and walked away from the gallery area. She kept walking for a block until she came to the old pier along the river's edge. There was a chain linked fence preventing her from getting any closer to the shore. She was sure, if she kept walking, she would eventually find a gate, but that was beyond her motivation level. She also didn't want to ruin the perfectly leveled snow surface that was forming. Except for her footprints, there were no other marks disturbing the snow around her and the nearby warehouses. It was a perfect plane.

She lit up, shivered from the cold and took a drag on her cigarette. As she exhaled, her smoke obscured her view of a ship, headed towards the ocean. She imagined, on board, people who had left their problems behind to work on a tanker; a way to forget about their petty lives.

"Erin?" Allen called. He walked from the gallery and joined her. His presence wasn't welcomed, but she could tolerate it a little.

"Whas-up?" she asked shivering a little.

"I'm thinking of leaving."

"Really? Why?"

"Where to start? My ex is here and your ex is hitting on her…"

"Don't mind him, he's just a big flirt."

"Besides that, our fake date plan was a bust–nobody's jealous of us…and, some other things."

"Tawnee?"

"Yeah…yeah, that too."

"Got the hots for her."

"I…I'm interested in many people."

"Allen I…"

"Please don't lay some, 'can't we be friends?' crap on me right now. I know where we stand. I can take it. At least I know how you feel."

"But it's good this way, right? Like you and Pam."

"Pam? Right. Apparently been buddy-buddy with Chris all this time. Why didn't she tell me they were still hanging out? What kind of friend is that?"

Erin looked away in embarrassment. "She probably didn't want to hurt your feelings."

"Whatever, another reason not to hang out here."

"Where are you gonna go?"

"Home. I need to go home. I need to go to that place where no one messes with you, put on my sweats, get some coco and Kahlua, pop in a bad video and just be …home."

"Sounds nice."

"Wanna come?"

"I can't."

"Why not?"

"Tawnee's my friend. I have to support her show, no matter what Steiner or Kevin do tonight."

Allen thought for a few seconds and looked at the lights across the river of the North side. "Yeah…I guess"

"You could stay too, keep each other company?"

"I could…but I can't."

"Why not?"

"Because it's too much work pretending not to care. I'll see you later." Allen turned and started walking to the complex's exit.

Erin felt sorry for him. She was in a worse situation than he was with more than one person to deal with this evening, and yet she was willing to suck it in and deal with it. "Allen!" she called out. He paused and looked back.

"Call me for brunch tomorrow!"

"Sure, it's a date."

"It is NOT a date!" she yelled back.

Part Three
The Dinner Club

Erin's feet were getting cold. She had let some snow leak into her boot. *I should have chosen another window to look through, perhaps one without so much snow under it.*

Pat had not yet been spotted. She erred on the side of caution and did not knock on the front door. The lights were on in the kitchen of the old, two-bedroom house. Someone was home. Mimi came into the kitchen, returning a plastic cereal bowl. Erin took the opportunity to get her attention. She frantically waved. Just as Mimi was putting the bowl in the sink, she saw Erin, shrieked and dropped the bowl. She put her hand on her chest and took a breath.

"What is it?" said a man's voice from the other room. It was Pat's.

"I thought I saw a rat," Mimi covered.

"Really?"

"No, it was just a sponge…rag—sponge-rag!"

"Sponge-rag? What the fuck are you talking about?"

"Yea-yes, don't worry about it!" She gestured for Erin to meet her at the back door. Erin uprooted her boots from the snow and walked to the back of the house, trying her best not to annoy the two barking pit bulls next door. She opened the back gate. Mimi kept looking back and forth between Erin and from where Pat could appear from.

"Oh, my god! Hi, Sweetie," Mimi whispered.

"Hi, what's up?" They tightly hugged for a few seconds.

"Oh, my god! Love your new hair! So nice to see you, but not a good time; Pats here!"

"I know. That's why I'm out here. How is he?"

"Not so good; lost his job, been really abusive."

"Oh my god! Is he hitting you?"

"No, not really, just verbal shit. But I really can't take it any longer. I mean, I love him, but I'm about ready to bolt."

"What! Oh, no, no-no! Break up? But you guys been together for six or seven years?"

"I know. But you don't understand. That Ned thing has been on his head since we last saw you. I thought the wake would help, but he's only gotten worse. Saying how he wants to get a gun now."

"Oh, no!"

"Exactly. What does he need a gun for? The guy that killed Ned is in jail and the rest left Neo 'cause they're afraid someone like Pat's gonna shoot them. But how are you doing? Did you have a good trip in spite of Mr. Grumpy Pants?"

"Oh, I had a blast: Drank, partied, saw some great art, met some new friends, hooked up with some old ones. I loved it. It's tough to be back. But enough about that, what are you gonna do?"

"I don't know." Mimi looked very sad. Erin hadn't seen her that low since her cat died. She gave her a hug. "Well, no matter what, you know you have a bed at my place."

"Thanks, but I don't know how long he can hold a grudge. I mean you were just the messenger, right?"

Erin was quiet and just as sad looking.

"What? What is it?"

"That's just it, I'm not just a messenger..." She sighed. "I knew Ned."

"So, we all knew him."

"But no, I sorta knew this girl that was in the gang that killed him."

"Oh my god...Really?"

"Yeah, and on top of that when I got arrested, the cops bought her in too, but I didn't rat her out."

"What?" Mimi put her hands on the side of her head.

"Yeah, so as far as I know, she walked."

"Erin? Why did you do that? Were you scared?"

"No...well yeah. But I did it because I had <u>had</u> enough: My car got totaled, Kevin the homosexual told me literally to fuck off and I slapped Steiner, all in one night. I had no interest in any more drama, ya know?"

"I guess. God, I hope you don't tell Pat that."

"Ain't gonna come from me."

There was the sound of walking coming from the kitchen. On automatic pilot, Erin started running from the back yard. It could have been Pat or their dog, Rufus. She was not waiting to investigate. When she made it on the side of the house, she heard Pats voice ask, "Why the fuck are you in the back yard?" to Mimi. Erin had lucked out. She made it to the street and tried not to slip on the black ice, covering the asphalt. This created a hazardous driving situation and even more so for running. She risked it and kept jogging away from the house. She slipped, fell back and landed on her butt and right wrist. She quickly got up and continued running. The pain in her wrist caused her to hold it. *I hope it's not broken! This would be perfect, right at the time I'm trying to get into art school and taking drawing classes, I break my wrist!*

She made it to the bus stop. Brushing the snow off of the bench, she was able to sit down and rest. She moved her right hand and fingers. There was no odd sensations, which put her mind at ease a little that it may not be broken, but it still hurt. She grabbed some snow and held it on the pain. *I probably deserved to be injured, deserve more than a broken wrist for betraying Pat. I should have my hand cut off. It's so sad to see two people I love in such a fucked up situation. Pat use to be a big, lovable teddy bear, and now he's a big grizzly. Mimi used to be so tough, now she's a scared little rabbit. My hands feel numb.* She tucked them under her armpits. *Smart Erin, remember things called gloves?*

It started to snow. The black ice was covered up, making it even more dangerous. She felt weird, not in an emotional way but nauseated and a little dizzy. "Oh, shit, what did you do to yourself now, Erin?" she asked.

#

It had been over a week since the Pat and Mimi visit. Erin finally felt okay—not good, but okay. She got out of bed and tried to clean up her room a little. Many wads of tissue paper were found in almost every part of the room from failed attempts at throwing them at the full garbage can. Empty soup bowls, teacups and spoons were gathered. She wiped off her bedside table, which had a sticky coating of purple cough medicine. The activity made her start to feel a little weak. She sat down on the bed and rested. *I wonder if my visit to Pat and Mimi's really happened or was it an elaborate fever dream? The bruise on my wrist is evidence enough. Should I take more, cold and flu drugs?* "No, let's see if I feel better after a nap," she said. She heard someone cough. It could be any of her other roommates who had also caught the Bangkok Flu. *I know I wasn't the one that gave it to them because Roger was sick first. I hate him even more. After he got sick, it took the pressure off him being asked to move out. If I were well enough, I'd move all his shit to the curb.*

Fabrianne should have done it. She's so dedicated to her job. She sucked down medicine and went to work anyway, giving her an extra week of suffering. Strong enough to do that, should be strong enough to get rid of Roger. Erin lay back down again and looked through the window. It was an unseasonably sunny day. *Great, it's always nice out when I can't go outside. If I feel better later, I should try to enjoy the day. I'm tired of being inside for so long, I'm tired of being sick.*

After calling her work number and telling Mr. Agnew's voice mail she was going to be out today, She called Allen to see what had been going on in the outside world. Unlike her, he had avoided the flu. She had seen him briefly, through her window, when he dropped off a pot of homemade chicken soup on the front stoop. The gesture was greatly appreciated by all, in spite of Erin's weak stomach throwing it up later. *He was a little insulted when I asked if it was all part of an elaborate plot to get Tawnee to break up with her new boyfriend, Zack.*

"Hi sweetie," she said before coughing.

"Poor thing, are you still sick?"

"No, just phlegm."

"Gross. How about the rest of your gang?"

"You mean Tawwwww-nee?" she teased.

"Shut-up. I like Fabrianne too and I'm not interested in her."

"They're still sick. Matter of fact, I want to get the hell out of here before they get me sick again."

"Bet Mr. Greasy Hair didn't bring over soup."

"Ah-ha! You are still interested!"

"I never said I wasn't interested. I'll always be interested… until she gets engaged or something like that. Besides, I have a date, so in your face!…Or her face–whoever."

"Date! With who?"

"Don't act so shocked, Erin. There are people out there who do find me attractive."

"That's not what I meant. I mean, this is a surprise. You didn't tell me about anyone else."

"Yes, I did. Remember the girl at Last Chance Records?"

"But I thought that was a dead end? How did this happen?"

"I was buying a S&M&M Eminem album and we got to talking and she invited me to see her friend's band play at Stickers, tonight."

"Stickers? That's a frat boy bar! Maybe she's not as 'alterna' as you think"

"Bands gotta play somewhere, Miss Negative."

"I'm not being negative."

"Jealous?"

"Oh, please, let's not get into that again."

"Then you should be happy, instead of ragging on my date."

"I'm not trying to harsh you. I'm just concerned for your well-being."

"If you say so."

"I am—damn it! So when are you meeting? Are you having dinner?"

"Actually, no. I'm meeting her at the club at 9. I was going to get a snack at Tea-V, first."

"Where?"

"It's that tea house in U. Circle. It's pretty good, they sell a zillion kinds of tea and sandwiches. Everybody goes there 'cause it's cheap."

"I should go there. Get some warm tea. Get out of this sick-ass house."

"Well…if you're sure you're not contagious, I could meet you there?"

"If I'm still sick, I'll try not to kiss you."

"Any excuse, huh?"

"Shut up! Pam joining us?"

"She ain't home. She actually has a date too."

"No way! With that guy she met at the concert?"

"No, he was a pervert. This is some guy I haven't met; think his name's Ogden or some shit like that."

"Wow. Everybody's getting laid but me."

"You can't tell over the phone, but right now, in response, I'm gesturing to my bedroom."

"Guess how I'm gesturing right now?"

"I'm sure it involves a middle finger."

"Bingo. See you in an hour."

#

When Allen said: 'tea house,' she expected an old English building with antiques decorating the walls, and intellectuals sitting on old leather chairs playing chess and smoking pipes while Mozart was being played on a violin. Instead it was more modern than most dance clubs she'd been to. All of the chairs and tables were shiny, brushed metal, as were all the teapots. Instead of people playing chess, the black-clad students not self-absorbed in their own laptops were talking loudly about fashion or their philosophy classes. As for Mozart, 48-RPM, bass-filled, lounge techno music replaced him.

Tea-V boasted of over 200 varieties of tea flavors and 12 varieties of finger sandwiches. Erin flipped to the herbal section again and tried to decide between Fennel or Sage with lemon. *The rumor of Tea-V being cheap is half true. Yes, the sandwiches are cheap, but you're only paying for 1/4 the size of a regular one. In order to fill yourself up, you have to buy at least four of these little treats. If you add in dessert, you might as well have gone to a really good restaurant.*

Erin and Allen sat next to one of the many 30x40 neon colored, silk-screened portraits of Asian people involved in tea-related actives such as: harvesting, brewing or how to perform a Japanese tea ceremony.

"This place is dope. How did you find out about it?" Erin asked, rubbing her hands across the metal tabletop.

"Sal quit her job at the art supply store to work here..." Allen looked around for her "...somewhere."

"Oh, I finally get to meet the infamous Sal. I swear, she looks so familiar to me but I can't figure out from where."

"Hmm, she's never worked at the pizza place or hung out with your crowd that I know of."

"So why didn't you try to hook up with her? From what I've seen of her in those videos you guys made, she's cute."

"In spite of what you may believe, I don't hit on every single female friend that I know. Besides, she was my boss when I met her—hard to get over that barrier as is...and she's married, now."

"Ah ha!" Erin said pointing at him. "Acting all Joe Noble and it's actually because she's already taken!"

"Shut up and order your tea."

Erin giggled and followed his request. Their server came by to check on their table. Like the other two servers, she was dressed all in black and bore no resemblance to anyone involved in a tea ceremony, but more of a goth-raver ready to hit the dance floor. Before she left, Allen asked her if Sal was working tonight.

"Who?" she asked.

"Oh, I'm sorry, Salome," he corrected.

"Wait! Who?" Erin asked

"Oh, she's over there," The girl informed, pointing to the far right corner near the restrooms.

"Wait! Who?" Erin asked Allen.

"Salome Jolly. I call her Sal. Why? What's up?"

"Oh-my-God!-Oh-my-God!-Oh-my-God!" Erin said holding her head.

"What? What is it? Is she an enemy or something?"

"No! I know her!"

Allen's eyes widened. Erin looked around for Salome, she was where the waitress said she would be. Although the tall girl with short blonde hair had a different appearance, Erin was able to mentally revert her looks back to when they first met. Erin waved and tried to get her attention. Salome looked around to see if Erin meant someone else.

"Salome!" Erin called.

She finished dealing with her customers and walked over to Erin's table. "Hello?" she said with uncertainty in her voice.

"Oh-my God! Salome, you don't rem…"

"Erin? Erin!" she yelled, hugging Erin. They laughed and rocked back and fourth, like wrestling an invisible alligator. "Oh My-God! Bob said he saw you at an art show!"

"Hold on, how the hell do you know each other?" a very confused Allen asked.

"Europe!" Erin answered.

"Last trip, or when you first went?"

"First went. She was on that plane! She was part of the group: Her, Bob and Larry!"

"And you just now figured it out?"

"You kept calling her Sal. I didn't even recognize her in your videos. When I met her, her hair was black and long."

"And yet, she recognized you—immediately."

"I knew she was around because Bob told me," Salome informed. "Why didn't you tell me you knew her?" She hit Allen's shoulder with her note pad.

"I'm still coming to grips that she seems to know everybody I know. She even dated Monroe."

"I-did-not-DATE-Monroe!" Erin said, through clinched teeth. She added a punch to his arm to emphasize her point.

"This is so great! Have you seen Larry, yet?" Salome asked.

Erin looked at Allen. "Have I?"

"What are you looking at me for?"

"In case you know Larry. Do you call him something else? Fred? Barney?"

Salome laughed. "I don't think he knows him–well he does, but not personally"

"Come again?" Allen asked.

"You know E.F. Laura?"

"That drag queen columnist in What Weekly?" Erin asked

"Yeah, that's Larry!"

"Holy fucking shit! That's Larry!" Erin yelled. She realized she was standing and starting to draw attention. She sat down. "No wait! That mean's...Larry's gay?"

Salome had a confused look on her face. "Well...yeah... You didn't know that?"

"Erin's not that good with the gay-dar," Allen said before receiving another arm punch. "Ow! I find it amazing that you know E.F. Laura and didn't know he was gay."

"To be fair, Larry was still playing it straight back then," Salome defended. "Didn't want to be cut out of his trust fund. This is great, we should get together after work and hang out."

"I can, but Allen has a date." Erin pointed at him.

"You're getting over the flu, you shouldn't be running around to some bar," he said to Erin

"Whatever, Dad! It's just one drink."

"Famous last words."

"What date?" Salome asked him.

"That girl at Last Chance Records invited me to come see her friend's band play."

"What friend? That's not a date! Skip it!"

"Took me weeks to get this far."

"What time do you have to be there?"

"I told her 9 but I'm sure the band doesn't go on until 9:30 or 10."

"Perfect! You don't have to be there until 10. That's like, three hours from now."

"But..."

"No buts, she can wait. Oo-oo! I should take you to Gold Fish!"

"What, in River Mill? That's nowhere near where I need to go. "

"No problem, I'll drop you off there after we get some drinks."

"But I was saving my money for Stickers."

"Come on, Allen. We can all catch up. I haven't seen you in like, weeks and Erin in...years, is it?" Erin nodded. "I'll tell you what, I'll get Janet to cut you a deal on your bill." Salome started to walk away.

"But-but," Allen protested

"No buts, it'll be fun." She walked back to her station, leaving Allen speechless.

"Wow! She doesn't take no for an answer," Erin acknowledged.

"You have no idea."

The best deal Janet could give the pair was a couple of free, low-end priced sandwiches. Salome's shift ended shortly and the trio hopped into her Audi SUV and drove to the North East neighborhood, known as River Mill. Allen kept fidgeting and asking what time it was as Salome tried to steer with one hand while talking to her husband on her cell phone and Erin spent her time trying not to feel sick. She preoccupied herself by thinking of how much she knew about Salome. She had only spoken to her for a total of about four hours on the flight from New York to London. She would never have imagined the girl with nothing but a bike and a backpack would have an SUV and have a hostess job at a trendy eatery. As far as she was concerned, there was no connection to the girl she met back then.

"Erin, how did things turn out with that boy you were running away from?" Salome asked.

"I wasn't running away from him, we were supposed to be on that plane together."

"Oh, right, right. What happened when you got back?"

"Nothing much. I saw him last year for the first time at a Halloween alphabet party and just recently at that gallery thing when I saw Bob."

"This guy stiffed Erin before she went to Europe," Salome explained to Allen. *She doesn't know that Allen knows more about the story than she does.* "Did you have a good time any way? Sorry we haven't been in touch. I moved as soon as I got back and lost your number. I'm surprised Larry and Bob didn't call you."

"Never gave me their numbers."

"Really? That's rude."

"No biggie. I had a great time. So much so, that I went back and had an even better time."

"Really? Even after that guy tried to rape you in Italy?" Allen asked

"S-say what?" Salome asked.

Erin felt a little embarrassed. "No one tried to <u>rape</u> me. He was just coming on to me."

"Very strongly I might say. This guy kept rubbing on her all night," Allen added more information, angering Erin.

"Eww, really? Did Bob tell you what happen to us in Prague?" Salome asked.

"No, I didn't talk to him that much. He was out on a date with my roommate."

"No way! Small damn world. Did it work out?"

"You mean: did he score with my roommate? I guess, they're still hanging out. Funny thing is, her homeless ex boyfriend has been on our couch for at least a month."

"She dated a homeless guy?"

"No!" Erin laughed. "He's couch surfing. He can't find a place because the market is so bad right now."

"That's bullshit. Me and Brad found a place in a week."

"You and Brad are professionals my dear," Allen informed. "I think he delivers pizza's, right?"

"Oh no," Erin said with slight sarcastic anger. "He got another job working as a driver for a local TV station. He has a real job now."

"And yet he's still on your couch? Sweetie, you guys are getting used," Salome said

"Yes! And, Fabrianne won't get him to leave. I'm so sick of coming home and seeing him there, eating all of the leftovers, drinking all of the beer. And Fabrianne's like, 'Well, he <u>is</u> paying into the rent a little now.' And I'm like, 'Who gives a fuck, this was supposed to be our house, and he moves in and is becoming permanent?' It's not right. I don't feel comfortable there."

"And he whacks off to porn videos when you're not there," Allen added

"Yeah, that too."

"S-say what?" Salome asked

"Yeah, I thought he stopped and Fabrianne thought it was like some desperate cry for help, but the thought of him doing God-knows-what on the couch makes me never want to even be in the living room again."

"That's not right, that you can't be comfortable in your own home."

"Exactly! And if the other two girls aren't going to ask him to leave, then I might as well start looking for another place. The problem is, I like them and it's in a great neighborhood… minus the Neo yuppies."

"Where, exactly?"

"Grandview."

"That is nice."

"Yeah, but it's expensive buying groceries and shit there. The cafes all charge what you can buy a bag of coffee for, for one cup."

"You're the only person to complain about living in a house in Grandview," Allen mocked.

"There's more to a home than yuppie shops and cafés. I'd trade it all for a cool funky neighborhood where I can be myself."

"Well…" Salome thought for a second. "My friend Bethanie owns this two-unit duplex in East West River Valley and one was for rent. We didn't take it because we need a third bedroom for Brad's weights and shit."

"Weights?"

"Brad is a fitness trainer at Stone Cold Gym."

"I call him Brad the Bod," Allen teased. "They have a room that looks like a gym."

Erin imagined Brad as a large muscle-bound goon. *How had he and Salome hooked up? It's hard to picture.* "I'd like to live in East River. Even though this friend of mine already bought a freak'n loft there. There goes the neighborhood."

"Her block isn't built up like that part. It's further west. You should check it out, very artsy fartsy."

"I just might do that." *I wonder what would happen if I moved out of the fancy Grandview neighborhood just to get away from Roger. It's obvious he's becoming a part of the furniture and ain't going anywhere. But no matter what, there's no fucking way I can afford a two bedroom anything, even with the extra cabin money and my job. Maybe I can talk Tawnee into going with me. I really like Fabrianne, but I wished she would take a stand against Roger. After all, he was the reason we found our own place.*

Salome made a right into Chinatown. Erin thought about the secret Alphabet party she had gone to in its hidden underground spaces. Instead of looking back on it as a horrible night of running into ex boyfriends, peeing her pants and waking up next to a downtown fountain, she looked at it as a crazy night where she stretched the limits of sobriety. *I actually found the galley night more stressful. I did my best, trying to stay away from Kevin and Steiner, but Steiner of course hung around me. It was like the more you push him away, the more he wants to be near you. Maybe he was just interested in hitting on Chris or Pam, but after they left, he still hung around me. Even after I told him why I slapped him, he agreed he deserved it. Don't think we'll reach the level of close friends but I think I can tolerate him in case he shows up at the house or an event. Kevin and Peter are another story. Kevin can rot and as for Peter, the Erin you knew died two years ago.*

Salome parked the car the way she drove, which was badly. While driving, she would wait until the absolute last minute before completely depressing the brake, bringing her bumper an inch away from an insurance claim and making Erin stomp an imaginary pedal on her side of the car. When she parallel parked, it was so close to the yellow Citron in front of them, the only way anyone was going to depart their parking space was by hitting the other person's bumper at least three times.

The über-hip River Mill area created an inviting welcome mat with its trendy boutiques selling clothes costing more than Erin's current debt, and its newly restored restaurants. This area used to be the garment district until someone discovered it was cheaper making garments in China. It's huge, red brick buildings had remained closed and in some cases rented by artists until the building owners kicked the artists out, inserted yuppies, and like a designer-labeled bomb had gone off, the area became what it is today. On the walk to Gold Fish, they passed by such restaurant names as: Au! Blue, Cenoté and 99.

"The reservations for 99 have to be at least a month in advance, and as soon as they're open, the phone line is <u>always</u> busy," Allen said

"Who the hell would wait so long just to get into a restaurant?" Erin complained

"Apparently we would," Allen said gesturing to the 30 person deep line coming out of Gold Fish.

"Shit!" Salome complained. "Where did all these people come from?"

"Apparently, your little feed bag has been discovered," said Allen. "Whelp, anywhere else to go?"

"Ahhh! No!" Salome whined. "I want to go here. I have to have their Bo Nuong again."

"Bo what?" Erin asked

"Bo Nunong Goi, its like a barbecued beef salad."

"Beef salad? What kind of restaurant is this? Is this Chinese?"

"Vietnamese."

"You mean like dogs and stuff?"

Salome laughed.

"For fuck's sake, Erin! How racist is that?" Allen complained.

"I don't know anything about Vietnamese; I've never had it before."

"With an attitude like that, you won't!" Allen crossed his arms.

"Now we have to go in. We can't have Erin running around thinking they all eat dogs," Salome said. Allen silently agreed.

They went to the front of the line to put their names on the list. The blonde, White woman dressed all in red at the front desk informed the current wait for a table would be 45 minutes. *I find it amazing that people would tolerate waiting this long for anything that doesn't involve a ticket.*

They took their position at the end of the line, behind a couple who, although together, were having separate conversations with other people on their cell phones.

"Maybe they're talking to each other?" Allen silently joked.

Erin smiled. "Gotta do something to pass the time." She lit up a cigarette.

"Let's catch up!" Salome suggested. "How was Europe the second time?"

"A lot of fun; more relaxing...sorta."

"Sorta?"

"Yeah, some stuff happened in Italy...France..."

"France?" Allen interrupted. "You didn't tell me about France."

"Why would I? Who are you, my therapist?"

"No, your therapist would have jumped through a window by now."

"Ha-bloody-ha." Erin sneered.

"I'm curious. What happened in France? Is this about Marie?" Salome asked.

"Sorta...not really. Do you know her friend Henrí?"

"No, but go on."

"You have to promise me, this won't get back to her."

"I'm not really on good terms with her right now."

"Really, what happened?"

"It was...it's complicated. Go on, tell your story and I'll tell you my Spain story and we'll see which is the worst."

"Is that the one with that guy with the plaster?" Allen asked

"Yeah-yeah. Erin's story first," Salome interrupted. "And leave no scandalous stone unturned."

"All right. Me and Marie went to this fancy hair salon in the Bastille and it's like a hair salon here—you know, fancy women getting their hair cut by gay guys. Marie knows the owner, Henrí, and he's this cute guy, about 30 I think, and they're all chatting, people are bringing us glasses of wine, everybody's being friendly. I don't know what the hell anyone is saying but apparently, later on, Marie tells me that Henrí says I have a very cute face, he just wish I didn't have those awful dreadlocks."

"Ahhh, so you cut them off for a man," Allen guessed.

"Yes—well, not really. It was a way to erase the past. I got them when I went the first trip. I figured I'd get rid of them this time. When I passed through Paris the second time, I got my hair dyed. That was actually to erase his work."

"Oh, oh, I know where this is going," Salome said.

"Right. So literally, at that moment they all sit me down and just cut my dreads off and gave me my buzz cut—I had dreadlocks for a couple of years, by the way," Erin informed Salome and Allen. They nodded comprehension. "After that, even though I couldn't understand anyone, I could tell that even the customers were saying: Oh! She looks so much better. When I went to lunch, guys were checking me out and shit. It felt great. Later that night, Marie throws this dinner party. She invites a couple of friends, Henri's there. We're all hanging out at her apartment. People are asking me about American politics and I'm like: I've never even voted, how the hell should I know."

"You've never voted!" Allen asked angrily.

"Stop interrupting!"

"Yeah, Allen." Salome hit him on the shoulder with the back of her hand.

"So, I'm talking to her about some shit and he's like: How long are you gonna be here? Blah-blah-blah? I tell him a couple of days and he asks me if I've ever seen the Eiffel Tower at night, and I admit I've never even seen it up close, 'cause I just like to hang out in cafés…"

"Brasseries," Allen corrected. Salome hit his arm again.

"Thank you. Brasserie—whatever! That and check out small museums and just hang out. I'm not a big fan of hanging out at tourist areas. So he's like: 'Oh, you have to see it. It's beautiful.' So just the two of us take the subway there and he's right, it's really cool, the lights on it making it all orange and stuff, no fat American tourist hanging around."

"So, is he hitting on you or anything? 'Cause that sounds like a romantic setup?" Salome asked. Allen hit her in the shoulder for interrupting.

"No, he's being a perfect gentleman. We stop by this bar on the way back…"

"Brasserie!" Allen corrected.

"No! Le bar! As in <u>alcohol</u> and music! So we talk a little. I talk about Kevin and Steiner. He says how it was wrong for Kevin to tell me to fuck off..."

"Wait, who's Kevin and Steiner?" Salome interrupted. Allen hit her arm again. "Hey! It's important to the story!"

"Boy trouble. I'll fill you in later. He's like sugar coating me with: a woman as beautiful as you should be lavished with kisses and gifts every day, yadda yadda yadda, and I eat it up. We're heading back to the apartment on the subway; I'm talking about something and these guys—teenagers, start mumbling something in French. I guess they didn't know that he spoke French and Henrí goes off on them. They're cursing, doing hand gestures. I thought there was going to be a fight. He tells me that they were calling me a dyke and him a fag and I flipped them off and said: 'I got your dyke right here asshole!' They get off. I ask him: does being gay in Paris get you as abused as it does in America and he tells me that he's <u>not</u> gay. See, I thought he was because of the hair salon thing and he hadn't hit on me."

"In Erin's world, any man in a beauty shop is gay, and Vietnamese eat dogs." Allen laughed.

Erin gave him an evil eye. "Anyway!...So, I'm like: You aren't? And at that moment, he kisses me."

"That'll learn you!" Allen's interruption was met by double arm slaps.

"We end up at this motel nearby, 'cause he says his place is being remodeled and we go at it."

"Go at what? Board games? Twister? Mouse Trap? Chutes and..." Allen moved away fast enough to avoid getting hit again.

"We have sex!" Erin said angrily, causing the couple in front of her to turn around and look at her. She scowled. "Afterwards, he says he has to meet the contractors in the morning, but I could stay at the hotel if I wanted. The next day, I go back to the salon. He's not there..."

"Wait! Don't tell me. A French urban legend! There was no Henrí! He was a ghost that worked at the salon 50 years ago!" Allen joked.

Erin and Salome laughed. Erin swung and missed him, again. "No! It's his day off or something. But I'm cool with it. Even cool with a one-night stand thing; I don't want no relationship, I'm on vacation. Days go by, I occasionally go by the salon…"

"Occasionally? As in, stalk?" Allen asked

"Just to say 'hi', God damn it! He's never there. Turns out the motherfucker is hiding in the back from me."

"How did you know that?" Salome asked

"I saw him. I went in. He wasn't there. I went across the street to buy some cigs, and his ass appears from the back."

"You should'a kicked his ass," Salome said.

"I should have, but still, I'm like: Whatever, I'm on vacation. I talk to Marie later and she's saying how much she likes my new hair, and I say, 'Too bad the guy that cut it is such a womanizing scumbag.' And she's like, 'Henrí? Do you think he's having an affair?' I'm like, 'affair?' And she's like, 'Oui, Henrí's married!'"

Salome put her hands on her mouth. "Oh-my-god! You had an affair!"

"Well… technically, he did. I'm not married."

"That's true," Allen agreed. "You're the other woman."

"Yep, that's me. La whore de Paris."

"Whoa! That is scandalous! I don't know if my plaster story can top that one," Salome said.

"Go ahead. Try me," Erin said in a challenging way.

For the remainder of their 40-minute wait, Salome told her plaster story. Apparently while in Spain, she and her traveling companions had met up with an artist and sculptor, whose work consisted of plastering people's private parts and casting them in bronze. After much wine and coaxing, this resulted in a bronze cast of Larry and Bob's dicks and Salome's butt displayed somewhere in an artist loft or perhaps even a gallery, somewhere in Europe.

The inside of Gold Fish resembled Vietnam even less than Tea-V represented an English teahouse. It was as dark as a bar, with most of the light illuminating from an eight inch wide glowing aquarium tube recessed inside the wall. It ran the entire length of the restaurant. Goldfish were free to swim all the way from the front, to the men's' room and back again.

"Holy shit!" Erin said, summing up what most people felt when first seeing the aquatic instillation. "This is fierce."

"I'm just amazed I don't see any dead fish," Allen said. "You know how when you go to a cheap pet stores, they always have at least two dead, floating fish?"

The hostess, another blonde White woman dressed all in red, showed them to their seats. The area was cramped and crowded. Erin barely had enough room to move her seat back without hitting the chair of the guy in a suit behind her. He was gracious enough to stand and let her get situated before sitting back down. She said thank you, but she wondered if the rumbling noisy conversations all around them and the techno music drowned her out.

Yet another blonde White woman dressed all in red came by and handed them their menus: Shiny, yellow pieces of paper attached by an elastic band to a thin, grey piece of slate. As usual, instead of looking at the items, Erin immediately scanned the prices. *This is in the tier three range for prices. This means I'll be sticking to shared appetizers and one drink. Just as well, I have no idea what vegetarian 'Ga Xao Xa Ot' is.* When the waitress returned, Salome ordered her Bo Nuong Goi; Allen ordered Canh Chua, a sweet and sour fish soup; and Erin, a vegetable juice martini, which she assumed would be like a bloody Mary.

"You're not getting anything to eat?" Salome asked.

"I thought we were coming for drinks. I'm surprised Allen ordered food. Aren't you gonna miss your date?"

"It's okay," he said. "As long as I get out of here within an hour, I'll be okay. You should get something."

Erin took another look at the menu as the waitress, impatiently waited for her to order. As Erin read what was in the vegetarian Cha Gio, she heard her name being called. It took a second time before she looked up and realized it wasn't part of the music.

Like an urban-jungle explorer with a social machéte, Donna Etcheverria squeezed between tables and people and made her way over to Erin.

"Oh-my-God! How are you?" Donna yelled.

Erin stood up and did her best to hug her over the obstacles. *I have to admit, it's not surprising to see her here. Donna is, after all, the litmus test for all that is hip.*

"I came here with Amber." Donna gestured to the table near the kitchen. Amber Little Feather was the only one seated at the six-person table. She waved hello.

"Why do you have such a big table if it's just the two of you?" Erin asked.

"Oh, I always expect more friends to show up, so I always book a large table."

"That's optimistic," Allen said.

"Yes, yes it is. I'm Donna Etcheverria." Donna reached out her hand, palm down. Allen looked uncertain about how to shake it. He introduced himself, reached down and kissed her hand as if she was royalty. Donna laughed. "How delightful!"

Salome introduced herself.

"So why don't you guys come and join me?" Donna asked. The group looked at each other. There seem to be no objections. *I like Donna's table location better, anyway. I'm sure she knows the owner or someone else high up. There's no way anyone would sit just two people at a large table until the rest of the party showed up.*

After introductions to Amber, they all sat down.

"What did you guys order?" Donna asked. They shared their individual orders with Donna. "Is that all? Did you order the Chao Tom?"

"What's that?" Erin asked.

"It's pounded shrimp wrapped around a sugar cane and then barbecued." Erin looked confused. "No? Kelly!" she called out. A waitress came to their table. "I want to order some Chao Tom for us. Oh, and some Cha Gio, and maybe later some Xoi Nuoc Dir for dessert. Oh, and Erin, you're still a vegetarian, right?"

Erin nodded.

"So, bring us the vegetarian Bun Bo and Cha Gio, too." After Kelly took the order and departed, Allen leaned over to whisper to Erin while Salome and Donna talked.

"Who is this girl?" he asked

"She's one of the Etcheverria sisters. Her sister owns that Café: Psychicmondo–whatever."

"Never been there."

"Oh. Well, they're loaded. I think her parents were old school rich. Both died in a plane crash. Left them a bunch of money."

"How do you know all this?"

"Roger went to school with her and she had a crush on Steiner when I was going out with him. Speaking of school, did I tell you I signed up for Geometry and life drawing class at the community college?"

"You mentioned you were going to…So, how is she going to pay for all this extra food?"

"She won't have to. She probably knows the owner. When I went with her —"

"What are you two talking about?" Donna asked

"Allen was asking me how I know you." Allen looked embarrassed.

"Oh, me and Erin go waaay back." The way she spoke gave an inkling she had been drinking for a while. Erin noticed an empty bottle of Champagne on the table. "I met her and… Lashell? At the same time. What ever happened to Lashell?"

"Oh, she's around." *I haven't heard from or contacted Lashell in a month. I'm unsure if we're still friends. I refused to call her about Allen, just out of cruelty. After a week, it just slipped my mind to call her back at all. Then I got sick.*

"You're on that cable TV show: Shut Up…something, right?" Salome asked Donna.

"Oh that, I haven't done that show in a year."

For some reason, the mention of Donna's past project reminded Erin of Monroe. "Oh! How could I forget? Allen knows Monroe," Erin volunteered.

Donna's look was both pleasant surprise and one that said: 'How do you know him, and is it as a close friend?' "Oh, Really? How's that?"

"I work with him, Salome used to as well," Allen answered. "Actually, we also had some stuff on Channel 57; some videos with Sal and Monroe. How do you know him?"

"Are you kidding?" Erin said. "Donna knows everybody. Even more than me. She even knows Steiner and my ex boyfriend, Peter."

"What a small, incestuous world," Allen said. "No wait, is that the right word?" Donna laughed.

"She's not sleeping with them!" Erin said, slapping Allen's arm. "Actually, I have no idea if you're sleeping with any of my ex boyfriends—are you?" Erin asked

"Gee-zus! Erin," Allen complained. "Paranoid <u>and</u> nosey!"

"Hey, I'm just curious. I don't really care. She's free to do whatever she wants; it's America."

"That's right," Donna agreed, raising the last glass of her Champagne. "God bless America...and no, I'm not sleeping with them. I actually haven't seen Monroe in a long-long time...after our...talk."

"Oh really?" Erin said intrigued. "What talk? He put the groove on you?"

"Yes...is that too personal? Is he a good friend of yours?" Donna asked, looking at Allen and Salome.

"We like him," Allen answered. "But he's his own person. So did you devastate him or let him down easy?"

"Al-len!" Erin complained.

"Hey, I'm just joking...and curious."

"I thought it was easy. But is it ever easy?"

"I guess not"

"I liked him. But you know... I just like to have fun. Can't men and women just be friends, hang out without someone wanting a relationship?"

"It depends, Allen answered. As long as there's an understanding of what they're getting into."

"Bullshit-loney," Erin disagreed. "I had one of those relationships with Steiner, and things got messy anyway. No matter how <u>casual</u> you try to make it, one of you always tries to want more."

"And was that you?" Donna asked.

"It was me, sad to say. Well, that and I was chasing after a gay guy."

"Oh! How did that turn out? You mentioned that when we first met."

"Donna—he's gay—the end."

"<u>His</u> end!" Allen joked. Erin hit the back of his head. "Will you stop hitting me!"

"Will you stop saying stupid shit?" Erin answered.

Donna laughed.

Donna ordered another bottle of Champagne for the table. Along with their bottle, the food they had all ordered arrived, presented on square, red clay tiles. They were warned the tiles were heated to keep the food warm. Erin liked everything she actually could eat. It was tempting to try the Chao Tom, accurately described as pounded shrimp wrapped around a sugar cane and then barbecued.

Amber wasn't speaking much. Erin realized this and asked how she was doing.

"Poor Amber." Donna interrupted. "She got her heart broken today. That's why we went out."

"Ahh, that sucks," Erin said.

"It's okay," Amber said. "He was a jerk."

"Wow, this is the table full of broken hearts...'Cept you," Erin said to Salome."

"Yep. I do love my man," Salome bragged.

"What about you, Allen? Did you have your heart broken recently?" Donna asked.

"Only by me," Erin said. *Oh, oh, that was kind of a rude thing to say. But, thanks to Champagne, it's already out there.*

"Ahh." Donna said, almost laughing.

"I'm just kidding," Erin said rubbing Allen's back. We're still good friends, not like your Monroe thing."

"Yes. It was sad. I mean, he's a nice guy, but—you know."

"Doesn't own a Mercedes?" Allen asked, defensively.

"Oh, my, no," Donna said. Her tone was of a person accused of something cruel.

Erin whispered to Allen, "Dude, she's paying for this meal!"

"I don't care. She dissed my friend!"

"Then let him pay for this. Have you seen the prices on the menu?"

"Life is more than free meals, Erin!"

"Whatever." Erin took a bite of vegetarian Ga Xao Xa Ot and drank some more Champagne. She lowered her voice so only Allen could hear her. "Have I ever told you how I know Monroe?"

"Not really. You said you met at a club."

"Yep. We met, kissed a little. I wanted to leave; he wouldn't leave me alone, so I gave him a hand job in the car and he left."

Allen's response was silence.

"Now...whatever Donna did to him, I can totally understand why she did it."

Allen was angry. He shook his head in disbelief.

"Don't worry Amber and Allen, we'll find you two new loves," Donna said, raising her glass.

"Maybe they should go out on a date together? Salome suggested."

"Hey! That would work," Erin said pointing to them both.

"No, thanks," Allen said.

"What? Why not?"

"You shouldn't put her on the spot like that," he responded.

"What about you Amber? What do you think?" Donna asked.

"I don't date Black guys."

"Oh, my," Donna said.

"Really? Why not?" Allen asked.

"I just don't. I prefer White guys."

"That sounds racist," he responded with his face in a scowl.

"No, it's not—I'm not a racist!"

"You only date guys based on their skin color!"

"That doesn't make me a racist! How dare you accuse me of that!"

"Hey, you're the one with the prejudiced attitude!"

"I'm not prejudiced just because I prefer a certain type of guy! That doesn't mean I want to keep Blacks out of my neighborhood or won't stand up for equal rights!"

"Whatever you say."

"Hey! You can—"

"Okay! All right!" Donna interrupted. "This is supposed to be a happy night out. No one is allowed to talk about anything bad anymore." Allen and Amber ended their heated discussion. Both simmered in bitterness and anger.

Erin wished to calm the waters at the table for fear Donna would get up and leave them with a big bill. "So, Donna, how's that loft working out for ya?"

"It's great! I got a large painting by Wyatt Davis hanging over the fireplace."

"I know his wife," Salome said.

"You know Delesia?"

"Yeah, she used to come into the art supply store where I used to work. You remember her, Allen? That Black chick with the long braids?"

"Sure," he said, still sounding angry with Amber.

Donna and Salome continued talking. It turned out they also both knew E.F. Laura. Salome asked Donna if she knew Bethanie. Donna said no.

"She had a TV show like you on cable access about Wiccas or something—I think you'd like her space Erin, it's all old and stuff," Salome said.

"Really, where?" Donna asked

"East West River Valley."

"I thought that was still projects?"

"No, Wait!" Erin interrupted. "You don't know about East West River Valley?"

"I know, I must be out of it. I live right near there, yet haven't gone over in that part recently."

"Donna! I thought you were the queen of all that was hip and new? Yet how can you miss something right next to you?"

Donna laughed. "I'm not the queen of all that is hip and new. I've been so busy with work and travel; it's sad. The last time I was over in that part, I didn't see anything interesting."

"It's not that big yet. Just a bookstore, a produce store and I think there's a café opening up," said Salome.

"Then we should all go visit East West River Valley..." Donna said before taking a sip of Champagne. "...Right now."

"What?" Allen asked

"Yes, after dinner, we should go by East West River Valley and then we can end the night at my place."

"I can't go. I have a date," Allen said.

"No, you don't," Erin said.

"Yes, I do and..." He checked a fish-shaped clock on the wall. "...and I have 35 minutes to make it."

"Allen is meeting some girl to hear her boyfriend's band play," Salome said.

"It's not her boyfriend!" he said.

"Of course he is," Salome replied.

"And how would you know?"

"Because no one invites a guy out on a date to be with other people that they know. She's either interested in a guy in the band, or she's inviting you out as a buddy-buddy thing."

"You don't know that."

"Gee, I never thought of that," Erin said. "She's right, Allen."

"Hey! Just because you girls can't get a date, don't go ragging on mine."

"Maybe she's a racist," Amber said. Erin and Salome laughed.

"Oh, my," Donna said. "This conversation has become bitter, let's talk about something else."

"I'm cool," Allen said. "You guys are the ones who are bitter."

"I'm not bitter!" Erin said.

"Sure you are: Steiner, that other guy. You just don't want to see anyone else happy but you."

"That's a load of crap! I'm quite happy without either of them!"

"Sh-yeah, right."

"I—"

Donna clapped her hands twice and interrupted Erin. "Okay, okay. Enough of this! Let's move on. After dinner, we go to my place to look at my new painting, okay?"

"Sure," Erin agreed. "Maybe we can swing by East West, and have a look."

"Of course, Allen?" Donna asked

"I'm still going out on my date—and shouldn't you be resting up?" he asked Erin. "You just got over the flu."

"I feel fine."

"Such concern, how sweet," Donna cooed. "Come on, Allen. Just for a little while. I have chocolate truffles and a 20-year-old port for dessert. You can be fashionably late. She'll know that you're not desperate; girls find that sexy."

"Yeah, Al. You like Wyatt Davis stuff. I'll drop you off just in time for the band to start," Salome added.

"Whatever," he agreed. "Don't call me Al."

"We should actually go to my house, first," Salome said. "I live near here."

"You live in River Mill?" Donna asked. Her voice hinted of excitement.

Salome just scored 10 Donna points.

"Sure. We just got a place near 12th and Jackson."

"Isn't that part crack addicts and drug dealers?"

"Not since we've moved here–no more than where you live."

Ouch!

"Oh, then by all means. Let's all go to Salome's place first."

"Rowl!" Allen whispered to Erin, impersonating a catfight

"I can't believe she challenged Donna and won," Erin whispered back.

"I told you. Doesn't take no for an answer."

After the meal, as Erin had predicted and hoped, Donna cut them a deal with the waitress. Half of what they had ordered was missing from the final tally.

Erin elbowed Allen as she showed him the bill. "Better than free sandwiches," she said. He seemed unimpressed.

#

They loaded back into Salome's SUV and drove four blocks to her apartment. *This isn't an apartment, this is a loft! Salome said apartment to prevent herself from sounding like a yuppie!* As they entered the old brick building, Donna looked like she was taking notes, comparing this building to hers. To Erin, they all looked alike—giant boxes.

The inside was different from Donna's. Instead of one big room with just the bedroom area separated by its own level, each section of Salome's place was separated into three different floors. Each floor had its own entrance and they all shared the same view of the East Side bridge.

"Fuck'n awesome view!" Erin commented as they took the spiral staircase from the kitchen/dining room level down to the living room/weight room level. In the living room was a large plasma screen TV. On the screen were the Neo Tech Bulldogs basketball game. Watching the game, the husband named Brad. He wasn't as built-up as Erin had thought he would be, but from what she could tell by his physique in his Stone Cold Gym sweatshirt, he did seem to be in great shape.

"Well, hello!" he said cheerfully, turning down the volume of the TV. He walked over to greet them. The closer he got, the older he seemed. Erin pegged him at least 10 years Salome's senior, in his mid to late 30s, and tanned with well-chiseled features. Erin shook his hand.

"I brought them here to show them the pad," Salome said before kissing him hello.

"Oh, then by all means. Can I offer anyone anything?" he asked, smiling. His teeth were perfect. *If I didn't know any better, I would swear he looks like a famous actor.*

"Not for me, I'm not staying," said Allen.

"You have any cognac or brandy?" Donna asked.

Brad looked a little confused. "I think we may have brandy left over from Christmas, I'll have to check."

Erin asked for a beer. Brad left for the kitchen and Salome led them around to the weight room area. Erin recognized the standard equipment: Barbells, bench and a treadmill, but not some electronic machines, which resembled torture devices with elastic attachments. Each member of the group took turns trying out the different devices, each received ridicule and laughing when they couldn't lift a certain amount of pounds or pull the elastic bands far enough. Allen surprised Erin by lifting more on the bench than she had expected. *He's apparently stronger than I thought.* Salome confessed she never used the exercise area. If she had to work out, she preferred to use the dance aerobics kickboxing class at the gym. It turned out Donna also took those classes on a different night than Salome. *Perhaps those classes are more of a social scene than an actual workout.*

After the dispersal of drinks, everyone returned to the living room area. Donna spent her time walking around, looking at different objects and asking Salome about them.

Salome clued her husband in on how she knew Erin. The mention of Europe lead to how Brad, who used to be a male model, had met Salome in Belgium. Erin mentioned she stopped there briefly on her way back from Amsterdam. "I was in Antwerp, saw some castle called Het-something…It was okay, too much medieval stuff for me. If I see too many castles and stuff like that I get bored."

"And yet, you like to go to England," Allen criticized.

"I don't hang out in Buckingham palace. I told you, when I travel, I just like to hang out where the locals are."

"I hear ya," Brad agreed. "That's how I like to travel."

Donna stopped looking at a lamp to give her opinion. "But if you hang out with just the locals, you don't have access to a lot of things. Like I found out about this fabulous local celebrity party in Madrid from a friend that works at a TV station there. Now, you think some local is going to get you into that party? I don't think so."

"But if you hang out in fancy parties, you miss a lot of the local scenes and <u>realness</u>," Salome countered.

"I believe that the best way to observe the whole world is to fly over it. That way you get the big picture."

"That sounds kind of shallow," Allen said.

He beat me to what I was about to say.

"Oh really, Allen…" Donna walked over to the couch and put her hand on his shoulder. "…Tell me, what would you rather do: go to that local club and maybe, just maybe, meet some girl, or hang out with me, drink port and eat chocolates in front of a fireplace until the sun rises?"

"I don't know…I've already made plans."

"You see, locals on the ground beat the high flyers every time," Erin gloated.

"He said he didn't know," Donna corrected.

"He basically said no."

"Did you?" Donna asked

"I don't know…you guys are freaking me out, putting me on the spot and shit! Of course I'd like to hang out drinking port, but I can't flake out on that girl from Last Chance Records—"

"Last Chance? How appropriate is that?"Amber commented.

"No one asked you!"

"Oh give it up! You know you'd rather hang out with Donna than some grimy music groupie!"

"How little you know me."

"Will you?" Salome asked him.

"What?"

"Are you going to hang out with Donna or that girl?"

Allen stood up and did a mock scream. "You guys are still freaking me out. This conversation is over!" He walked to the window. Donna and Amber laughed in victory.

Erin walked over to Allen to check on his mental state and the view. "Well?"

"Well what?" he asked her.

"You know. Sure thing with Donna or chance it with grime girl."

"She's not a grime girl! Spike's really nice."

"Wait! Spike's the girl at Last Chance records?"

"I know it's a weird name. It's her nickname, 'cause her last name is Lee and…" Allen looked at the expression on Erin's face. He took a guess on what it meant. "Please don't tell me you know her."

"Well, sorta. I worked with her friend Tracy and we all snuck into a rave one night and shared a bottle of wine at an art show."

Allen placed his forehead against the window and sighed. "Why God, why? Do you know everybody I know?"

"I told you, F.J. Pizza. She's cute though…a little young."

"Really? What do you mean? How young is young?"

"19 I think."

"19!" he yelled. Everyone looked at them. "I thought she was at least 21! How the hell does she get into bars?"

"Tracy and them never pay to get into places, they sneak in everywhere and get their drinks for free."

"But 19! Shit! You guys are right. She's probably after some guy in the band."

"Oh, don't be like that. We don't know any better. She may like you."

"Sh-yeah, right. A 19 year-old likes the 29-year-old guy. That's 10 years!" Allen appeared very frustrated and upset.

Erin tried to give him hope. "Well, there's still Donna."

"I don't think so. Her racist friend doesn't date Black guys, I'm sure she doesn't either."

"I'm not so sure."

"How so?"

"Well, Donna is like one of those rich people that wants to experience the world. She might be into you just for the experience."

"Oh great, the Mandingo experience."

"I have no idea what that is, but okay, whatever works." Erin patted his shoulder and walked back over to the couch to finish her beer.

After another beer with a brandy chaser, Erin started to feel woozy. It wasn't the kind of woozy she liked or was used to when she was drunk or high, but more like one that meant if she indulged in anything remotely challenging, she would throw up. *I have absolutely no interest in Donna seeing me throw up.* She would back out of the second leg of the adventure to Donna's loft. After announcing her intentions, she asked Allen what he was going to do.

"I don't know, I guess I'll stick around these guys. I'm kind of curious what a 20-year old port taste like."

"Is that sex lingo for going after Donna?"

"No, but that would've worked. There's no way a girl like that is gonna date a guy like me."

"That's the spirit!" Erin said sarcastically, patting him on the back.

Amber also announced her intention of backing out of the next journey.

"Ahh, you too?" Donna whined.

"I have make sure my roommate didn't let her coke-headed boyfriend move in." Amber said

"Think I can bum a ride to the station?" Erin asked Amber.

"Sure. Is Kenwood okay?"

"S-sure," Erin agreed with reservation. *I expected her to take me home. Kenwood, is closer, but it's in the opposite direction and not the safest place at night.*

Goodbyes and hugs were exchanged. Salome said she'd call Erin and try to do something tomorrow.

While they were walking back to Amber's car. It took Erin a second to realize Amber had started a conversation with her. Erin was busy worrying she had relapsed back into the flu, thanks to her venture out.

"What?" Erin asked

"I said, what is the deal with Allen?"

"Huh? I don't know what you mean."

"Accusing me of being a racists and shit? What's up with that?"

"He's not as militant as you think. He's just been going through some relationship things. We ran into his ex a while ago and this girl he likes started dating this guy…"

"So, what does that has to do with him thinking I'm a racist? I'm not a racist! I believe in people having rights. I just ain't attracted to Black guys!"

"Well, I think you should be open to anything. I mean I'm attracted to people. I don't care what they are…as long as they're cute…and tall…and are into something like art or a musician. But they can be any race."

"But see! You wouldn't date a midget!"

"Well…I don't know. I guess not."

"Ah ha! See! That's what I'm talking about. You wouldn't date a midget, but you'd let them live in your neighborhood."

Erin had nothing to say. Amber may have scored a point for her opinion, but Erin didn't care to discuss preferential philosophy. She just wanted to go home and crawl into bed. Amber kept talking about the subject, in spite of Erin's lack of input. *Apparently, Allen struck a cord with Amber. I wonder if it has anything to do with the formally Jewish girl who changed her last name to Little Feather and now considers herself an Indian—Native American—whatever.* Erin was now glad Amber was going to drop her off after a short drive. *Any longer and I'm so close to telling this bitch: either go out and fuck a Black guy or shut the hell up.*

Kenwood station looked a little different from when Erin lived in the neighborhood. It was cleaner, like someone had taken a high-powered water hose and sprayed the whole block. There was also a lack of drug dealers and prostitutes around the station. *The new inhabitants in the nearby loft must have objected to the view.* There were still a few homeless people milling about, pushing shopping carts or sleeping next to a grate. Erin quickly tried to make a hasty entrance into the station. Someone yelled something. *I have no time or patience for a crazy homeless person or a drug dealer.* Again, someone yelled something, it sounded like her name. She rumbled through her jacket looking for the last train token. This time it sounded like her name had been called. She looked to see what the person wanted. It was Jeff, from F. J. Pizza. He still sported a Prince Valiant haircut and wore a black leather jacket with red sleeves. He was wearing eyeglasses, which may have been real or just for fashion.

"Erin!" he yelled.

"Oh, oh, wow, Jeff." He approached her. She considered hugging him but remembered she really didn't like him. "How's it going?"

"It's cool. What's up with you? I like your hair!"

"Thanks. Nothing much…hanging out."

"Where are you working?"

"At the university, in the Medical department."

"Great. Nice to see you moved on from F.J.P."

"Of course. How about you? You still there?"

"Me? Yeah, but I'm at the new one. You should drop by."

"Sure." *I need to cut this short, so I can go home.* "Well, I gotta go. Don't wanna miss my train. It was nice seeing you."

"Yeah, definitely—Hey! You should give me your number, we should hang out."

"Uh–I'd love too but I'm moving soon."

"Really? Where?"

Erin had to think of a lie fast. "Paris."

"Paris?"

"Y-yeah."

"What are you going to be doing there?"

"Art…I have a friend who runs a thing, a fabric shop type of…thing."

"Really? I didn't know you did art—"

"Jeff!" she interrupted, "no more questions. I have to go—bye!" She found her token, turned around and paid her way into the station.

"Okay. Call me!…" he yelled, "…at F.J. Pizza…The new one!…3-6!"

"Bye!" she yelled without turning to look at him. "God, I hate F.J. Pizza," she muttered.

#

The train ride was a short one, only two stops, and she was back in her neighborhood. On the walk back, her thoughts turned to Jeff and his relentless pursuit of a gathering with her. *Although I find it annoying and it reeks of desperation, I wish Allen had perhaps a small part of Jeff's behavior. In truth, Allen was right—he really doesn't have a chance with Donna. Not because she shares Amber's opinion on race, but because Donna would never go after anyone who I wouldn't go after; just like Steiner. The thought of me and Donna having the same taste in men makes me feel a little sick.*

There was laughter as she entered the apartment. It wasn't aimed at her but it might as well have been. Roger was apparently entertaining two male friends. She didn't recognize them but it didn't matter. When he saw her, it was a look of defiance mixed with a little fear. He was right to feel both. Erin lowered her eyelids at him and went to her hallway bathroom. Someone was in there. This was odd because there was an understanding this was pretty much Erin's bathroom. Even Roger was warned by Fabrianne to go upstairs. This was one of the few perks of living in the room under the stairwell, without a view.

"Hey! Who's in there?" she said knocking. There was silence then the toilet flushed. Out came another guy Erin didn't recognize.

"Sorry," he said unconvincingly. The smell of his bodily functions trailed behind him like a smelly cape. This created a force field to which Erin had no desire to cross and enter her bathroom. She turned around, huffed back to her room and slammed the door shut.

For a while, she didn't hear any more laughter. She hoped Roger had conveyed the message she was not one to be messed with; she was wrong. Eventually a few comments could be heard, some chuckles and eventually, she was able to pick out entire sentences, followed by laughter. She opened her door, hard enough to almost rip it off of it's hinges and marched into the living room. All eyes turned and looked at her. "Hey!" she yelled, "Can you keep it down! I'm trying to get some rest!"

There was no comment. She about-faced and returned to her room. She didn't hear anything for a couple of minutes. Someone asked: "Is that your mom?" and then laughter. There was a rumbling of shoes on the hardwood floor. The rumbling continued to and out the front door. She felt vindicated she had scared Roger's friends off. The feeling of strength ended the moment Roger opened the door without knocking. "What the fuck is your problem!" he yelled.

Erin was speechless and shocked for a second. She quickly turned this into anger. "What the fuck do you think you're doing? Coming into my room without knocking?"

"Oh, I'm sorry," he said sarcastically. He walked back to the open door and knocked three times. "There, is that better?"

"Roger—get out," Erin said calmly.

"I'm not in your room!" He gestured he was actually outside the door.

"I'm not talking about my room! I mean get out of the house! I don't know why everyone else is pussy-footing around the issue, but your ass needs to go!"

"The other two seem cool with me here!"

"We had a perfect living situation and you just fucked everything up! You need to find your own place, now!"

"Or what?"

"Or what, what?"

"What are you gonna do? Tell the landlord? She knows I'm here. She knows how tough it is to find a pla—"

"Oh please..." Erin interrupted. "...don't pull that hard to find a place shit, I've practically found a two bedroom in East West River without even looking! You just like staying here 'cause it's cheap and you can stalk your ex girlfriend!"

"Fine! Then why don't _you_ move there?"

" 'Cause this is my house, asshole!"

"Fuck you! I ain't going anywhere!"

"Fine! Then maybe I'll call the cops and have you thrown out!"

"Sh-yeah right, and maybe I'll tell 'em about that skinhead girl that you knew that was in that gang that killed What's-his-face!"

A dark cloud of dishonor had entered the room. _How does he know that? I have no idea who would tell him: Tawnee? Fabrianne? Lashell? The bottom line is, he knows._ "Fucking masturbator!" she yelled before slamming the door in his face. She sat on her bed and simmered in anger. _What do I do? Telling the landlord is_ *apparently out if she knows that Roger is living there and has no problem with it. Calling the cops is out and my roommates are no help. I could at least try Tawnee. If I can get at least one person to vote Roger out, that'll leave a 1/3 vote against.*

Erin left her room and quickly ran up the stairs. Roger had already beaten her to the punch. Upstairs, he was talking to a bed-ridden Tawnee about what had just happened.

"...I don't know what she has against me," Roger complained to Tawnee.

"Besides the fact that you jerk off in the living room and are going to blackmail me with my past?" Erin complained.

"Hey! You just caught me getting dressed for bed," Roger explained.

"What? Dude you were fuck'n watching porno! Don't lie about it, now!"

"Whatever, I don't know what your problem is. You'd think you'd be more grateful to someone who <u>saved</u> your life."

"What! Saved my what?"

"Reeee-member? Lars? About to rape or kill your sorry ass? Pointed a gun at my head?"

"You weren't there to save my life! You were there to find him! You just came at the wrong or right time."

"Ah, great. Now you're so ungrateful, you dismiss when I do something nice for you."

"Oh please, do shut the fuck up! I—"

"Enough!" Tawnee yelled. She took some tissue paper and blew her nose. "I'm really not in the mood for this shit right now. Can you two go work it out somewhere else?"

"What's there to work out? He has to go! The end!" Erin complained.

"I'm not going—"

"Enough!" Tawnee cut Roger off. "I'm still getting over the flu."

"Right. The one <u>Roger</u> gave us all!"

"Erin! I gotta rest," Tawnee explained.

"It's gonna be <u>him</u> or <u>me</u>. I can't take this shit anymore!" Erin departed, elbowing Roger out of the way.

It's gonna have to be me. There's no way Fabe is gonna vote him out! I bet she's still in love with him! I bet she hasn't even slept with Bob yet! Tawnee's so fuck'n loyal that she'd never kick someone out into the street! Erin entered her room and slammed the door.

#

It was an unseasonably clear and sunny day outside. The radio announcer said the temperature was in the low 70's. Erin felt better. The cold drugs she'd taken had done their job of putting her to sleep and clearing her head. She could easily go to work, but the prospect of a nice day wasted in an office didn't sit too well with her. She called Agnew's phone number to leave a message that she was sick. She was quite surprised when he answered.

"Oh–hi," Erin said.

"Hello, Erin," he said. There was a serious tone in his voice.

"I just called to tell you I'm still nursing the flu."

"Okay. Well…when you're feeling better, I need to talk to you about something."

"Oh, okay." Erin's heart skipped a beat. *What does he want?* She thought about the workload piling up since she had been sick. "I guess I'll see you when I feel better."

"Yes–yes, you get better and I'll see you later. Bye."

Erin laid back in bed and worried about her future. Both work and home related. *Who told Roger that I knew Suzan?* She felt scared *If he'd rat me out to the cops, what would they do? How much jail time would withholding information get me? I have to get out of the house; I have to be around other people, not in this house, right now.*

She called Allen, forgetting he was at work. She hung up without leaving a message and called Salome.

"Hi! Erin, how do you feel?" she asked

"Much better. How did last night go?"

"It was a blast. We all ended up going to this club I like called Chocolate."

"You guys went out? After all that?"

"Of course. We had a blast. We even got <u>Brad</u> to dance, and he <u>hates</u> dancing."

"What about Allen?"

"He danced too."

"No, I mean any romance between him and Donna."

"Donna? Noo!" the way Salome said: 'No' was low, breathy and drawn-out. Like the bottom of all no's.

"Oh, too bad."

"At first, I kinda thought you guys were dating."

"Noo!" Erin said impersonating Salome. "Just friends. I was hoping to set him up with Donna."

"I don't think so. She's too...too tame. Have you met his ex?"

"Yeah."

"That's his type: rebel woman, kinda bossy."

"You think that's me?"

"Not in a bad way. I think you're pretty tough and very much a rebel."

"Ahh, thanks."

"No prob. So what are you doing for breakfast?"

"Bowl of oatmeal, I guess."

"Yuck! Let's go out."

"Where?"

"Buck-Buck Oink?"

"I haven't been there in ages."

"Me neither."

"Can we check on your friend's rental afterwards?"

"Sure, why not? Meet you at noon."

Erin hung up and got dressed. She ran into Fabrianne and Tawnee in the kitchen. They were discussing the incident last night.

"So, I see Tawnee filled you in about the argument last night," Erin said.

"Yeah, this all sucks." Fabrianne took a minute to blow her nose into a paper towel. "How come you guys just can't get along?"

"Fabrianne! He doesn't live here! He masturbates in the living room! He threatened to go to the police with the fact that I knew that skinhead girl in the group that killed Ned! Which, by the way, why the hell did you tell him?"

"Wasn't me," Fabrianne said.

"Nor me," Tawnee also confirmed.

"Hmm, must've been Lashell—that bitch! Anyway, Roger has got to go, now! I can't stand having him here anymore!"

"Erin, can't you at least try to get along with him?" Tawnee asked

"No! This is my house!"

"Well, technically…it's our house." Fabrianne said rather smugly. "And if Tawnee and I want him here you're out voted."

"Fine! You guys vote to have him here. 'Cause that just votes me out!" Erin stormed out of the room. She forgot she left her house keys on the microwave. She stormed back, got them and stormed out again.

"Erin!" Tawnee called, running after her. Erin stopped. "Don't go off like this, nobody's voting you out!"

"Might as well—I'm not staying here!"

"Where are you gonna go?"

"I'll find a place."

"But you can't leave!"

"Then you guys need to get rid of Roger!"

"I'm on your side. I think he should go, but I don't want him to go under bad circumstances."

"You know, just 'cause you guys dated Roger doesn't mean you have to be all loyal. He's an asshole—get rid of him!"

"Speaking for myself, I just want to keep the peace in the house. I don't know what Fabe's reason is."

"Maybe she's in love with him?"

"I asked her twice about that."

"You did?"

"Yeah, and she swore to me that it's over and she has no feelings for him, whatsoever."

"Fine! You guys can deal with him! I'm gonna start looking!" With that, Erin put on her leather jacket and departed.

"Oh, Erin," Tawnee said with sorrow.

\#

Buck-Buck Oink was so packed Erin and Salome had to wait outside for at least 30 minutes. Luckily, it was so nice outside they didn't mind. It also gave Erin a chance to light up a cigarette before going in. During the wait, she filled Salome in on her Roger situation.

"Wow! That's weird that they would choose him over you," Salome stated.

"Yeah, I know. I mean, we got the house in order to get away from him, to have a place where it was just <u>us</u> girls."

"Are you sure one of them's not sleeping with him?"

"That's what I asked, but they said no."

"It's nice that they can be so loyal, but that's going a little too far."

"I agree."

"So, do you think you'll be able to afford to move out?"

Erin took a long drag. "I don't know. I may have to just find someone with a place. I wonder if Chris still has a room for rent?"

"Chris?"

"Allen's ex."

"You would move in with <u>her</u>?"

"Sure, why not?"

"When I knew her, she was a little...unstable...I wouldn't trust her."

"That's what everyone says. She told me she was going through a bad time for a while, but now she's sorta cleaned up."

"Sorta?" Salome rolled her eyes.

"Well, I saw her still drink and stuff, but I guess that's better than drugs."

"Yeah...yeah."

Someone came up and tapped Salome on the shoulder. It was a 32-year-old White woman. She had long, black unruly hair and displayed more jewelry on her body than Erin had ever seen anyone wear—mostly silver pieces: pentagram necklaces, hoop earrings, at least 15 metal bracelets on each arm and two nose rings

"Hi, hon," Bethanie greeted.

"Bethanie!" Salome yelled and hugged her. Erin noticed Bethanie's hand, briefly exposed from under her layers of black clothing, showed a tattoo of vines. By the look of the design, it probably continued from her knuckles and ran all the way up her arm, if not further.

"This is my friend Erin."

Erin quickly looked for a place to extinguish her cigarette, so she could shake her hand. "Sorry," Erin said, switching the cigarette to her other hand.

"Don't worry about it hon, you take your time," she said with a Baltimore accent and smiled, exposing many gold teeth.

"Erin is interested in your room for rent."

"Oh, good, I haven't had many takers. Everyone is still afraid to live in that part of town."

"Me and Brad weren't," Salome complained. "We just needed better space for his weights."

"What's wrong with your part?" Erin asked.

"East River Valley is becoming all the rage but you go to East West, and everyone's afraid to live there, 'cause they still have those projects there."

"Projects? I thought they tore those down?"

"They did in the other part. The one near me is still—don't pay them no mind hon, things are changing so fast that that project is going to be torn down by next month. We already got a new cafe and a book store—can you believe it?" She turned her attention to Salome. "Last year, there were no White people anywhere, then—boom! A Coffee Barn and loft up in East River, and now it's spreading to my side."

"Then...why are you having so much trouble renting?" Erin asked.

"I told you hon. People see one Black person standing on the corner and they go running back to Upper Heights. They're too stupid to realize how fast it's changing."

"...And you could be one of the pioneers," Salome told Erin as she put her arm around her.

I feel like I'm being sold a timeshare condo. I understand Salome's trying to help her friend, but maybe the weight room excuse isn't accurate. What did B. L. O. W. U. P. stand for again?

Salome and Bethanie spent most of the breakfast playing catch-up. Erin spent hers eating a very good Greek omelet. From what she would occasionally pay attention to, they use to work together at the art supply store. Erin asked Bethanie if she knew Allen. She didn't. For the rest of the meal, the girls talked about crystals and herbal medicine. Bethanie fancied herself as some type of pagan witch goddess. Erin mentioned she had just got over the flu.

"I avoided getting it by wearing a jade necklace, which wards off illness." Bethanie said. Erin mentally rolled her eyes and nodded in comprehension.

When the meal was finished, they rode to Bethanie's house in Salome's SUV.

As Erin remembered from the last time she was in this area, East River Valley was slowly turning into and probably surpassing 10th street as the new hip hang-out of Neopolitan. Donna's loft was now getting another loft right next door to it. There was also a new restaurant called El Poco Lo Taqueria and a comic book store called Comet Comics. They crossed over into East West River Valley. *This is literally on the other side of the railroad tracks.*

Signs of progress were hard to spot, Although the houses were of the same architecture—Victorians and Brown stones —they were run-down or had bars on the windows. Prevalent on the corner were the Black people Bethanie talked about. They didn't seem to be anything out of the ordinary for Erin: kids played in the playground, people sat on their porch talking to each other and old people walked the street. She didn't see any gangs of youth, drug dealers, prostitutes or cars with booming stereos like she did while living in Kenwood. *What's the big deal?* A few businesses had daringly set up shop: a café called Ethiopia Utopia and a bookstore called Malcolm Text, which advertised Afro-centric literature and poetry.

Bethanie's townhouse was a Victorian duplex. She lived on the right side and the left one was for rent. It, too, had bars on the windows, along with a little metal gate with sharp points running along its top. "Do you get robbed a lot?" Erin asked. Bethanie ignored her question and unlocked the door of the rental. The living room had a high decorative ceiling, fancy molding and hardwood floors. There was an old smell to it, like this place was from the 1800s and should be haunted by ghost. Erin found this creepy, but it also fascinated her. The kitchen gave her a similar feeling. The white gas stove looked very old and would probably be considered dangerous by today's safety standards.

The back door led to an enclosed area. There was no grass, just a concrete slab surrounded by the other apartments and houses, forming a walled-in space with no escape except for an alleyway just big enough for rolling the garbage bins through. *I can totally imagine throwing a party in this space: a barbecue, a DJ and perhaps some little hanging lights would be perfect here.* Looking up, she could see a lot of people were hanging their laundry on clotheslines. *They probably wouldn't appreciate a barbecue grill smoking their sheets.*

They went back inside and toured the rest. The upstairs, where the bedrooms and bathroom were located, felt kind of cold and dark. The bathroom had a black and white checkerboard patterned marble floor and a claw foot tub. Erin liked it and imagined spending hours in it. One bedroom faced the back alleyway they had seen earlier while the other had a view of the other apartments and houses. Across was a view of an old fat woman walking around in some type of 1950s bra and girdle. Erin had never seen the type before. It added to the illusion of this neighborhood being a step back in time. *I like that, being able to come home to a different time zone and go out again to the future, just by walking a couple of blocks to East River Valley. This could be an escape route, a sanctuary?* "How much are you charging?" she asked Bethanie.

When they had finished their tour, the three women stood outside of the townhouse. Bethanie and Salome talked about a flea market they wanted to go to. Erin thought about the rent on the space. *It's twice as much as I'm paying to live in Grandview. But the advantage is this is a two-bedroom unit and the Grandview is a three-bedroom unit. Basically, with a roommate, I would be paying the same rent for double the space and less people to deal with.* The prospect of this gave her goosebumps as well as a little fear about just packing up and leaving her roommates, whom she liked. *I would have no problem leaving Fabrianne, who seems to prefer having Roger stay, but Tawnee might feel betrayed. I left for Europe soon after moving in without telling them I was going, nor arranging to pay my share of the rent. They didn't kick me out and waited an entire month until Dad sent them any money. They could have easily put my shit on the curb and gotten a new roommate. That loyalty, that gives them points, now pisses me off!*

"Hey! We should visit your friend Donna while we're here," Salome suggested. All three rode the few blocks back to the popular area of East River. It was uncertain Donna would be home; the time was around 2:30 PM and most people would still be at work. Because Erin had no idea what Donna did for a living, it was worth the gamble to ring her loft's buzzer.

"H-hello?" Donna answered.

"Hey Donna, it's Erin, Salome and her friend Bethanie."

"Hi, Erin…hold on."

"Everything okay?"

"Everything's fine. I was just taking a nap…give me a few minutes."

The three girls looked at each other.

"Hangover?" Erin asked Salome.

"Probably. We cut out of Chocolate at around 3:30. She mentioned that she wanted to go to Club Röt afterwards but I didn't think she'd do it."

"Club Röt?" Bethanie asked.

"German for red. It's over on 5th. Brad and me went home, didn't realize she was such a party girl."

A guy exited the loft's lobby. Erin assumed he was one of Donna's neighbors. He was very attractive, unshaven, with longish black hair and wore a black suit with a red shirt.

"Bonjour," he said to the ladies in a deep French accent.

"Bonjour…" Salome answered. "…Comment ça va?"

"Ça va bien, merci. Et vous?"

"Très bien. Vous habites ici?

"Non, je suis visiter juste. Bonjour," he said and then departed.

"What was that all about?" Bethanie asked.

"I was just asking him if he lived here," Salome answered.

"And?" Erin asked. *I should have been able to translate what they said, I suck.*

"He doesn't. You can put your tongue back in your mouth." Salome laughed.

"Hey! He was cute!"

The girls waited a little longer than expected. Donna eventually buzzed them up. The absence of an elevator made Bethanie complain as they trudged up flight after flight of stairs. Donna answered the door in a forced yet cheerful manner. She hadn't bothered to get fully dressed and wore some type of Japanese Kimono housecoat.

"Hi, guys," she said, letting them inside.

The loft was in neat order but there was a smell of pot and wine in the air.

"Hmm...something smells like a good night," Erin joked.

"Yeah, sure...There's some left on the table if you want. I'll be back...Anyone want any coffee?" Donna mumbled.

Bethanie accepted a coffee. Erin went to see what Donna was talking about. On the black, slate coffee table lay a small, white ivory pot pipe etched with Chinese dragons. Next to it, about an ounce of cannabis in a small round matching container.

"Whoa!" Erin announced. Never being one to turn down free pot, she took it upon herself to prepare the paraphernalia for the group. "So...you had a good time, I guess?" Erin yelled to Donna while cleaning the pipe.

"Yes, Allen and me went to Röt and danced. Then I met up with my friend Jean Luc and we came back here around four or five."

Salome walked around the loft, looking at everything, as Donna had done to her loft the other night. "Is he a tall French guy with a red shirt?"

"Yes."

"So, Allen bailed on you?" Erin asked.

"Yes." Donna had a sound of confusion in her tone. "At the club, he left unexpectedly—like, was he mad or something?"

"Mad? At what?"

"Maybe he was still mad at what Amber said? But I didn't say it, why did he leave like that?"

"Beats the hell out of me, Donna." Erin looked at Salome. Salome shrugged.

The four females took turns sucking on the pot pipe and relishing in the euphoria it created. *I didn't expect Donna to take part in this. Apparently her night of partying has zero effect on her morning activities.*

The pot also caused an expected hungriness. As fancy as Donna's stainless steel refrigerator and cabinets with frosted glass doors were, they were all quite empty of any type of snack food. After laughing about that fact for at least five minutes, the group left to go find food.

Like a group of hunters looking for meat, they searched around the neighborhood looking for that one food item which would satiate their hunger. El Poco Lo was chosen after Erin yelled "Nachos!"

Before they had even received their entrees, the girls had consumed three baskets of nachos and dip. Erin was so full, she could only nibble at her vegi-buritto.

"This is so good," Salome said, taking a bite of her tequila prawn burrito.

"This would go better with a margarita," Donna joked.

"After your night, I don't see how you can even go **near** booze," Erin said.

Salome had a serious look on her face. "We should do it!"

"Do what?" Bethanie asked. She took a bite of her vegi-taco

"Get a pitcher."

"Are you kidding? Don't you have to go to work or something?" Erin expressed concern

"Who cares? All I do is take people to their tables and take reservations; I've done it on 'shrooms one time."

"That must have been an interesting workday," Donna commented.

"It was. So let's do it. Who's in?"

"Me." Donna raised her hand.

"Why not," Bethanie said raising her taco.

"Erin?" Salome asked.

"Sure. Why not get a round of tequila shots too?"

"YEAH!" Salome yelled.

"I was just joking."

"Too late!" Salome got the attention of the waitress and ordered a pitcher of margarita and four tequila shots.

#

When Erin woke from her nap, it took her a few seconds to realize she was not in her house. The large, graffiti-style painting of a foot in a red, spiked-heel shoe by artist Wyatt Davis told her she was in Donna's loft again. On the large couch next to her was Salome, and across from her on a chair that looked like an updated beanbag chair was Donna. Bethanie was not around. *Did she leave? Was it after the second tequila shots?* Erin stood up and went to use Donna's bathroom.

She sat on the fancy Japanese style toilet, which included a bidet, and looked at the recessed and inset lighting illuminating the various framed, black and white photo prints of shells. She was a little envious Donna didn't have anyone to answer to as far as decorating.

Man. I can't stick around Grandview. I need to have my own space; get more into being creative. If only I had some dough for a security deposit; I would be sooo out of there—fucking Roger! Comes in and takes over our place. Could I borrow some money from Dad or Josh? Naw, I have no desire to push it with them.

By the time she had finished and flushed, Salome and Donna were up and discussing what to do later.

"Well, I have to go to work, but I get off at 9. We should all meet up again for a late dinner," Salome suggested.

"That sounds marvelous." Donna agreed.

"Whoa. After all that booze and weed, and you guys want to go at it, again?" Erin asked.

"We don't have to get booze...or weed. I was talking about another dinner together," Salome corrected.

"Bilbo?" Donna suggested

"Yeah!" Salome agreed. "Oh! We should invite Amber and Allen."

"What about Bethanie?" Where is Bethanie? Erin asked

"She left. She's going to some Wicca meeting thing tonight."

"9:30?" Donna asked. They all agreed on the time and parted to different destinations: Salome to work, Donna to check her e-mail and Erin to home to get ready for her geometry class.

#

She showered and then called Allen; Pam answered.

"Hi, Pammy!" Erin exclaimed.

"Errand girl! 'Ow's it going, lov?"

"Okay...well, not so good. My fuck'n roommates won't get rid of that guy so I'm looking for a new place to live."

"Bummer...Well, you know Chris is still looking for a roommate and shit."

"Yeah? Thing is, I found this great place near East River Valley, so I'd rather move there instead of North Depot."

"I hear ya, man."

"Allen tells me you had a hot date the other night."

Pam blew a raspberry of disapproval through her lips. "I did. I think I'm gonna break up with him tonight, though."

"That sucks. Why?"

"He's just not cut'n it for me, ya know what I mean? He's nice and all, but I'm just not feeling it."

"Feeling his dick?"

Pam laughed raucously. "That's hilarious—but no. Just ain't got that zing."

"Right, right. Bummer. Well, me and some girls are gonna go out to eat tonight, you wanna come?"

"Naw, I'm sure this breakup thing is gonna take longer than I think, but thanks anyway."

"Can you tell Allen about it?"

"Why don't you tell him? He's fuck'n eavesdropping on my conversation."

"I am not!" Erin heard Allen's voice say. There was a rustling noise like the phone was being wrestled away from Pam.

"'Lo, Erin."

"Hi, sweetie! So, what happened last night after I left?"

"Oh, that. We went to Chocolate, which was fun. But then Donna and me went to some trend-bot club called Röt where everyone looks better than you."

"Better than me, personally?"

"Correction, better than <u>one</u> looks. We danced a bit. Things were going pretty good and then this fuck'n <u>total</u> Euro-trash bastard goober shows up and starts hanging around Donna. He's slobbering all over her and shit and I was like, whatever. I'm outta here."

"I saw Donna. She was all confused that you left."

"Really? I thought for sure Mr. French Goober was gonna slip her the baguette."

"Ew! I'm not sure if he did or not. I know he spent the night there."

"Ah-ha!"

"That doesn't mean anything. She said that she wrapped things up by 5:00. Nobody goes to bed at five, drunk, gets up with a hangover, fucks and then sleeps until 2:00."

"Why not? I would."

"Cause I'd fuck him at 5:00 while I'm still drunk and then go to sleep. Were they making out when you left?"

"No, not that I can tell. I mean he was hanging all over her but, there was no kissing."

"Well, there you go."

"You're very optimistic."

"I chased a gay boy for a year, <u>that's</u> optimistic."

181

"True."

"So, we're all going out again at 9:30, you wanna come?"

"I don't know, is <u>Frenchie</u> gonna be there?"

"Fuck him! If he shows up, you can be the goober this time. You be the one hanging all over her, scare his ass off." *I totally believe Donna had sex with Jean Luc. If it were me, that's what would have happened no matter what time it was. But I don't want to discourage him.*

There was silence, like Allen was thinking about it. "Who else is gonna be there?"

"Just Salome, Donna and me. Oh! And maybe Amber. I was hoping this chick Bethanie was coming. She has this dope pad for rent and I was hoping to get into it."

"So, you're moving out?"

"It's heading that way. They've pretty much chosen El Masturbat-O over me."

"Are you sure about that? I mean, you live in a prem-o location, two hot girl roommates…"

"It's not like I'm fucking my roommates, that's <u>your</u> fantasy."

"Yes…yes it is."

"Anyway, you perv! 9:30, some place called Bilbo. You know where that is?"

"No, but I'm sure the phone book will tell me."

"Okay. And remember, be more aggressive. Eye of the tiger! Fuck Frenchie!"

"No, that's <u>your</u> fantasy."

"You're such a perv. Bye."

#

Neopolitan Community College, where she was going to be taking both of her classes, was located in University Circle with the other schools: Neo Tech, The College of Fine Arts and Neopolitan State. She felt like she was going to one of the major universities for a Ph.D., as she climbed the stairs of the block-like, glass building. She had to sign in because ID cards were issued only to full time students. This put a little damper on her fantasy of thinking she was a college student. She rode the elevator to the 5th floor. *I wonder if the other three people in here are also taking my class.* Two of them got off on the 3rd floor, but a Latina girl remained. Erin took a chance and asked her: "Are you taking the math class?"

"Yeah—Hey! Don't I recognize you?"

"Huh?" Erin panicked. She went over her list of all the people that would want to do her harm. The girl's appearance didn't ring a bell. "Uh…not that I know of."

"No? Yeah, you were at Poco Lo earlier," she said in a heavy Hispanic accent.

"Oh, yes I was. I didn't see you there."

"I was your waitress."

"Oh, my god! Really? I didn't even recognize you. I'm sorry."

"It's all right. You guys were pounding them back pretty hard."

Erin laughed. "That we were. We went a little overboard."

"That's all right, at least you didn't act like assholes, and you left a good tip."

Erin wiped pantomime sweat off her brow. "Whew! Thank God for that. I don't even remember how we got home."

"You made it here, so you couldn't have been feeling too bad."

"Believe me, it was a struggle."

The girl laughed as the elevator door opened. They walked down the fluorescent lit white hallway and entered room 507. There were four other people already in the classroom, a boy and girl who looked like they were still in high school, another girl around Erin's age and one older man. Erin sat behind the girl around her age.

The Latina girl sat on Erin's right.

"Were you celebrating something, or just out for lunch?" she asked Erin.

"Oh, sorta a celebration, just meeting new friends; bonding, that kinda thing." Erin looked around the room. It was a standard classroom: desk, blackboard, slide projector, window blinds.

The final addition to the class, the teacher, entered carrying a stack of papers and a book. She was a 37-year-old brunette White woman. She looked like she could be nothing else but a teacher, with her horn-rimmed glasses and conservative fashion.

"Hi class, I'm Sue Berkeley, welcome to Geometry 101. I hope everybody is here, 'cause I don't believe in waiting."

She proceeded to call roll. The Latina girl's name was Chita. There were three names which no one responded to. Sue seemed kind of perturbed by that, especially after one of them, a teenage guy, came in late. She handed outpapers; they were lesson plans for the course, for weeks one through six. Erin had a slight anxiety attack. *It's been four years since I've even stepped foot into a classroom and now she's handing out something that looks like a pop quiz?* Sue started to talk about points, lines and planes and how they extend indefinitely and were intersected. *I'm completely lost. Not sure if it was the pot I had or Sue's going too fast for me.* At one point when Sue was describing how 'point C lies on plane X and J intersects X at point P,' Erin turned to Chita and asked her if she understood.

"I lost her at Plane Y," she admitted. Erin panicked even more. Even when someone asked a question, Erin neither understood the question nor the answer. *I have to do something. If I fail this class, I won't be able to get into The Art Academy.* She took a deep breath and relaxed. She looked at the drawing on the blackboard and tried to figure out what was going on. She tried to visualize what Sue was talking about. *The planes are like pieces of paper and lines are pieces of strings. Where the string's poked through the paper, the hole is a point. If the strings were laying on a piece of paper, the paper or plane contains the string or line.*

"Erin?" Sue asked. "Where does line J intersect plane Y?" She pointed to the diagram on the blackboard.

Erin thought for a second. *Strings and pieces of paper....* "Point P?"

"Correct," she said.

Wait, what? You mean I actually got a math question right? It was an odd sensation. She understood something. *Life and men have escaped me, yet basic geometry is within my grasp?* Her visualization technique continued to aid her. Even when they moved on to space, collinears and coplanars, if Sue asked Erin a question, she got the answer right. By the end of class, she felt smart for the first time in her life.

At the end of class, Sue handed out homework assignments and everyone filed out. Erin and Chita waited for an empty elevator.

"You get all that shit?" Chita asked.

"Most of it. I'm sure it was a fluke." She looked at the sample question on the homework assignment: *Are points A and B collinear? Well they're both points on the same line, so I guess so.* She looked at the answer key; she was right. *Gee, maybe I should smoke pot more often.* "Are you taking classes to get into one of the colleges?"

Chita thought for a second. "Naw, I'm just trying to finish getting my GED, how about you?"

"Trying to get into the Academy."

"Cool. You an artist?"

"Me?…Not really. I just like making jewelry."

"You're taking geometry to make jewelry?"

"Yeah, apparently it's a pre-rect."

"For jewelry making? Wow. I see girls selling that shit at art fairs, that what you gonna do?"

"Well, no…kinda—no! I don't know."

Chita nodded her head and said "huh."

What the fuck was that 'huh' for?" Was she judging me?Miss G-E-D! You're like the same age as I am, least I graduated high school! I did good today! I'm not gonna let her ruin my good mood—Screw you! I was gonna offer to help you with anything you didn't get, you're on your own!

#

It was a little early, but she went on ahead to Bilbo. It was back in the River Mill area, a little past Salome's loft. The word 'Bilbo' was glowing in pink neon on a rusty metal sign. The building was shiny, unsymmetrical, metallic and curved, like a melted 50's diner. There was no line of Yuppies coming out the door, an advantage to coming early. Erin went in. She felt like celebrating. *I need to acknowledge I have done well in something.*

The inside of Bilbo was also stainless steel and curved. It reminded Erin of the inside of a submarine. Hanging little lights on thin wires were everywhere, providing barely enough light to see the food you were eating. A waitress reached under each table as she walked by and hit a switch, activating the lights underneath their tabletops. These light tables, all in diffident colors, gave an eerie, upwards glow to all who sat down.

Erin went up to the bar, which also had a light table effect in white.

"How much is a glass of your best wine?" she asked the bartender.

"$55," he answered.

"Ooookay, give me one step up from cheapest."

For what she paid for a glass of wine, she could have bought a bottle at the Super Bottle liquor store. She didn't care. She sipped and savored it like the $55 one. As she looked around the room, she practiced what she learned in school, looking at lines intersecting each other on the wall patterns; planes meeting other planes where the doors met the floor. She thought about space. "The set of all points," she said to herself, "not limited to one point or plane."

Allen came into the restaurant 35 minutes after her. He looked around. *It's like he's checking out the bizarre architecture more than looking for me.* When he spotted her at the bar, she waved him over.

"You the only one here?" he asked.

"What am I, chopped liver?"

"That's not what I meant—a little sensitive, are we?"

"Sorry, I'm all jazzed up. I did well in my math class."

"That's great!" Allen gave her a hug. "Maybe you've found your niche."

"I'd rather be good at other things."

"Sometime you choose greatness and sometimes greatness chooses you."

"Don't start quoting Star Wars on me."

"Star Wars?"

"Or whatever. So, how was work?"

"The same: Customers are assholes, the pay sucks, there's no future."

"Oo-kay. Did you use that attitude on your date last night?"

"That was no date, no more than that one with Spike was."

"Ahh sweetie, don't be all negative." She patted him on the back. "Maybe tonight, she'll only hang out with you. Just don't let some guy muscle in on her."

"Sh-yeah, right."

"Have some wine." Erin handed him the glass and he took a sip. "Speaking of you and relationships…"

"I don't like where this is going."

"Oh, don't worry, I'm just curious. How would you feel if I moved in with Chris or she moved in with me?"

"What? What's going on?"

"I'm trying to get the hell out of my house, that's what."

"So, you have to live with her?"

"She's the only person I know who needs a roommate. I can see that it would bother you if I moved in with her."

"No, you can do what you want. I just find it weird that, more and more, you entangle yourself in my life."

"Don't flatter yourself. I've lived here a lot longer than you, of course I'm going to know some of the same people…if not more."

"Fine, Miss Social. Maybe you can think of a woman who isn't dating, 19 or hanging out with goobers."

"I'll have to think about it. It's a pity that Tawnee is dating, she'd be perfect for you."

"Yeah, thanks for bringing that up. I feel much better now," he rolled his eyes.

"Well, you know, even if she breaks up with…Zack? I think that's his name, she always tries to be all buddy-buddy with her exes. So he'll still be around–just like Roger."

"Tawnee dated Roger?

"You didn't know that? Yeah, before Fabrianne."

"And they all live in the same house together? That's nuts! No wonder they won't kick him out."

"Probably–whatever, I gotta get out of there."

"You sure?"

"Man, when I was looking for a place to live, I had to fuck'n spend the night in my car, 'cause Roger wouldn't kick this heroin addict out—and they hadn't seen her in months!"

"Well, you gotta admire his loyalty."

"Loyalty, my ass. She was a cute Japanese girl. I bet he was sleeping with her or something; whatever the reason, I've had enough."

"Well, who's to say that living with Chris is going to be any better?"

"My ex roommate never cleaned the litter box for three or four cats, walked around naked sometimes, had a drawer full of condoms and...AND she had a garbage bag full of pot!"

"When you say garbage bag..."

"The big green ones!"

"Wow! That's like a thousand years in prison."

"Oh, yeah, and Chris knew her!"

"Hmm, as a customer?"

"I don't know. What-ever. Chris can't be worse than her."

"Yeah, I guess. I mean, she did some crazy shit when we were living together: Snuck into abandoned buildings, went to dangerous clubs, was in a rock band. But she never did anything that would land me in jail...well, not intentionally."

Erin saw Donna, Salome, Amber and Kim Yee making their way over to the bar. "Show time."

"Who's that Asian guy?"

"Kim. I think he's Korean...and maybe gay. I'm not sure."

"About the Korean or gay?"

"Both."

"Airrr-runnn!" Donna said while hugging her. She then hugged Allen. "Allen? Where did you go last night?"

"I had to go to work early," he lied.

Introductions to Kim were made. Allen and Amber didn't even acknowledge each other. They all sat down at two small, pushed-together brushed metal tops tables. Donna went ahead and ordered a bottle of something called Txakoli for the table and a plate of elvers.

"What the hell is that?" Erin asked

"Baby eels."

"Eeww, gross! I'm not eating that!"

"Er-ah, they're for me. Why? Did you want me to order something for you?"

"Oh, no…I thought…Oh, no, nothing."

"She thought you were going to pay for dinner or something. Now we know why she likes you," Amber accused and laughed.

Erin felt angry and embarrassed. "It's not that…I thought you just knew more about what to order here," she lied.

"Oh, okay."

Erin quickly picked up the menu and tried to find out if they served something besides baby eels. There were lots of meat dishes: blood sausage, pork roast and quail. She found something called Potatoes Riojanas. It was more of a side dish of potatoes and onions cooked in red wine. She ordered it with a fava bean gratin. "Not much on the vegetarian choices," she mumbled to Allen.

"I noticed. What kind of food is this? Stuffed squid in ink sauce? Zikiro? Salome! What kind of food is this?" he asked her.

"Basque," she answered.

"Well, Basque to you to!"

"No," she laughed. "Basque region of Spain. Bilbo? As in Bilbao Museum."

"Ohhh, I see. That explains the architecture."

Erin was confused as to what they were talking about. She made a mental note to look up Bilbao.

The Txakoli arrived as did some bread. The waiter poured a little olive oil in a plate and added some balsamic vinegar to it. *I have no idea what that was about.* The rest of the group started dipping the bread into the oil; and eating it. Erin joined in. The wine gave her a little buzz and when combined with the warmth of the bread and the aromatic olive oil, she felt good. *I wish I could feel like this always.* Donna's Elvers were bought out.

Erin had to turn away as Donna ate the four inch long, white, spaghetti-like eels.

"So…Amber, how did that roommate thing of yours turn out?" Erin asked to distract herself from thinking about the elvers.

"What, you want to live with her, now?" Allen asked Erin.

"What are you talking about? I'm curious."Erin said.

"What <u>are</u> you talking about?" Amber asked Erin.

"Oh, he thinks I'm sizing you up for a place to live. I'm trying to get out of my house and he's just mad because I may want to move in with his ex."

"I'm not, you can do whatever you want," Allen complained.

"My only complaint about my roommate is her boyfriend. Besides that, she's pretty flawless," Amber said.

"Whelp, it looks like it's Chris then," Erin joked, poking Allen's shoulder.

"Again, what…ever," he responded.

"If I could get that place that Bethanie is renting, it'll be perfect. That way I wouldn't have to live way the hell out in North Depot."

"I wouldn't worry about that. Bethanie likes you. That place is as good as yours," Salome said.

"Sweet!" Erin exclaimed. "You should see her place, Allen! It's like five blocks from Donna's!"

"We'll be neighbors!" Donna said raising a glass of Txakoli. "We need to celebrate Erin potentially becoming my neighbor!"

"Let's go to the Acid Pit," Kim said. *I had almost forgotten he was at the table. His presence is always so invisible and non-threatening. Maybe that's why Donna hasn't axed him, like Monroe.*

"Excellent idea," Donna said. "Salome, Erin, Allen, Amber? I can get us in free. I know the manager."

Everyone agreed to go to the dance club except Erin.

"Er-ah, I have to go home and check on my own roommate situation," she lied. *In truth there's no way I would step foot into the Acid Pit ever again, after I quit like that.* "You see…" she said to Amber. "…I don't like Donna because of all the free stuff."

"Hey, I was only joking, Gaaaw-lee," Amber said defending herself. "Man people think I'm everything from a bitch to a racist."

Allen cleared his throat as a sign of agreement.

"That's enough out of you," she protested.

Allen laughed. It wasn't the reaction Erin expected out of him. *Must be the Txakoli.*

Their dinners arrived. Erin loved her Potatoes Riojanas. "This is better than sex," she said to Salome.

Salome tried them. "That's pretty good, but not better than sex," she corrected.

"Maybe with Erin," Allen joked. Amber laughed. Erin gave him the evil eye. "I kid you because I love you," he said, giving her a gruff shoulder hug.

"No more wine for you," she said.

For dessert, Erin had the green apple sorbet. It was very refreshing and had some kind of Apple-flavored vodka in it. This pushed her from buzzed into tipsy. She had to go to the bathroom. When she stood up. The full force of all of the alcohol she had sloshed around in her brain and almost made her lose her balance. "Whoa," she said. She grabbed a chair and then laughed. "No more for me."

Allen laughed. "You look like I fell—I mean feel—Man, maybe I shouldn't have had that martini."

"I don't remember you having a martini."

"Because you were so busy looking away from Donna's eels—which were good by the way... although I wouldn't have salted them so much."

"I agree. I also would have like to have seen a different white wine go with it," Amber agreed.

"Something heavy?" Allen asked.

"With lots of oak, like a Mountain Valley Springs chardonnay."

"That would have been perfect!" he agreed. "Or even their light reds!"

It took Erin a second to come to grips with Allen and Amber conversing and actually agreeing on something. *From hating each other to wine aficionado buddies in one day.* "Off to the bathroom I go." She tried her best to walk a straight line to the ladies room but found herself bumping into a couple of tables. "C'mon geometry—straight line!"

When she made it back, the group were getting up and putting on their coats.

"What's going on?" she asked.

"We're going to the Acid pit. Hel-lo," Allen said sarcastically.

What I meant to ask was the fact someone must have paid my part of the bill. I'll let the matter fade and hope they do too.

"So, are you going?" Salome asked her.

"No, I'm going to go home and yell at my roommates."

"Sounds like fun," Amber stated.

"But first, my place…for things," Salome announced

"Oh, yeah, that too," Donna agreed.

"What things?" Erin asked.

As they were walking outside, Salome whispered in Erin's ear, as best she could over the techno music which had recently started playing: "I went to this alphabet party on New Year's, and you know how they take all the drugs, A-Z, and they dilute them into shots of energy drinks?"

"Uh, sure. I actually had no idea what that liquid was, I assumed it was just water."

"So they put them all into these tiny little plastic bottles on lanyards and had them in this box behind the counter. And my friend—well, he's not my friend anymore, grabbed the entire box and bolted with it."

"Holy crap! Really?"

"Yep, so to make a long story short, I have 12, tiny little bottles of God-knows-what in my fridge."

"You don't know what they are?"

"Nope. They didn't have time to put the letters on the bottles."

"So if you drink one of those, you could be drinking liquid pot…"

"Or heroin."

"Oh my god! Salome! That sounds dangerous!"

"It's fine. You know how they dilute the hell out of that stuff."

"Still."

"So we're going to go to my place and share a bottle of mystery juice."

"Really? <u>Allen</u> is going to take part in that? There's no way he's gonna participate!"

"I don't know–maybe–whatever. He doesn't have to–we are, you want to?"

"Man, you guys? I'm still reeling from the pot and margarita's…and that weird Spanish wine."

"C'mon Erin." Salome elbowed Erin in the ribs.

"Fine, why not?"

#

The sun shone through her window and illuminated a small kewpie doll Allen had given to her during her illness. Fear of the doll's wild green hair and grimacing smile caused Erin to lift her head out of the drool, which had collected on her pillow. *I don't know how I made it home. I remembered going to Salome's house and taking a sip of one of those bottles and Donna asking if there was any Champagne in the house. After that, it's a Technicolor blur.* She heard ringing. It wasn't a tinnitus type of a ring, but a nice steady tone, like a phone; it was the phone. Erin cleared the phlegm out of her throat and picked it up. "H-hello?" she said.

"Hi Erin," Mr. Agnew said rather cheerfully.

"Hi Mr. Agnew." *I feel like I've been caught holding a severed head in front of a policeman.*

"Hi! I was wondering if you were going to come in, today?"

She looked at the Japanese cartoon clock, shaped like a blue cat. The time showed it was almost 12 noon. She was horribly late. "I'm still feeling a little down—Maybe tomorrow."

"Oh…" The way he said: 'oh' sounded like he actually expected her to attempt to come in this late. "Is there anyway you can swing by, even briefly?"

"I'll see how I feel later. If I come by, I'll call first." *There's no fucking way any of that is going to happen.*

"Oh, all right…You make sure you come by as soon as you can."

"I will." Erin hung up and rolled her eyes at Agnew's relentlessness. She lay back down, lit up a cigarette and thought about her night.

I don't have any memories of a wild orgy or saying something stupid or offensive, just lots of laughing and clowning around. I remember seeing Bethanie there—why was Bethanie there? She panicked. *If Bethanie was there, something might have been said to ruin my future plan of moving out.* Moving out reminded her of where she was, not physically, but socially. *No one in the house is on my side. It's depressing, the girls are siding with Roger. Perhaps I'm not giving Tawnee the benefit of the doubt. After all, she just wanted us to shut up and get out of her room.*

She got up went to the bathroom and shat and showered. During the shower, she tried to recap any conversations with Bethanie. *I remember Bethanie laughing at a joke Allen had made. Being that he's so paranoid and goodie-two-shoes, I know that he wouldn't have taken a vile of mystery drugs and will have the best memory of last night. Friday is his early day at the art supply store. I'll call him there and hope he hadn't left, yet.* After the shower, as she was drying off, the phone rang. By a coincidence, it was Allen. "Oh my God! I was just about to call you," she said.

"You must be psycho—er-ah I mean psychic."

"Mr. Fuck'n Funny Man. What's up?"

"Well…I slept with Amber."

Erin paused for what must have seemed to Allen like hours. "…Okay…speak to no one! Meet me at the Cafe Across the Street in one hour!" Erin hung up and got dressed *I can't figure out how a supposedly racist, formerly Jewish, Native American girl could end up in bed with a Black guy.* She pondered what Lashell called the Mandingo fantasy scenario. *But that would involve a large muscular Black guy—not* Allen! "Drugs. It must have been the drugs," she concluded.

Before she left the house, she checked the mail bucket next to the door. It was filled with the usual junk mail but there was an actual letter for her. It was from her father. "What the fuck?" she said opening it as fast as she could. Expecting to see a greeting card or family photos from some event she had recently missed, she was taken aback to see instead, a note and a check. Skipping the note, she read the check first. It wasn't from him but someone called Super Fidelity Car Insurance. It was made out to her for $10,000. "Holy Fucking shit!" She quickly read the note:

Skipper;
This is the settlement check from your car accident, I guess they sent it here because you listed this as your permanent address. If you ask me, your insurance company should have got more out of them. I guess they figured it ain't worth it. Expect your premiums to go up.
Dad

P.S.
You can always use some of this check to pay off your Brother and me. (Just a suggestion)

"Woo hoo!" Erin yelled. "I'm rich!" She put the check into her back pocket and threw the note into the trash.

#

An hour after depositing the check, Erin sat across the table from Allen. They had yet to get to his story because Erin was so excited with her financial improvement. She rambled on about everything she could get done: "Besides paying off my brother and my dad for Europe, and my math and art classes, I can erase my credit card debt, put a security deposit on Bethanie's apartment, buy a cheap used car and still have enough to help with a couple of semesters of art school, and if I don't get into art school, fuck it! I'll just use the rest for another kick-ass trip to Europe."

"Europe?" Allen asked. "After all the crappy things that happen to you, there?"

"Maybe not those places—'cept Paris 'cause I love my friend, Marie, but we keep eating out at places I've never heard of: Bung Bo? Bilbao? Where the fuck is that?"

"Upper-left Spain."

"Yeah-yeah, whatever. My point is, there's a lot of places I still haven't gone yet."

"That is, provided that you have a job when you come back."

"I'll have a job. If I stay where I am, I get fuck'n two weeks paid vacation after a year!"

"But, you haven't gone to work in a week?"

"I also get like a million hours of sick leave. They can't fire me for being sick."

"But aren't you still in probation?"

"I'm not worried about it. Everyone there loves my mom, they have to hire me. Besides, my boss never shows up most of the time. If anyone should be fired, it's him."

"Sounds like you have it all worked out."

"Yep."

"You know, if you don't move out, you'd have even more money to spend."

"Sh-yeah right. You just don't want me blocking your access to Taaaw-neee," Erin mocked him in a silly voice.

"Well...after last night..."

"Oh, my god! I totally spaced! How could I forget why we're here?" Erin got up, walked to the other side of the table and gave him a hug and a kiss on the cheek. "I'm so sorry! I'm such a flake!"

"That's all right. You're excited about the loot."

"Yeah, and all I had to do was have my car totaled and get arrested to get it." She returned to her seat.

Allen laughed. "Anyway, after we dropped you off..."

"Wait! I'm sorry, let me interrupt you there. Last night, did I say or do anything stupid that might jeopardize my hooking up with Bethanie's apartment?"

"Nothing more stupid than usual."

"Fuck'n ha-ha—I'm serious! I don't even remember you guys taking me home."

"Believe me, of everyone in the group—minus me—who took those mystery drugs, you were the least offensive."

"Really? Also, where the hell did Bethanie come from?"

"She was already there, visiting Brad."

"Visiting Brad? What, are they having an affair?"

"Y-yuck! Anyway! As I was saying, you were just making jokes and shit. We dropped you off at your house after we performed anal on you..."

"What! You did what?"

"Just joking," He laughed. "Man, you really did black out."

"Don't joke like that. I believe everything you say!"

"So we drop..." Allen suddenly looked out the window.

"What? What is it?"

"What is she doing here?"

Erin looked outside to see what he was looking at. Pam Barlow walked in, took off her leather jacket and hung it on the coat rack. "Oh my gosh! I don't believe it? What are you doing here?" Erin hugged her.

"I know, long time no yo, ho," Pam answered. She lightly poked Allen hello on the shoulder.

"Aren't you supposed to be at work?" Allen asked. He seemed a little perturbed by her presence.

"Lunch break."

"Kinda far to come for your lunch break, ain't it?"

"I know, but I kept thinking about that fuck'n banana cheese cake."

"It is good," Erin agreed.

"But won't you get in trouble for taking a long lunch?" Allen asked.

"Dude, unless you're fuck'n my mom, you aren't my dad! Lay off 'ight!" Pam said frustrated. "Ain't anybody keep'n tabs on me. I mean, look at Erin. She ain't at work. You ain't busting her ovaries about it. What are you doing here, anyway? Are you guys on a date or something? That why Allen's all super freak?"

"No!" Erin laughed. "I called in sick. Allen was actually just about to tell me how he got laid last night."

"Whoaaaa-whoa-whoa!" Pam yelled "Hold all calls, I'll take this in the office! What? When did this happen?"

Allen buried his face in his hands. "Last night."

"High five, muh-man!" Pam raised her hand for him to slap.

"You hate high fives."

"I do." She put her hand down. "So, when? How? And muy importante, who? Was it that girl at Last Chance?"

"No! That girl's barely out of high school! No, this was someone me and Erin know, who I thought was a racist."

"Guess she learned you," Erin said.

"Yeah!" Pam laughed. "Wait, she wasn't calling you nigger during sex, was she?"

"No! No, that's just sick!"

"I'm just say'n, maybe she gets off on sleeping with the enemy."

"She's not like that. I only say she's a racist because she prefers White guys only. I don't really think she's a racist, just closed-minded."

"But apparently not. I mean, if you prefer white meat only you don't settle for dark meat... unless that's all there is in the fridge...or you're ripped and looking for a snack."

"That's what I was going to ask," Erin said. "I know I was boomed, but is that how it happened? Allen! Did you take advantage of a drunk girl"!

"For Christ's sake! No! If you let me finish my story, you can make up your own mind."

"Sure, spill it!"

"So we drop your drunk 'n high ass off and head on over to the Acid pit. There's a line coming out the door 'cause of some big shot deejay guy or something, so we end up going back to Chocolate."

"Back to Chocolate? Is that your way of saying, sex with a Black guy?" Erin joked. Pam laughed; Allen did not and continued his story.

"So we're at Chocolate and guess who shows up?"

"Christine, your ex?"

"No, Frenchie, that guy that cock-blocked me from Donna the other night."

"I hate to tell you Al, but I think they slept together," Erin informed.

"Whatever, and don't call me Al."

"Okay, Al."

Allen stood up and started to leave. Erin and Pam both grabbed his arms and pulled him back into his seat.

"Oh, chill out and finish your story," Erin pleaded.

"Anyway, I ignore Donna and Pepe le Pew and I'm dancing and hanging out with Amber, Sal, Brad and Bethanie...." Erin started to interrupt but Allen stopped her: "...And no, Bethanie didn't mention you all night. So we're talking about boobs because Amber asked Bethanie about the tattoos on her tits of Chinese goblins."

"She has goblin's on her chest?" Erin asked.

"Yeah, nice ones too...the tattoos not the tits...actually she does have nice tits—big ones!" he clawed his hands in front of his chest and shook them.

"Oh, my god, Allen! You're such a pig! She showed you her tits?"

"Hey! Me and the other 10 people in the VIP lounge," he said defensively. "Remember, everyone else but me is on something. I think Bethanie and Amber got Ecstasy 'cause they kept feeling stuff."

"Like what?" Pam asked, "your thigh?"

"No, like the silk curtains and the pillows on this big couch we were sitting on; they were all into it. So we're all talking about tattoos and piercings and Amber shows us her tongue piercing."

"Her tongue is pierced? I didn't know that," Erin said before taking a sip of Allen's latte.

"It's waay in the back."

"Back for blow jobs, as I'm sure you found out." Pam nudged Allen's arm.

"Well...not really."

"No blow job? Well, that sucks," Pam complained.

"But she doesn't!" Erin added. Everyone laughed.

"So, no B.J.? She went straight for the humping?" Pam asked.

"Well...not really."

"What do you mean, not really? No fucking, no head? Did you or didn't you have sex?"

"You decide. So we leave Chocolate, Amber gives me and Bethanie a ride to her home and me the station. And she's like: 'I'm not a racist you know!' And I'm like, whatever, goodnight. And she's like: 'just because I don't sleep with Black guys doesn't make me a racist', and I'm like, jump over it, Evel Knievel."

"You said that?"

"No, but I should have, 'cause then she starts tearing up and saying how you don't know me and it's a terrible thing to accuse someone of, blah, blah, blah."

"Oh-me-god. You must'a totally struck a cord," Pam said.

"Yeah 'cause she's telling me how the Black guys in high school called her rich White bitch and were so mean to her and I'm still like, I'm sorry, I don't think you're a racist...crazy as a loon but not racist...I didn't say the last part."

"We know. So how do you get from that to sex?" Erin asked. She took her fork and cut off a piece of Allen's chocolate brownie cheesecake and ate it.

"I tell her to drop me off at River Mill station and she's like: 'No, I'll give you a ride home.' But first she has to stop at her place to feed her cat. I tell her don't worry about it because she lives in Central City, not exactly on the way but she insists, like she wants to prove how nice she can be."

"Soo she fucked you to prove how nice she can be?" Pam asked. Allen shrugged that he didn't know.

"But how did you even get to that point?" Erin asked.

"We stop off at her place—beautiful neighborhood, Erin, even better than Grandview. Beautiful old Edwardians and yet, we get inside her apartment and it's a fucking mess."

"She invited you inside?"

"She just said: 'You can come in, I may be a while.' But you missed my point. Her apartment is a mess—like her, pretty on the outside and a mess on the inside."

"I don't think she's pretty," Erin said.

"Dude, guys think all girls are hot if they sleep with you," Pam said defending Allen's statement.

"Yeah, so she feeds her cat and we're literally stepping over garbage: clothes, old pizza boxes, and newspaper, <u>tons</u> of junk mail. While she's feeding her cat, I look through some of her stuff: lot-a horse related stuff, she's apparently use to be into riding—I'm talking contest, professional stuff! She sees me looking at her old stuff and she freaks, like I've just discovered she use to be a hooker or something."

"Hold on, I gotta go get my cheesecake" Pam got up and went to the counter to order.

"Go on," Erin said.

"What about Pam?"

"You live with her, you can fill her in later."

"True. So once again she's near tears about her past or whatever, this time assuming I think she's a rich bitch just because she lives in Central City and used to ride horses. I comfort her. You know: 'There-there', nothing more. We're sitting down and I pat—just <u>pat</u> her leg—like this:" Allen patted Erin's leg on the thigh." But when I do that to her, she quickly closes her legs on my fingers."

"Was it a defense thing?"

"That's what I thought, but she smiles and jokes like: 'Getting fresh, are we?' And I joke back like: 'Sure.' And I playfully grab her shoulders and act like I'm going to push her back on the bed, like in those romance novels."

"Bed? What are you doing on the bed?"

"I think it was a bed...it must have been a couch...it was so messy. But there's <u>no</u> resistance. She goes back by herself and laughs. But I'm Joe Noble and I ain't gonna do anything, and she jokes: 'Time to get even with my ex boyfriend.' But you know, still I do <u>nothing</u>. I really don't, because I think she may be drunk or whatever with the way she's acting."

"Of course."

"But the hand is still on the leg, she's laying back and it's like we're frozen in time deciding where this is going to go. So I joke back: 'Revenge sex. Is there nothing better?' She laughs, fucking <u>tightens</u> her thighs around my hand, sighs and says 'you don't move your hand we may find out.' So as a joke and just as a joke..."

"Lotta jokes going around," Erin said.

Pam came back to the table with her cheesecake and an herbal soft drink of some kind. "What'd I miss?"

"Allen's hand is trapped between her thigh and she won't let it go."

"What? Does her pussy have kung-fu grip or something?"

Allen laughed. "Pretty much. So my hand is on her leg, she tells me to move it. I do that old joke where the guys hand is on the woman's leg and she tells him to move it and instead of taking it off, he rubs her leg and says: like this?"

Erin laughs. "That's funny. You did that?"

"Yes, but once again…"

"I know, it was a joke," Erin finished his explanation.

"So I say: like this? And I move my hand up and down her thigh, expecting her to slap it away…" Allen paused as if what happened next was not real and hadn't happened. "…She comes…"

"What?" Erin asked.

"…She comes."

Pam and Erin looked at each other and then back to Allen with their mouths open.

"What do you mean she comes?" Pam asks.

"As in, orgasm."

"You sure?" Pam asked.

"She moans, she kung fu grips my fingers more, closes her eyes, winces shivers, relaxes, exhales, over"

Again, Erin and Pam looked at each other.

"Oh, my God! Allen, you're the love god!" Erin commented.

"Dude, you made her come without even trying? Can you come into the bathroom later, just for five minutes?" Pam joked.

"I know. That was the easiest orgasm ever, without even trying."

"She must have been really edging the whole time," Erin explained. Pam nodded in agreement.

"I guess. I had no clue."

"Dude, so after that, the others must have been a walk in the park," Pam said.

"Well...that's just it, that was it."

"What do you mean that was it? After that you didn't keep going? Guy makes me come that fast, I'd throw a saddle on him!"

"I guess it was kind of an awkward moment. She was embarrassed, I assume. I didn't know what to do so I try to do the gentleman thing and lay down with her. She cuddles up with me but doesn't try to advance things. I don't do anything else and we lay around in silence for at least half an hour. Eventually I say: 'I guess I should be going,' she agrees and we part company. So. You tell me, was that sex?"

"Yes," Pam said.

"No," Erin disagreed.

"What do you mean, no? He made her come, the end."

"But there was no intercourse."

"Intercourse? What is this? Discovery Channel? What more do you need for the definition of sex?"

Erin kept thinking about her hand jobs in cars scenarios. "For one thing, he didn't get anything out of it. After she got hers, she should have least gave him a hand job or something."

"I'm with Erin, I like my sex with more insertion," Allen

"You men, it's all about getting back to the womb!" Pam took out a cell phone and started dialing.

"When did you get that?" Allen asked.

"Got it yesterday. I'm gonna use it for my business." Pam ate while pressing different buttons.

"Are you checking messages? How rude," Allen complained.

"Fuck!" she muttered.

"What?" Erin asked.

"This guy I like has to work tonight."

While Pam checked more messages, Allen and Erin continued to talk.

"So, what should I do?" he asked her.

Erin was caught off guard. *No one has ever asked for my opinion on relationships before.* "Er-ah, well...I think you should call her, try to get together and see if it was a fluke or not."

"But I don't want to ruin my chances with Tawnee."

"Tawnee? What are you talking about? She <u>has</u> a boyfriend!"

"No, she doesn't. She has that greasy guy who didn't even visit her when she was sick."

"So? Allen—if you mess this up 'cause you're pining for Tawnee, then you're a jackass!"

"But I don't want to date Amber. She's annoying and overly sensitive."

"And she has push button orgasms! If you—I can't believe we're even debating this!" Erin slapped her forehead in disbelief. "I thought guys were all about getting laid? What kind of man are you?"

"Eats you up, doesn't it? That somewhere out there in the world, there are nice guys."

"You're not nice! If Amber had been Tawnee, drunk or not, in that situation there wouldn't be a debate about fucking her!"

Allen didn't respond. Erin knew she was right.

"Hey, check it out…" Pam said, while she put her phone away. "…We got a call from Sal. She said that she, some girl named Donna and Amber—is that your insta-cum girlfriend? —are going to eat at some place called La Mouche and they want you to come, no pun intended."

"Holy shit! How can they go out again? What is this? The third night in a row?" Allen complained.

"Da' matter, old man? Can' hang?" Pam teased.

"That mean you're bailing?" Erin asked.

"I don't know. On the one hand, Donna does seem to know a lot of restaurants where people give us mad discounts. On the other, I feel lately like I've been drinking more alcohol than water."

"Me too," Erin agreed. "It seems I haven't been to work all week."

"You gotta go, dude. Finish what you started," Pam said to Allen.

"I guess. Are you going? Erin?" Allen asked unconfidently.

"Me? What's today? Thursday? I have my first art class tonight."

"When do you go?"

"7-10."

"Fine, then you can be there by 10:30."

"I guess. Pam?"

"I'm there. I wanna see the girl with the instant orgasms."

#

After she finished her cheesecake, Pam went back to work. Erin and Allen traveled back to Allen's job so Erin could get some supplies for her class and use his 40% discount. Erin thought it was nice of him to travel all the way back to Downtown North, and thanked him more than once.

"No problem, I have no other plans," he said getting off the bus.

"That's not true, you could be home, grooming for you date."

"Date? What date? It was a fluke."

"That's the spirit!" Erin sarcastically said, patting his back.

They crossed the street to the two-story building with the 'Van-Go's Art Supplies' sign over its entrance, next to a giant three-dimensional ear. Allen waved hello to a couple of people goofing off at the front register. One joked how Allen couldn't stay away from the place. Erin hadn't been in the store for a year. The last time she came in was for polyform clay she used to make some earrings shaped and painted like fingers. She found everything here kind of overbearing. *So many different kinds of brushes: What's the difference between the $100 Sable and the $3 hogs hair? Why is there an entire section devoted to just Japanese paper?* She took out her list and tried her best to pick out items she was familiar with. She did pretty well with the fine arts materials, but some graphic ones stumped her.

"Utility knife?" she asked Allen. "What is that? An SUV of knives?"

He laughed. "Basically. It's one of those large razor blade knifes." He retrieved the item off the shelf.

"Bow compass? What's that?"

"It's behind the counter. I'll get one for you. I assume you want something cheap?"

"Don't assume anything, Daddy-O. I got ten G's in the bank. You get whatever you think is good."

"Yes, Ma'm," Allen said heading off.

Erin looked at a bunch of sketchbooks. Some were labeled 20lb and others 80lb. She picked them up to see if their weight was any different; they were not. "Weird," she muttered. She looked at some of the hardcover versions. As she put one into her shopping basket, she saw Monroe. Her heart skipped a beat. *How could I have forgotten he worked here? He seems to recognize me.* He quickly returned to sticking labels on a stack of tackle boxes. *Damn it! I need one of those boxes to carry my stuff in.* She waited until he'd left the section and grabbed the closest one.

Allen's situation came to mind. The situations were similar, both involving awkward sexual events and people you wouldn't have slept with.

She turned around and headed toward the canvas aisle.

Allen returned and put what he judged to be a good yet affordable compass into her basket. "Guess who I ran into?" he asked her

"Monroe? I escaped from him earlier."

"No, I see him all the time. Steiner!"

"What's he doing here?"

"Buying spray paint. I guess he and his friends are gonna bomb the West side bridge."

"Bomb?"

"As in, tag?"

"Oh, of course. Whelp, I hope they don't get caught."

"Oh, and also, Chris is going with them!"

"Why?"

"To take pictures or participate I assume."

"Really?"

"Yes. Apparently they're all buddy-buddy, now." Allen said sarcastically.

"That so? You think they're dating?"

"Don't know—don't care."

"You're not curious?" Erin poked him in the ribs. "Not even just a little?"

Allen grabbed her finger. "Not in the least—her life. She can do what she wants. Besides, I have other fish to fry."

The chance of our exes dating each other feels weird, especially if they're trading secrets about Allen and me.

With Allen's help, Erin quickly checked off the rest of the items on her list. As a thank-you gift, she proposed buying him a drink when they met up later.

"Ugh," he protested. "I may take it easy on the booze tonight."

"Me, too. Can you <u>believe</u> they want to go out, again?"

"That's Salome. She likes to do lots of things all at once and if you say no to her she cuts you off and you don't hear from her for weeks."

"Is that what happen with you? What did you do?"

"Nothing, she just wanted to go out a lot and after a week of that, I just wanted to take a break. You know, just chill: Draw, e-mail, watch TV?"

"Right, right."

"But nooo! She wanted to go to Pink 32 once again."

"Pink what?"

"32. It's that club over on 3rd. Anyway, after that, no more calls, no more invites."

"But you seem okay now?"

"That's 'cause I ran into her later at a Halloween party and she was all like: 'Oh, hi!' Like nothing had happened."

"Man, if she cuts you off for saying no, then I must be on her shit list by now. I've backed out of club hopping twice so far."

"I think you still have a little wiggle room. You at least come to dinner."

"I better make sure I show up later."

"I wouldn't worry about it. I mean, what kind of friend blows you off like that?"

"It's not about friendship dearie, it's about connections."

"Ahh, the apartment."

"That's right."

"Are you sure you don't want to sit down and talk with them about it?"

"My talking days are over. I'm a girl of action."

#

Allen and Erin parted ways. Erin returned to her house to get ready. Only Tawnee was home, sitting on the couch watching TV. Because of her bathrobe attire, Erin assumed it meant she was still sick. They gave each other polite yet uncommitted "hellos." Erin went into her room and checked her e-mail. There was one from her brother Josh asking how much money she had received from her settlement. She knew the reason wasn't curiosity, but collecting. *Don't worry Josh, you'll get your dough...after I get a new car.* She moved on past the next three spam messages. The last was from Salome. It was some type of electronic invite to la Mouche. *Not content with just a verbal message?*

Erin felt even more pressure to show up tonight. She changed into an outfit which would give her the option of going out after her class: An all black ensemble with a leather Harley Davison leather vest and black, Converse tennis shoes. She looked like a biker chick, despite the fact she'd never even sat on a motorcycle. As she was exiting, she looked back at Tawnee, sitting alone on the couch. She felt like she had to be honest with her if their friendship was to survive any longer.

"Tawnee?" Erin called out.

"Yeah?" Her voice added a hint of 'what, now?' in it.

Erin paused for a second. She felt little angry, like she had become a pest in the house, a complainer. "I'm moving out." This is not what Erin wanted to say. She had no place to move to. She needed the weapon. A nuclear bomb which would give her a powerful edge.

"Wh-what?"

"I'm moving out...Well, not at this moment, but I guess before next month's rent is due."

"Erin! God damn—you don't have to do this!"

"Yes, I do! You guys have made your decision: Roger's in, I'm out!"

"Oh for fuck's sake! You know that's not true!"

"It's true to me!"

"Just 'cause we want you guys to work things out doesn't mean we've chosen sides!"

"And that's part of the problem! You guys deciding who lives in my house! I mean, I don't know if Fabe is still hot for him or you're still mad at me for going of to Europe..."

"Europe? I am so over that!"

"Well, for whatever reason, you guys are making all the decisions!"

"It's a democracy, Erin! We all decide on what goes on together!"

"Well, you decided to keep Roger! I decided I can't live with him!"

"What do you want me to do, Erin? Put him out on the streets? I've known him for four years?"

"Come on, Tawnee—God damn it! The guy was whacking off in front of me!"

"You caught him masturbating! Guys are horn dogs; they do stupid shit like that! It's not like he singled you out to get caught!"

"How do you know?"

"What?"

"How do you know if this all ain't some plan of his to make me move out, get my room?"

"You're giving him too waaay too much credit!"

"And you're giving him too much trust!" Erin started to leave again.

"Erin..." Tawnee said sorrowfully.

"I'm sorry, we moved here to get a place without him, remember? I can't stay with him, I won't, I shouldn't have to!"

"What else are you gonna do? You can't find another place, at least for what you're paying now? All those Neo yuppies are driving up apartment prices. People are actually bidding on apartments, now!"

"I've already found a place. All I have to do is sign a lease."

"And a security deposit?"

"Taken care of. So, see, it's not like I don't have options. It's you guys who can't decide how this turns out!"

"Erin! Don't put me on the spot like this!"

"Sorry, it's him or me, T!"

"Erin, you know I just want the both of you to work it out!"

"Him, or me! I'm going to go get the lease!" She turned around and walked out the door. She remembered she had left her back pack full of art supplies next to the door. She opened the door just wide enough to not be seen, grabbed the packing and shut the door.

#

Erin felt guilty about putting Tawnee on the spot. She also felt nervous she had made an idle threat. *What if Bethanie can't rent to me? Then what? I'll be a paper tiger, forced to stay in a house with no respect from the others. I have to do something to secure my position.*

When she came out of the University Circle station, she immediately ran to a pay phone and called Salome. She wasn't home, so Erin left a message: "Hi Sal, it's me, Erin. Listen, could you do me a favor and if you see Bethanie, tell her I want the apartment. I don't have her number. Tell her I have a security deposit and everything. Thanks, and hopefully I'll see you after class." Erin hung up and started walking to the community college where her Basic Drawing 101 class was going to be held. She felt very excited: The thought of her first art class since high school, the prospect of getting a new place to live and a chance to get out of debt all swam through her mind. With the money she had, she might even be able to live by herself for a while. Erin sighed in pleasure over that fantasy.

Her art class was taught in an old, small, lime green structure which could easily pass for a grammar school, circa 1970. She could see inside. There were several cafeteria tables, a few wooden easels and what appeared to be a kiln. *The last time I used a kiln was to make a dragon-shaped pot pipe. Miss Hicks waited until it was perfectly glazed and fired before smashing it yelling "I told you guys, no pot pipes!"*

Once inside, she looked for a place to sit. She was the youngest attendant among the eight. Two were women, around her mom's age. They chatted about some BBQ chili cook-off in Tucson. Erin had no interest in listening to that, so she sat between the lanky creepy guy with a beak-like nose and the overweight 30ish woman eating an energy candy bar. To pass the time, Erin took out her bow compass and tried to figure out how it worked. The only thing she could figure out was once extended into an upside down V, it could be bent into a "U" shape.

"That's a nice compass," said the guy in a heavy Russian accent.

"Thanks. I just got it," Erin said, giving a polite smile.

"Are you married?"

Erin was taken aback by the question. "Er-no."

"You want to get coffee, after class?"

"What?" She found his directness shocking.

"You and I get coffee after class."

"Huh? Oh no, I can't. What I meant to say was, yes, I'm married."

"Oh, you're married? What's his name?"

"Steiner." Erin had no idea why his name came to mind.

"Steiner? Is that German?"

"I don't know, I guess."

"You guess? You don't know? You marry man and not know about his name?"

Erin felt like she was being interrogated. "No, you can't know everything about everyone."

"How long you married?"

"Uh, five years—oops, I see someone I know over there." Erin pointed to the two women. She quickly gathered her things and switched chairs to the one out of his conversation range. She mentally breathed a sigh of relief. The two women were still talking about a garlic meatball festival in Tucson. Erin ignored them and started playing with her supplies again.

Mrs. Watts entered the room. She was a short Korean woman in her late 40's. Her hair was pulled into a tight bun which, combined with her black horn-rimmed glasses, gave her a domineering aura. There were no friendly hellos or introductions, just a proclamation: "This is basic drawing 101. I take this class a lot more serious than you might expect for a community college class. We're all adults here and therefore we should be expected to be a lot more thick-skinned than children. This means I will tell you exactly what I like and dislike. No candy coating, no bullshit. Now, take out your sketchbook and a pencil or charcoal stick and draw something —anything, I don't care what. As long as it's something you can draw from memory and can render pretty well. I want to see what I'm working with."

Erin tried to think of something. She took out a charcoal pencil and put it to paper. *Birds! I've always like to draw birds. There's something about them and their sense of freedom.* She started drawing an indistinct bird. The feathers looked like large scales, its beak appeared as a cone, its mouth fused together. The only thing she felt she had rendered correctly were the legs and feet: sharp talons, gripping onto a branch for dear life.

When they were done, Mrs. Watts walked around the room and collected the drawings. She then stood in the front of class and, one by one, presented each drawing. Everyone seemed to be a better artist than Erin, especially the Russian guy. His woman's face looked like it was drawn from a model, standing near-by. It was hard to find anything wrong with it but with each drawing Mrs. Watts manage to come up with something she disliked: "The eyes are too close, the hair looks like a wig, the teeth look like doll teeth." A drawing of a tree by one of the women: "This looks like a cartoon drawing of a tree." And finally, Erin's: "Are you planning to attend art school?"

"Uh, yes?"

"You seem hesitant. Yes or no?"

"Yes!"

"Your hesitancy is part of what's wrong with this drawing. It's childish and simple. There's no life to this bird—it's a drawing of a dead bird." Erin was insulted. *For someone who rarely sketches, I don't think it was that bad.* She scowled her face at the back of Mrs. Watts. The teacher returned to her table. She put a black portfolio case onto the nearest table and opened it up. "Gather around, please."

Everyone stood up and surrounded the table. The first page was a drawing of a woman's face. It was very crude. The eyes weren't lined up and the hairs looked like they were done one at a time, like black spaghetti. The next set of drawings were just as amateurish: tree, cowboy, elephant, vase and flowers, all equal to if not worse than Erin's bird. Mrs. Watts then flipped to another section. Erin assumed it was to demonstrate the way it should be done. The drawing of the woman had shading and depth. The features were proportional and more dimensional. The other drawings were also better versions of the previous set: The cowboy could have been a Marlborough ad, the flowers drawn by a young Pablo Picasso. "Now…" Mrs. Watts said closing the book, "what you saw was the work of my last class. From the first drawing I just made you do, to the redone version, three weeks into the class."

"No way!" Erin said.

"Yes," Mrs. Watts said. "So there is hope for all artists. Even you." The group chuckled. Erin wasn't amused.

For he next exercise, the teacher had them drawing the basic geometric shapes that compose all of life—squares, circles, triangles, rectangles and ovals—over and over again. Next she had them add dimension—cubes, pyramids, elongated tubes, eggs—and showed them how to add depth to them with shading. With each exercise, Erin's drawings were raked over the coals: "Your lines aren't straight? Can't you draw a straight line?" Or, "Your shading looks like a smudge. That's not shading, that's dirt." By the end of class, Erin felt like quitting or strangling the teacher. As they departed, Mrs. Watts told them to draw every day and she would check their sketchbooks to make sure that they did.

On the walk to the main entrance, the Russian guy hit on her again. "So, do you want to practice art together?"

"No, thanks," she answered as coldly as she could.

"We could share pointers?"

"Dude! I'm a lesbian!" she yelled. She remembered the problem with using that excuse. As predicted, he tried to interrogate her more. "So, maybe you and girlfriend come over for vodka?"

"For fuck's sake! Dude! Back the hell off!" He quieted down for the rest of the walk and only let out comments under his breath in Russian.

Erin hurried away from him, back to the train station, as fast as she could.

At the train station, she again had to use a pay phone, to call Salome.

Allen answered. "Allen?" she asked

"Ja?"

"Why are you answering Sal's phone?"

"Because I'm drunk."

She heard laughter in the background, as well as accordion music. "Where are you guys?"

"Not there!" he laughed.

"Not in the mood, dude."

"What's wrong? Bad day at class?"

"We'll talk about it later. Where are you?"

"Still at La Mouche."

"Where?"

"Little Paris."

"Where?"

"You know, where all of those French restaurants are in River Heights, on Noble?"

"I rarely go up there. I can't even afford to be spat on up there."

"Yeah, anyway, that area's now called Little Paris."

"Check. So, why are you drunk? I thought you'd had enough?"

"I couldn't resist. Bob and Salome kept ordering Champagne."

"Oh, wow! Bob is there? That's great! I felt so bad, I feel like I sabotaged his relationship with Fabrianne at the gallery... No, wait, is she there?"

"Nope."

"Good. I don't feel like getting into it with her right now. How about Amber? You guys making out in the bathroom?"

"Noooo, she's blowing me off..." Someone at the table made a joke, everyone laughed. "...Blowing me off, as in snubbing!" Allen repeated.

"Can she hear you?"

"Oh, she and Donna are at another table. I think we're embarrassing them or something."

"That's too bad."

"Well, it could also be because the tables are too small for big groups, but still, she hasn't said a word to me all evening."

"That sucks, I'm sorry."

"Whatever. You already know who I'm holding out for, so fuck her..." Again, someone said something and they all laughed. "Pam is a dirty drunk."

"Tell me about it. So listen, don't you guys leave without me, I'll be right there."

"I'll save you an amuse bousche—Pam, grow up!" More laughter was heard.

#

The interior of La Mouche was almost an interior decorator's nightmare. There were frequent representations of the common house fly: Paintings, sculptures and napkin rings all incorporating the insect's image.

In Paris I saw lots of tour boats labeled: 'Bateaux Mouches.' I thought that 'mouche' meant ugly, but apparently it means fly. Fly boats sounds a lot better than ugly boats.

In spite of the association of the fly with dirty insects and bad health standards, the tables were all packed with patrons. It was as small as Allen had stated, making it easy to spot the different groups within the larger one: Pam, Salome, Bob and Allen sat at one table, laughing loudly at a crude joke, and Donna, Amber, Kim and music columnist, Quincy Zeitheit sat quietly at another, on the opposite side of the room.

"Erin!" Donna called out, waving at her.

"There she is!" Salome called out to her.

She was caught in a sudden custody battle. *Which table do I sit at? At one table, I like every single person sitting there, at another, only one person. But that person could get me into clubs for free and cheap meals.* Both tables gestured her over. *Both groups probably wouldn't like me sitting at the other. I have to decide. If Allen was right, and I snub Salome, that would be it! If I snubbed Donna, it would be yet another thing I've done to be banned. But, if she can forgive me for dating Steiner, who she had a crush on, or that argument with Peter on Halloween…but will there be a punishment this time?*

She played it safe, waved to both groups, and then hit the bar and ordered a glass of water. Before long, Allen joined her and gave her a shoulder hug. "Hey! You can order a drink at the table," he suggested.

"I can't."

"What do you mean, you can't"

"If I sit at one table or another, someone's gonna get snubbed. If that happens, no apartment and no free meals."

"That's kind of shallow."

"I know, but I rrrrreally want that apartment, but I rrrrreally like going out to eat for cheap."

"Yeah, well you gotta choose."

"Fuck! Why do I always have to choose between friends,? Why aren't you guys sitting together?"

"Cause those stupid yuppies assholes took the big table in the middle." Allen gestured to the six people at the middle table.

"But why the hell should I have to choose between groups of people? Or rather, person—Quincy, Kim and Amber can fade."

"Whelp, I don't envy your dilemma." Allen returned to his table.

Erin stood for a minute and looked at the two groups.

"There has to be a way to make both groups, happy."

At Donna's table, they were receiving more food. At Salome's, more Champagne. *Hmm, Food versus booze.*

"Erin! Fuck'n sit down!" Pam yelled loud enough for some people to look around to see who 'Erin' was. She felt mortified. *I know if sit at the other table, Pam is gonna yell or do something worse.* She quickly sat down at Salome's table. *In a way, I feel relieved—Pam unintentionally made my choice for me.*

Erin reached over and hugged Bob. "So good to see you! Thought you'd be on a date with Fabrianne?"

"No chance of that," he responded.

"What?"

" 'Bout fuck'n time! Why were you at the bar?" Pam asked

"Getting some water."

"Here, have some French water!" Pam sloppily poured Erin some Champagne into an empty water glass.

"Do you guys have any food?" Erin asked

"We should order more cheese turds," Pam suggested.

Everyone except Erin laughed.

"Wait-what?" she asked.

"She means gougère—little cheese puffs," Allen answered.

The puffs were ordered, served and quickly devoured. Bob ordered French fries. Erin ordered leek and potato soup, and fig and olive tapanade. Everything was perfectly cooked. She noticed at the other table they were finishing their dessert. "So, did you guys decide where you're going after this?"

"Home," Allen answered.

"Me too," Salome agreed.

"I'll probably go crash at Oggie's," Pam said.

"Last Chance Records, if they're open, then home," Bob answered

"Oggie?" Allen asked.

"Ogden!"

"Aren't you breaking up with him?"

"I like to give them one last fuck. To make sure I want to break up and to let them know what they're missing."

"How charitable."

"You guys aren't going to Chocolate or Pink 32?" Erin asked.

"No way," Allen protested. "There's no way I'm going there; watch some French goober pick off my date."

"You're not going to get any further with her, sitting over here," Erin advised. *I wonder if their proximity has more to do with Allen's bitterness at Amber and Donna, than the tables between us.*

"Fuck'n forget about her," Pam suggested. "One minute she's a racist, the next she's hot for you? Fuck that!"

"Well, we should at least find out if they have any plans" Erin said.

"Fine, you go check, then," Allen said with a bit of hostility in his voice. Erin got up and walked over to the other table.

"Erin! So nice of you to join us," Donna said.

Is she being sarcastic? "Hi, Donna, how's it going over here?"

"Lovely, we were just having dessert. Do you want to try my profiterole?"

Erin looked at the ultra-rich dessert of puff pastry, chocolate and ice cream. *That desert is very Donna. Decadent and sweet, but probably bad for you if you have too much of it.* "No, thanks. We're still working on the main course stuff."

"You sure?" Amber asked. "It's free?"

"Whoa!" Erin said. *Another comment about me being some kind of free loader?*

"Amber, be nice," Donna scolded.

"I'm going to hold off on the dessert, for now," Erin said coolly. "I just came over to see if you guys were going out after this?"

"That's free, too," Amber said.

"Listen, bi—"

Before Erin could say the word: "Bitch," Donna interrupted. "Erin, do you want to join me for a smoke outside?"

"Uhh, sure."

Donna got up and headed to the door. Erin followed. "Wait, I didn't know you smoked."

"I don't," Donna said, opening the front door.

When they got outside, Erin interrogated Donna about Amber's comment. "What the hell was that about?"

"Do you have a cigarette?"

"Oh, so you do smoke?"

"No, but it looks better than if someone sees me out here and I'm not smoking."

"Right."

Erin handed her the cigarette and lit it.

Donna took a forced drag on the cigarette and sloppily exhaled and coughed. "These must pair well with alcohol."

"Lotta that this week."

"I know. I was late for a client meeting."

"Sooo, getting back to Amber—"

"I'm not good with people arguing," Donna interrupted.

"I wasn't going to argue with you Don, I just wanted to know what's her defect."

"My parents were arguing before their plane went down, about fish, of all things."

"What? Really?"

"Yeah. The black box, you know the thing that records all the sounds in the airplane?"

"Uh-huh.." Erin lit up her cigarette.

"It recorded them arguing right before they ran into trouble and...you know."

"Wow."

"Wow...I mean, my parents argued a lot, so more than likely they would have gotten a divorce, but can you imagine going out, arguing about stupid stuff like fish."

"Donna, seriously. I only wanted to know what her 'tude was about."

Donna took a drag on her cigarette and let out a long exhale. "She says that Allen tried to take advantage of her."

Erin's mouth hung open and felt like it could hit the ground. "Wha-wha-what! Allen? <u>That</u> Allen?" She pointed to the restaurant.

"That's what she told me."

"And you believed her?"

"She's my friend, I have to."

"What did she say happened?"

"Just, she was bombed on that stuff we took, she offered to give Allen a ride home, she stopped off to feed her cat and he made a move on her."

"Oh my god! There's so much detail missing from that story! I can't believe she left out so many details!"

"What details? It sounds like she was high and he tried to take advantage of her."

"Donna! You make it sound like he tried to rape her! All he did was put his hand on her leg, she had an orgasm and he left!"

Donna looked confused. "He gave her an orgasm, just by putting his hand on her leg?"

"Yes! So there was no taking advantage of."

"And you believe him?"

"Of course, look at the way Amber treated him with the 'I don't date Black guys' stuff. Why would he want anything to do with her?"

"But that could also be a motive for raping somebody? Revenge?"

"Donna!" Erin grabbed the sides of her head. "Don't say rape! There was no rape!"

"Okay…perhaps you're right. There was no rape, but she was taken advantage of."

"No, she wasn't! She was all hot for sex the minute she invited him up there. She's just pissed that he didn't stick around—I can't believe she would lie like that!"

"But what if she's not lying? Have you considered the idea that she's not lying?"

"Oh, please," Erin said sarcastically. "If Allen took advantage of anyone, he'd get his ass kicked! He's too much of a wuss to hit on a girl."

"If that's true, that's more of a reason to take advantage of a drunk girl."

"Donna! She's a liar."

"Erin, what's more realistic, that a guy gives a girl an orgasm with just a touch or a guy tries to have sex with a drunk girl he hates?"

Erin was speechless. *What if Donna is right? Could Allen be capable of something so disgusting?* "He couldn't have…It's not like…I've known him for almost three months."

"And I've known Amber for two years."

Erin puffed on her cigarette and tried to think of a retort. She had none. *Donna makes a good case and I really don't know Allen that well.* "So, are you guys going to cut him off now?"

"I don't know. There's a part of me that says Amber is exaggerating. I mean, she did spend two months in a mental institution."

"What? Donna! There you go! Case closed!"

"But...so did I"

"Wha-what?"

"Yeah, that's where we met."

"Donna? You were in a crazy house?"

Donna laughed. "Well, no, It wasn't a crazy house. It was one of those rehab spa places where celebrities go when they go crazy."

"And you went crazy?"

Donna laughed again. "I had...stuff to deal with...I'm okay now." She took her index finger and jostled her lips while making a funny noise, her impersonation of a crazy person. She laughed again.

Erin nervously laughed. She was a little afraid. "What was Amber in for?"

"She actually never told me."

Lying?"

"Possibly. But until I know otherwise, I'm believing her."

Erin squatted down, smoked and thought. *If Donna was a lawyer, I might return a guilty verdict, even with the evidence of Amber's past.*

They smoked without speaking until Donna finished her cigarette. "To answer your earlier question, we're going to La La's. You wanna come?" Donna asked, snuffing out her cigarette with the heel of her Balaniks.

"Naw. I'd probably just spend the evening interrogating Amber, and what fun is that?"

"Not much."

"Yeah, so I guess I'll head on home."

Donna went back inside. Erin stayed outside for just a while longer. She tried to put on a neutral attitude before she returned to the table.

When Erin returned, Allen immediately picked up a weird vibe coming from her. "Everything okay out there?" he asked.

"Everything's fine," she lied. She poured herself a glass of Champagne and sulked and sipped in thought. Donna's group got up and left. Donna was the only one to come over to their table to say goodbye. She hugged and kissed Salome and Erin on their cheeks. She gave Pam and Bill polite hugs. Allen received only a pat on the back and a 'See you around.'

After she was out the door, Allen again asked Erin if anything happened between them. Erin again denied any problems. She changed the subject by asking Bob about his relationship with Fabrianne.

"What relationship?" he answered.

"What? You guy aren't dating? Am I imagining things?"

"No, we did date, for a week. But when I was gonna make a move on her she's all 'I can't, I'm not over my ex.'"

"What!" Erin yelled"

"Yeah, I know. Like I thought things were progressing along nicely, but it turns out she's still carrying a torch for the guy she calls rude and obnoxious."

"Ain't love grand?" Pam said.

Erin started to bang her head on the table. "Oh—my—God—I—was—right—all—a—long!" Allen put a cheese puff between her and the table. When she lifted up, it stuck briefly to her forehead and then fell off. Pam laughed loud and hard. Erin threw the bread at Allen. It hit him on the neck. "Stop fucking around! This is serious!"

"So your roommate is letting her ex stay with you guys because she's in love with him?" Salome asked.

"Of course," Erin answered. "All this fucking time she's been pining for that pervert asshole!"

"Unless she was using that as an excuse for blowing you off," Allen said to Bob.

"That's true," Salome added.

"I thought about that, but it's true. I saw them at the Mofo Dojo concert."

"Hanging out or making out?" Erin asked, wondering if he was over-exaggerating.

"Hugging, maybe a little kissing. I tried not to pay too much attention. I was a little pissed at the time."

"Son-of-a-bitch!" Erin muttered while hitting the table repeatedly with her fist.

"Wow!" Allen stated. "What are you going to do?"

"Well, first I'm going to tell Tawnee, and if this doesn't convince her to kick his ass out than nothing will."

"Wait, what about Fabrianne? It doesn't bother you that she's been sneaking around with him behind your backs?" Allen asked.

"That's her problem. I can totally understand going back to your ex."

"But that guy?" Bob asked.

"I wouldn't have been with his ugly ass in the first place so that's her fucking problem," Erin answered before taking a sip of Champagne.

"That mean you're still in love with Steiner?" Allen asked her.

"That mean you're still in love with Chris?" Erin mocked.

"Whelp, should I call Bethanie and tell her you're coming over for a midnight lease signing?" Salome asked.

"Not just yet. Who knows, maybe this will actually work." *I doubt it's gonna make a difference.*

Their bill came, and after paying, the group split up. Allen walked with Erin to the nearest bus stop. She ran scenarios through her head about what was going to happen: Everything from, Fabrianne and Roger move out together to Tawnee is also sleeping with Roger. A question from Allen shook her out of the ridiculous scenario. "What? she asked."

"I said, what's up with Donna and them. I can understand Amber being a freak-out, but what's Donna's damage?"

"No idea," she lied, looking at the sidewalk.

They passed by some French restaurants and a pastry shop. "Patesserie" Erin said to herself.

"Hey look, a bus!" Allen said pointing to the bus at the stop. Both Allen and Erin knew a bus in this part of town was a rare and endangered species. If they missed it, the next one would be around in another hour. "Go for it!" he yelled. They started jogging. Erin was feeling a little woozy from the Champagne. She ran a little sideways, being pulled by the weight of the art supplies in her back pack and corrected herself. When she did it again, the last thing she remembers is her right foot stopping, the sound of wind and a 'hope no is watching me at this moment' feeling. Allen stopped running the second he heard the thud. "Oh my god! Are you all right?" He ran back to help pick her up.

Erin looked up at him. When she tried to lift herself up, she felt pain in her wrist. It was the same spot as when she had slipped on the ice, but this time it was different; it hurt more.

"Ow! Ow-ow!" she yelled. She tried to wiggle her fingers and move her wrist. "Ow! ow-ow!" she yelled again in pain.

"Oh shit, what happened?" Allen asked, trying to help her up.

"My fucking wrist. I fell on it, again!"

"Again?"

"Yes, I thought I b—Ow-ow!" She complained about the pain.

"Okay, we gotta keep your wrist still." They stood up. "Keep it close to you and up so all that pumping blood doesn't make it hurt!" He took off his belt, wrapped it around her neck and under her forearm and made a makeshift sling. "We gotta get you to a doctor!"

"Doctor? No way! I gotta go home and bust Roger and Fa-Ow!"

"I think Fa-ow can wait until tomorrow." Looking around, they discovered the bus they were so desperately trying to catch was long gone. "We need a cab!" Allen started waving to a couple of taxis. One made an illegal u-turn and stopped to pick them up. Allen slowly helped Erin in the cab. She complained with every other step. "To…" he looked at Erin, "…which hospital?"

"University, only place I got coverage." The destination was given and the taxi sped off.

The driver, preoccupied with listening to a loud, right-wing radio station, weaved in and out of traffic and magnetically aimed for potholes. With every bump and thump, Erin complained. "Ow-ow, Dude! Take it easy—arrive alive!" The driver ignored her and ran a stop sign. "What's up? You speak English?" she asked.

"Now, that's a stereotype," Allen complained.

"Dude, I'm in fuck'n pain here, don't go all P.C. on me now!"

Every time the driver stopped he would pump the breaks sporadically. Allen tried to brace Erin but her cries of pain told of his failure.

Her cries combined with the weaving and five glasses of Champagne, started to make her feel like vomiting. "Dude!" she yelled, "take it easy on the driving or I'm gonna throw up!"

"Ne!" he responded in a foreign accent.

"Did he say no?" *I have no idea what his problem is. Perhaps he's a foreigner who hates American international policies or maybe he's a local who's had a bad day and is taking it out on me.* He weaved around some construction material in the road and over three metal street plates. This action unplugged the nausea control in her throat and made her puke onto the back of his seat and onto the floor.

"Ewww!" Allen complained.

The driver slammed on the breaks, sending Allen's head into the Plexiglas separating passenger from pilot. "Get fuck out of cab!" yelled the driver. He started to get out of the car. As fast as she could, Erin used her good arm to open the door. Allen regained his composure and helped push the door open.

"Get fuck out of cab!" repeated the driver. He was now standing outside, holding a baseball bat. He tried to grab Erin. She shook away from him causing her pain to intensify."Ow! You dumb motherfucker! I told you I was gonna puke!"

"Get out! Get away from cab!"

Allen and Erin made a hasty escape from the scene and onto the sidewalk.

"Did I not tell him to cut it out?" Erin yelled.

"You did," Allen answered.

Erin looked around for a clue to where they were. "Ow-ee-ow! I think it's broken!" She felt her pulsating swelling wrist.

"Just hold on for a few more blocks."

"What are you talking about? We're in the middle of fucking nowhere!"

"Not quite." Allen pointed to the University's Campanile. The driver had bought them within a half mile of the hospital.

"Son of a bitch," Erin said almost laughing.

"Free cab ride."

"Thanks to puke."

"How do you feel?"

"Ow! Except for the pain, no longer nauseous."

"Lets go, I'm sure there's a Vicodin with your name on it." Allen supported her wrist and they began to walk.

#

Erin had never been to the emergency ward of the hospital, at least in Neopolitan. When she'd broken her arm playing softball, her father bought her in. The way he ran around trying to recruit help for his daughter, you would think she had more priority than the guy who had cut his finger off playing with a weed whacker. There were no weed whacker guys or parents, but Allen was very attentive and made sure she was as comfortable as she could be. It took almost an hour before they were moved from the front desk area to the waiting room, then another wait just to get into the main hall where all of the sick and injured moaned and groaned and sat on gurneys and chairs. Eventually, a young intern name Phil showed up and started treating Erin. She wasn't sure if he was a doctor—he wasn't much older then she was—but she didn't care; her only concern was he was doing something. He moved her wrist one way or another and asked her to move one or more fingers and gave her an ice pack for the swelling. She wanted drugs but he was leery after he'd discovered she had been drinking and puked in the back of a cab. He escorted her to a room to take an X-ray.

Erin walked in, sat in a chair and set her wrist under a big white machine.

"Should I wait out there?" Allen asked gesturing to the hallway.

"Only if you want children," Phil said. It wasn't clear if he was joking or not.

"Uhh, I'll wait for you out here" Allen said, stepping back into the hallway.

"Don't go!" Erin pleaded. She felt very vulnerable.

"It's okay, I'll be right were you can see me." He stood in the doorway.

Phil left to get an X-ray Technician.

"You want kids, huh?" Erin asked Allen. She thought about the awful way he'd treated Chris when she got pregnant.

"One day, maybe…with the right person."

"Tawww-nee?" she mocked.

"Who knows? I can't see her and kids in the same picture."

"Chris?"

"Chris? Same thing."

"Me?"

"Strangely enough, I can see you more with kids."

"Me?" Erin blew a raspberry through her lips. "Sh-yeah right."

"No, I'm serious. I mean, not with my kids, but I can see you raising a brat or two."

"What do you mean, not your kid?"

"Well, I think we'd have to at least have sex in order to have a kid, and since that's not going to happen…unless you've changed your mind?"

"No, I haven't!"

"Then I guess it's Whatshisface that left you at the airport, Steiner or that gay guy?"

"Yuck to all of them! Hopefully there's' a cute guy in my future that will make me think about being knocked up for nine fucking months."

"Hopefully, both of us will reach that point...substituting the word guy for gal."

"Amen."

"Erin?" someone asked from behind Allen. He moved out of their way. It was Dr. Balboa. She came into the room.

"Dr. Balboa? What are you doing here?"

"Covering for someone. What about you? I love the new hair."

"Thanks. I fell down, I think I broke my wrist."

She furrowed her brown in concern. "That sucks. How was Europe?"

How does my OBGYN, know I went to Europe? Oh right, her friendship with mom. "It was great. I want to go back."

"Totally understand. I fell in love with Tuscany. So, you got my message on your test results?"

"I did, Thanks."

The radiologist came into the room. It was an attractive Black woman in her mid 30's. Erin caught Allen peeking at her butt, invisible under a lab coat. "Hi Sky," she said.

"Hi Tammy," Dr. Balboa answered. "They got you working late too?"

"Yeah." She went over to Erin and started positioning her wrist to take an X-ray. "Are you covering for Dan?"

"Yep."

Dan? How many other Dr. Dan's could there be at the hospital, besides my mom's boyfriend?

"He go to the conference in Atlanta?"

"No, I think he took his wife to Cancun for her birthday."

"Aww, how sweet."

Erin was floored. *Dr Dan is a married man! My mom is dating a married man! My mom is in an affair! My mom is the <u>other woman</u>! My mom is willingly involved with a married man with a kid my age!*

For the duration of the X-ray, Erin said nothing, even after both women had left. Allen talked about how cute Dr. Tammy was. Erin ignored him and tried to figure out what to do. *First, Mom gave birth to Josh when she was 16 and now she's having an affair. This combination could explain her weird behavior if she only just now found out that Dan was married, but it was unrealistic to think she wouldn't know by the first month.*

Someone came in and set her wrist and fitted it with some type of plastic cast. It was a lot more high tech than the old plaster ones. They gave Erin instructions on how to care of her wrist. She missed some of the washing instructions because she was thinking about her mom. Erin was so spaced out, Allen had to nudge her to ask if she was ready to go home.

"Huh? What?" she asked.

"Home? Are you ready to go?"

"Huh? Oh, my insurance card!"

"In your hand. You're done. What's wrong with you? They give you pain killers?"

"No, I have to fill a prescription, I'm fine."

"All right, lets go."

"No, I'm going to wait here."

"Wait for what? It's three in the morning."

"My mom. I think she comes in at six today."

"Your mom? I didn't provide enough support?"

"No, I need to talk to her about something. Geez it's all about you, all the time!"

"All right, all right. Where you gonna sleep? That horrible waiting room with the downtrodden?"

"Down what?...No, there's an employee break room on the 5th floor. They have couches and a Coke machine and everything."

"Yummy, Coke for breakfast."

"Whatever dude, just go! And thanks."

"You sure you don't need me to keep you company?"

"No, Joe Nobel. Just go! Don't you have to work tomorrow?"

"Nope, day off."

"Whatever. Just fuck'n go! Being all nice and shit already got you in trouble before.

"What are you talking about?"

"Nothing—just go home, have some fun—Merci—Beat it!" With her good arm, Erin pushed Allen to the exit. During the

goodbye hug, she added a kiss on the cheek. "I'll see you later."
Allen exited. Erin walked to the elevator, to go to the 5th floor.

#

She woke up on the couch. She was surrounded by noise.
She didn't expect to see so many people in the break room at 6
AM. They were talking loudly, slamming the microwave and
causing a constant metal 'ca-chunk' sound of breakfast sodas
being dispersed from the machine. Erin got up and headed to
the restroom. The hallway was more hectic than it should be at
6 AM. A window in the corner showed yellow sunlight. This
was a clue it was later than she thought. "Oh shit? What time is
it?" She found an employee in the hallway and asked.

"Uhh, 9:25," said a guy in a white dress shirt and blue jeans.

"Fuck!" She muttered. *Oh well, too late to talk to mom, but not
too late to go to work.* She went into the ladies room to clean up.

She was actually late for work. Her thought was: *If Agnew
ain't there, it'll be an opportunity to take a long lunch. If he is there, a
broken wrist as a good excuse for late.*

As it turned out, not only was he at work, but he was also
working at her desk. Agnew was a short, baldheaded, light
skinned Black man who wore gold-rimmed glasses that didn't
suit his face. He had piled a bunch of jobs up into two stacks.
Erin wasn't sure if they were 'in and out' piles. She hoped the
larger one was the 'out' side.

"Oh…Erin!"

"Hi Mr. Agnew, sorry I'm late. I had a little accident."

"I can see that. What happened?"

"I fell down. Must've been the flu. It's okay. I think it only
has to be on for a couple of weeks."

"That's good to hear."

"So, er-ah, are you caught up, since I was out?"

"Yes." He stopped working and swiveled toward her. "The
work load wasn't what I wanted to talk to you about."

Erin's stomach sank. She knew what was coming. After he
made statements like 'productivity' and 'efficient use of your

time' it was only a matter of time before she heard 'not working out' and 'not extend your probationary period.'

"You're firing me?" she interrupted his rambling speech.

"Well, you were not fully hired, so we're just passing on making you a career employee."

"Because I was out sick?"

"No, I would never do that. It's your output; you just weren't getting the data entered fast enough. It's like you were not coming in at all."

Erin thought about the day she went shopping instead of work. "But, can't we talk bout this?"

"I'm sorry, but I need someone who can get the jobs entered faster."

"I…" Erin was about to ask him for another chance. *That would be begging. I should tell him to go fuck himself, especially when he keeps saying: 'I'm sorry, but…' and 'this was very hard for me.'* "Not as hard as unemployment," she accidentally said aloud.

"I know, and I'm sorry, but the work has to get out," he repeated.

Say 'sorry, but,' one more time and I'll kick your <u>sorry</u> ass. "Okay then," she said sarcastically and left.

"Okay. Thanks Erin," he said.

She resisted the urges again. Instead she headed straight for the elevator.

"Thanks Erin? For what? What a fucking day," she said. She went to the 3rd floor, to her mom's office. She saw her in the hallway, just finishing up a conversation with a nurse. When she saw Erin, her look was one of happiness, shock and a bit of fear. "Erin!" she said. She hugged Erin. The hug was not returned.

"What happened to you?" She examined Erin's cast.

"I got drunk and fell down, and I then I got fired?"

"You got fired, why?"

"Some shit about not entering the work fast enough."

"What? Oh no! Well, don't you worry, I know some other people who need a…"

"Forget it, Mom!"

"You don't want my help?"

"I'll find another job."

"Not one with benefits like this one."

"I'm sure you get <u>plenty</u> of benefits, but I don't want to have any part of it!"

"What are you talking about? You're not making any sense."

"Dan's married, Mom!"

The look of fear and shock returned to Carolyn's face. She looked around to see if anyone was eavesdropping. She grabbed Erin's upper arm and tried to guide her to a more private place.

Erin pulled away from her. "Forget it Mom, I'm not going to ruin your reputation!"

"Erin, what's going on is between Dan and I," she whispered.

"Whatever! Just more secrets, Mom, got any more? Are you gay? Am I really adopted? Oh, here's one: You were actually 16 when you got knocked up with Josh!"

"Erin I can see you're upset, but..."

"Oh, please don't use the word 'but!" Erin grabbed the sides of her head. "No more lame-ass excuses and people pretending to be sorry while they keep doing the shit they're sorry for!"

"Erin..."

"Forget it, Mom! I need some fucking truth in my life! I want something <u>real</u>! No more <u>fake</u> roommates and jobs or parents <u>lying</u> to me!"

"I never lied to you!"

"Oh, that's right, you withhold the truth! You should work for the fucking government! You know, before, I blew you off and moved away without telling you, I felt really bad about that —this time, it's justified! I should have known I can't depend on someone that abandons her family in the first place!" Erin walked away.

"Erin! We need to talk about this!"

"No more talk, I have to tell my roommates that I'm moving out!"

Erin took the stairs exit. She knew if she took the elevator, there was a chance it wouldn't come the second she pressed the button. It was yet another thing in her life she couldn't depend on.

Preview

FLAMING
JACKASS
Detox

Alexander G. J.

Part One

Cabin Fever

Blam! Blam! Blam-blam-blam! The first two blams, b*ackfire?*
The forth—*firecracker?* But on the fifth popping sound, it was
evident the sounds were too even and planned. It had to be
man-directed. Erin stayed in bed with the covers up to her
nose. She was waiting for more popping, or anything else to
hint the noise wasn't what she thought it was. Buster's head was
lifted. He lay on the edge of the bed, his ears fully erect,
listening, like Erin for future sounds. Erin was never gladder he
was there. Chris came into the room. The door was open to
give Buster access to the kitchen. At 2AM, she would usually
hear the dog walk down the stairs and noisily slurp his water
dish.

"Did you hear that?" Chris asked.

"Yeah," Erin said quietly, afraid that any loud noises would
cause more popping. Chris walked over to the window.

"Stop!" Erin said.

"I'll be careful."

There was nothing careful about the way Chris walked
directly over to the window and looked out.

"Well?" Erin asked. There was the distant sound of sirens.
This was not unusual in this neighborhood. Chris poetically
called them the songbirds of East West River Valley. The
songbirds got closer and closer. Someone on the street wailed
in anguish.

"Oh-My-God!" Chris said.

"What is it? What is it? Is someone hurt?" Without
worrying about safety, Erin hopped out of bed and ran to the
window. There was a Black woman comforting a Black man.

He was very distraught and crying. "Oh my god! Is he shot or something?" Erin asked.

"No, but look." Chris pointed to a space between the apartments next door. Erin saw a pile of clothes next to a garbage can. "What? I don't see anything?"

"Next to that garbage can?"

"The pile of clothes?"

"Those aren't clothes, That's a guys leg!"

Erin realized she had been looking at the clothes at the wrong angle. When she adjusted her thinking, as her art teacher Mrs. Watts said, she was able to tell that yes, it was a leg, attached to a body lying in the alley. "Oh my God! Is he hurt? Why aren't those people helping him?"

"I think he's beyond help."

Erin stared at the leg. She expected to see some type of movement. She wanted to yell down to the two people to check his pulse. Her instinct for self-preservation kept the window closed. The girls stared at the leg without speaking for what seemed like hours. Eventually, a police car appeared and then another, and an ambulance. This raised Erin's hope that perhaps the guy was still alive. The milling about of the EMT crew was evident they were too late. The body was loaded up on a stretcher and put inside the ambulance. The police officers busied themselves with interviewing the man and woman.

They probably saw everything. What was it like to be near someone, perhaps a friend, who suddenly gets gunned down? Are your thoughts: Oh, no, my friend! Or are they: Oh shit! I hope I'm not next!

Assuming they had seen all they could see, the girls left the window. Erin got back into bed, Chris headed back to her room. Erin stopped her at the doorway. "Have you ever seen a dead body?"

"You mean outside of a funeral?"

"Yeah."

Chris thought for a few seconds. "No, I've seen plenty of people fucked up though."

"Me neither…

ABOUT THE AUTHOR

Alexander G. J. grew up in Charlotte, North Carolina. He moved to Atlanta, Georgia and studied graphic arts at the Art Institute of Atlanta, then to San Francisco, Ca and served as a cartoonist and editor on *Splunge Comix,* a humor magazine which featured the comic series *Flaming Jackass Pizza*, the inspiration for this novel. He currently lives in Richmond, California.

NOVELS BY ALEXANDER G. J.

Flaming Jackass, Sex, Drugs, and Pizza
Flaming Jackass, In Love
Flaming Jackass, Returns
Mary & I: the Real Story of Miss Mary Mack

Blog: flamingjackasspizza.blogspot.com

Facebook: facebook.com/rabbitstudiosbigpush

Author's page: amazon.com/author/alexanderg.j